DEVELOPMENT AND DISORDERS OF WRITTEN LANGUAGE

Volume Two

Studies of Normal and Exceptional Children

Also by Dr. Myklebust

Auditory Disorders in Children:
A Manual for Differential Diagnosis   1954

The Psychology of Deafness:
Sensory Deprivation, Learning, and Adjustment   1961, 1964

Development and Disorders of Written Language,
Volume One: Picture Story Language Test   1965

Learning Disabilities: Educational Principles and Practices
(with Doris L. Johnson)   1967

Progress in Learning Disabilities (Editor),
Volume I   1968
Volume II   1971

Diagnostic Test of Speechreading
(with Arthur I. Neyhus)   1970

The Pupil Rating Scale:
Screening for Learning Disabilities   1971

DEVELOPMENT AND DISORDERS OF WRITTEN LANGUAGE

Volume Two

Studies of Normal and Exceptional Children

HELMER R. MYKLEBUST

University of Illinois
at Chicago Circle

GRUNE & STRATTON • New York and London

Myklebust, Helmer R
    Development and disorders of written language.

    Includes bibliographies.
    CONTENTS: v. 1. Picture story language test.—V. 2.
Studies of normal and exceptional children.
    1. Children—Writing. 2. Agraphia. I. Title.
II. Title: Picture story language test.
[DNLM: 1. Agraphia. 2. Alexia. 3. Language
development. 4. Reading. 5. Writing. WL 340 M996d]
RJ496.A4M9   618.928552   65-23996
ISBN 0-8089-0335-7 (v. 1)   ISBN 0-8089-0714-x (v. 2)

Library of Congress Catalog Card Number 65-23996
International Standard Book Number 0-8089-0714-x
Printed in the United States of America

*To children
who have disorders of
written language—
that their way
may be made a
little easier*

Contents

CONTENTS

Figures and Tables

Table

Preface

SINCE PUBLICATION of *Development and Disorders of Written Language*, Volume One, *Picture Story Language Test,* a number of investigators, teachers, and clinicians have become interested in the written language form. Awareness is developing that knowledge crucial to understanding the processes involved in language acquisition can be gained through study of the spoken, read, and written forms, each in relation to the other. This is the emphasis of the present book—*Development and Disorders of Written Language,* Volume Two, *Studies of Normal and Exceptional Children.*

The studies reported cover a period of several years. Initially, the purpose was to develop an objective test, the Picture Story Language Test, to measure achievement in written language. This early phase—the norms, theoretical construct, and instructions for administering and scoring the test—is discussed in Volume One. The present volume includes further analyses of the results for normal children and comparative findings for exceptional children: reading-disability, mentally retarded, socially-emotionally disturbed, speech-handicapped, and learning-disability.

Because of wide interest on the part of various disciplines, and because the Picture Story Language Test can be given without translation, studies are in progress in several countries, notably Uruguay, Hungary, and Belgium. Comparative findings for Uruguayan and American children are included in this volume to illustrate the importance of cross-cultural efforts in expanding knowledge of language development.

The relation between language and cognitive functions is stressed, for it is in these terms that the data can further understanding of children's learning processes. The trend toward shifting criteria for educational grouping mandates review of the language-learning patterns of all exceptional children. The findings reported here seem relevant to these issues. Moreover, as knowledge is gained, there is greater awareness of the role of language in all learning.

Discussions in this book and in Volume One express a point of view regarding language acquisition: spoken, read, and written. This frame of reference may be of interest to students and investigators. The purpose is to present the material in a manner advantageous for advanced courses in language pathology, psychology, and special education, and especially for courses covering the disorders of read and written language. Developmental psychologists, school psychologists, and special educators may find the techniques and findings useful in ascertaining suitable educational programs for exceptional children. Also, remediation approaches for the classroom teacher are suggested.

Many students and colleagues have assisted with the research and, through critical discussions, with interpretation of the findings: I am indebted to them all. Special appreciation is expressed to Margaret Bannochie, who read the final manuscript and helped with collation of the data and with the bibliography. Dr. E. Milo Pritchett, formerly Head, Department of Special Education, Northern Illinois University, through his support made possible the completion of this research project. Joyce Lewis prepared the figures and typed the manuscript through its many stages. I am grateful to these friends and colleagues for their generous assistance.

HELMER R. MYKLEBUST

University of Illinois
at Chicago Circle

Part One

LEARNING TO USE
THE WRITTEN WORD

Chapter I

Learning to Read and Write

More than by any other attribute, physical or psychological, man is characterized by his use of language. Yet he is not born with verbal facility, but enters the world with potential for its acquisition. Every human infant is confronted with the unique task of learning the language of his culture. How he does so, and why linguistic behavior is achieved by man alone, are research problems of importance in psychology and education.

Psychologists, educators, and linguisticians, among others, often emphasize the ways in which language, thought, and social behavior are related. Sapir (1921) and Whorf (1956) contend that language not only is a means of communication but also influences the individual's manner of perceiving, categorizing, and abstracting. Vygotsky (1962) and Brown (1958) stress the interrelations among the language systems: spoken, read, and written. Clinicians and researchers involved with disorders of language are concerned with the interactions of inner, receptive, and expressive processes, the relations of input to output and to integration (Myklebust, 1971b).

In this volume the focus is on the written word, the development and disorders of written language. The spoken and read forms have been investigated by many workers representing a variety of disciplines (Money, 1966; Young and Lindsley, 1970; Travis, 1971). But only meager attention has been given to written language. As Gelb (1963) suggests, there is great need to develop a science of grammatology and orthography. This science should be inclusive, covering facets of reception, expression, and meaning. As this area of study develops, it will be advantageous to gain further information on *how* and *when* language originated. The time of origin has implications for the physical, mental, and cultural factors required for acquisition of each of the language forms. Determining the processes whereby a given verbal system is acquired permits identification of the phylogenetic period in which it was achieved. These questions are of more than theoretical interest; further knowledge concerning them

3

will provide insights into language development as it relates to all human beings: children and adults, normal and handicapped.

PHYLOGENETIC CONSIDERATIONS

Pei (1962) says that the origin and nature of language "are twin problems, linked yet separate" (p. 19). De Saussure (1931), who is especially concerned with the nature and function of language, states that the linguistic sign is both arbitrary and constant. A similar observation appears in many definitions of language. Linguistic signs are arbitrary in that there is no inherent connection between them and their significates; there is no underlying interrelation between the word *dog* and the animal it symbolizes. But all persons speaking a given language must use the same word for this animal if they are to communicate. The linguistic sign must be constant from one person to the next in order for the speaker's utterances to be meaningful, for language to develop. Pei states this fact cogently: "The link is not between the word and the object; it is between the word and the concept of the object which exists in the speaker's mind. At the same time, another link must exist among the various and varied minds of the members of the speech community" (p. 23). An essential of language is that the words, the linguistic signs, must be meaningful because, as Vygotsky (1962) has emphasized, a word without meaning is not a word. The primary purpose of language may not be communication with others. An even more basic purpose seems to be communication with oneself. When Langer (1957) suggests that the fundamental motive for acquiring language is to fill the mind, not the hand, she is making a similar observation. Nevertheless, communication with oneself, as well as with others, assumes meaningful symbolic verbal behavior. Meaning is essential to communication.

Spoken Word

Verbal language is of two types: spoken and written. Many theories have been propounded about the origin of the spoken form, but this system was attained so long ago that details surrounding its evolution remain speculative. Depending on one's definition of written language, there is agreement that man acquired ability to use the spoken form long before he learned to read and write (Diringer, 1962). This is of vital concern. Students cannot overlook the question of why man did not first acquire ability to read and write instead of first learning the spoken word. The sequence in which language was acquired phylogentically has not been stressed as a facet in understanding man's verbal behavior. This is unfortunate because forthcoming evidence indicates that the language systems can be understood intrinsically only in relation to each other. When the spoken, read, and written forms are studied interrelatedly, the development and disorders of language can be more fully comprehended.

If drawings, pictographic writing, and mnemonic signs are excluded, it is apparent that man acquired use of spoken language centuries before he acquired ability to read and write. Why he did so is a question that can be considered only cursorily. Compared with vision, audition is a more flexible, and hence more useful, modality for language acquisition. Hearing is mandatory (we cannot close our ears) and multidirectional. Vision is unidirectional, focusing only frontward. We can hear in the dark, through walls, and around corners. Myklebust (1964) stresses the impact of these differences in modality as revealed by the psychology of deafness. His studies disclose the severe limitations of the visual modality for initial language learning.

There are other considerations. Written language requires use of the hands, and because reading is unidirectional, we can neither read nor write while driving a car or while performing innumerable other routines. Primitive man found himself in similar circumstances. Hence, he evolved a language system through the most opportune sensory modality, the auditory. Audition, being the most efficient and practical sense, provided the means for evolution of man's most basic verbal system, the spoken word. Gelb (1963) states that speech is the fullest and most developed of all the systems of signs. It is the system that can be utilized in the dark, can be projected through and around obstructions, does not involve use of the hands, and encompasses the child's total directional environment. Moreover, developmental studies indicate that the spoken word is acquired ontogenetically at an earlier age than are reading and writing. Less developmental maturation is necessary for proficiency in use of auditory language. More evolution was required before man could attain facility with read and written language.

Written Word

The origin of written language is less controversial than that of the spoken. When the materials on which an individual writes are preserved, an inherent record is maintained. Also, the period of its origin is less obscured because ability to write is much more recent. Grammatologists and alphabetologists agree that writing has a short history. Diringer (1962) states: "At some point in the comparatively recent past, within those few thousand years which have seen the real intellectual development of mankind, writing, in the sense that we understand the word today, had its origins. An analysis of first causes here is an extraordinarily difficult and touchy affair, much like analyzing the 'causes' of war and revolution: in each case those present when the phenomenon had its birth have usually little or no concern with posterity, and posterity must, in consequence, tread warily. What can be said with certainty is that there is no evidence to prove that any *complete system* of writing was employed before the middle of the fourth millennium B.C." (p. 15).

Determination of the point of origin, however, assumes definition of what is meant by writing. Gelb (1963) concludes that "writing is clearly a system of human intercommunication by means of conventional visible marks" (p. 12). Drawings and pictographs are not included although these were forerunners of the written word. Diringer discusses five steps in the development of writing. First, the *pictograph* (picture writing), a process of conveying ideas through representational pictures; excellent examples are given by Friedrich (1957) and Clodd (1900). Second, the *ideograph*, which communicated meanings by using a part of an object to signify the whole and related objects; examples are the sign language used by the deaf and the ideography used in the Orient. To a degree the ideograph was intended to represent words. Third, *analytical transitional scripts*, the first attempt to associate the visual-written and phonetic-auditory aspects of language. Fourth, *phonetic scripts*, which for the first time provided a graphic representation of the spoken word. This script, highly systematized, represented syllables rather than individual spoken sounds, a syllabic form of writing. Fifth, the *alphabet*, was the last form to evolve and is the one in use today. Taylor's (1883) comment is pertinent: "To invent and to bring to perfection the score or so of handy symbols for the expression of spoken sounds which we call our alphabet, has proved to be the most arduous enterprise on which the human intellect has ever engaged" (p. 4).

In the alphabet the intent is for each letter to depict a single sound.

Previously it had been necessary to portray the object or to use a portion of it to represent the whole. Diringer (1962) indicates the significance of the evolution of the alphabet when he states that "enormous advantages implicit in using letters to represent single sounds are obvious—with its 22, 24, or 26 signs, the alphabet is the most flexible and useful method of writing ever invented, and, from its origin in the Near East, has become the nearly universal basis for the scripts employed by civilized peoples, passing from language to language with a minimum of difficulty. No other system of writing has had so extensive, so intricate and so interesting a history" (p. 24).

Linguists, alphabetologists, and grammatologists have made the study of writing an intriguing adventure. Nevertheless, there are other reasons for referring to this work. Little attention has been given to the sequence in which man first acquired verbal systems. Moreover, the importance of the read and written forms rarely has been recognized by scholars. Such recognition is essential for realization of the processes involved in language development and, accordingly, the effect of handicaps on these processes. Phylogenetic and ontogenetic patterns are not identical, but awareness of the phylogeny of man's verbal behavior encourages insights concerning its ontogeny. Fundamental relations exist among the spoken, read, and written forms of language, especially of the highly phonetic Western languages.

Written language originated by evolution of markings to represent spoken sounds.* A visual form was developed to represent the auditory. This process, referred to as phonetization, is described by Gelb (1963): "A primitive logographic writing can develop into a full system only if it succeeds in attaching a sign to a phonetic value independent of the meaning which this sign has as a word. This is phonetization, the most important single step in the history of writing —with the introduction of phonetization and its subsequent systematization complete systems of writing developed which made possible the expression of any linguistic form by means of symbols with conventional syllabic values. Thus full writing originated, in contrast to the feeble attempts grouped together as semasiography, which deserve no higher designation than implied in classifying them as forerunners of writing" (p. 194). Gelb also quotes Aristotle as having

* See *Development and Disorders of Written Language*, Volume One, *Picture Story Language Test*, Figure 1, p. 3 (Myklebust, 1965).

said: "Spoken words are the symbols of mental experience and written words are the symbols of spoken words" (p. 13).

Language development can be more adequately understood in terms of the reciprocities among each of the verbal systems, as indicated by both the phylogenetic and the ontogenetic patterns. Brown (1958), for example, stresses the phylogenetic perspective in a study of the processes by which children learn to read and write. The psychological and educational significance of these phylo- and ontogenetic patterns is emphasized throughout the discussions that follow, as are their implications for the psychology of language learning by normal and by exceptional children.

INNER, RECEPTIVE, AND EXPRESSIVE LANGUAGE

Vygotsky (1962), Mowrer (1960), and Goldstein (1948) suggest that language is more than reception and that expression is more than input and output. Mediation, or meaning, is essential. This aspect is minimized, if not ignored, by some workers, perhaps because *communication* and *language* are confused. Various forms of animal life are capable of communicating but not of utilizing representational symbols.

Language acquisition, as a cognitive process, can be understood as comprising three basic systems: inner language (integration), receptive language (input), and expressive language (output) (Myklebust, 1971a,b). The child first acquires an experience, and then learns the words that symbolize this experience; the word *dog* has no significance until the *experience* dog has been attained. Therefore, inner language is use of words to internalize symbolic meaning; it is the process of relating experience and symbol and precedes actual use of receptive and expressive language. A given culture has a *norm* of experience which must be learned and associated with the proper word if individuals are to communicate one with the other. Those using the verbal system must have associated essentially the same experiences with the words involved. They must have achieved similar if not identical *referents* for the verbal signs in question.

After inner language has been acquired to some degree, it is possible to comprehend what is said by others. As comprehension is initiated, a process critical to language development is established because reciprocal enhancement is fostered. When inner language develops, facility with receptive language increases, and likewise, comprehension augments inner language growth. In working with exceptional children one observes that the child's disability affects this vital cognitive process. Some children cannot comprehend, not because of receptive language deficits, but because development of inner language has been impeded. This may be true of a number of mentally retarded children. But impositions on receptive language, too, as in the deaf, restrict inner language (Myklebust, 1964). This restriction may also occur when receptive aphasia is sustained in childhood (Myklebust, 1971a); evidence of inner language deficits in other exceptional children is given in Part Two.

Expressive language, the third verbal function, follows acquisition of inner and receptive language; when the inner and receptive forms become operational, the child is ready to utter words. He does not engage in spoken language expressively unless he understands the words to be used. He does not understand these words until he has internalized them, associated them with the norm of experience determined by his culture. Neither does the child write until he comprehends the words he writes; he does not engage in written language until he has acquired facility with the read. Reading and writing entail the same verbal-symbol system, the printed or written form. As with spoken language, output follows input; the expressive form (written) assumes facility with the receptive form (read).

Man evolved two verbal systems: the auditory and the visual. The auditory evolved first, then much later the visual was superimposed. The interactions of these language forms have been more fully understood in recent years. Yet study has just begun of the importance of these relations to understanding cognitive processes in exceptional children. Initially, clarification follows when the primary processes are indicated categorically: inner language (integration of word and experience), auditory receptive language (comprehension of the spoken word), auditory expressive language (utterance of words), visual receptive language (reading), and visual expressive language (writing).

This classification is preferable in study of children ontogenetically, and it provides a frame of reference for analyzing verbal development phylogenetically. Man, before he used verbal symbols for communication, found it necessary to internalize and symbolize experience; he first acquired inner language. Presumably, this was accomplished by a few persons in a given group (Gelb, 1963). As agreement was reached on the *norm* of experience, other words could be acquired, much as the child who has gained a level of language usage can be told the meaning of words.

Centuries later, reading and writing evolved. But the study of the origin of language is largely, sometimes exclusively, in terms of expressive forms, the spoken and written. In language development, comprehension precedes expression. Hence, when man began to speak words, the words were comprehended by himself and at least one other person. Likewise, the first persons to use the written word understood what they were writing because writing assumes ability to read.

Only man reads and writes. In the chapters that follow, the major concern is with the written word. Nevertheless, the data are discussed in terms of interrelations of the spoken, read, and written forms. Developmental factors are emphasized, with attention to the ways in which they are modified in exceptional children.

Chapter II

The Written Language of Normal Children

The Picture Story Language Test (PSLT) was evolved to study the development and disorders of written language. Since its publication (Myklebust, 1965), it has been useful as an achievement test and as a diagnostic instrument. The ease with which it can be administered in cross-cultural investigations has been gratifying (Tuana, 1971; VandenBerg, 1971). Some researchers have found the test applicable also in studying the development and disorders of oral language (McGrady, 1964; Duff, 1968; Wilson, 1968; Myklebust and Boshes, 1969).

The primary standardization data, instructions for administering the test, and the scoring procedures are presented in Volume One,* as are the theoretical constructs and general frame of reference. Additional data that reveal the manner in which children acquire facility with the written word are considered in this chapter.

THE STANDARDIZATION SAMPLE

The standardization sample consisted of 747 normal children, ranging in age from 7 through 17 years in alternate age groups. To obtain as representative a group as possible, children were selected from three types of school systems: metropolitan, suburban, and rural. As anticipated, the results varied on the basis of type of school attended. Hence, results are presented for each of the subsamples (Tables 1 through 5).† (There were no suburban children at 7 years, and no suburban females at 15 years.)

---

* *Development and Disorders of Written Language*, Volume One, *Picture Story Language Test* (Myklebust, 1965).

† All tables appear in Part Four, pages 181–253.

Total Words

Length of the story, as indicated by the number of words written, varied substantially by group. The shortest stories were written by children from urban schools, followed by those from rural schools, and the longest stories were written by those from suburban schools. But these differences were greatest between the ages of 9 and 13 years. At 15 and 17 years there was considerable overlap of scores because the suburban and rural groups achieved a plateau by 13 years of age, whereas the urban continued to progress to the age of 15 years. Though the urban and rural children scored below the suburban at the early age levels, they achieved equal story length as they became older. The trend in all three groups was for females to write longer stories than males.

Total Sentences

The pattern for total words also appeared for number of sentences. The suburban children wrote the most sentences at 9, 11, and 13 years, but at 15 and 17 years these differences essentially disappeared. Although the growth patterns varied, there were no deficiencies comparable to those found in children who have language disorders. On the other hand, educators in the urban and rural schools should be aware of the need for development of written language during early school years.

Words per Sentence

The three groups were more similar in number of words written per sentence. Sentence length, as an indicator of facility with written language, has proved remarkably stable. Whatever the reason for the variations in story length, the number of words written per sentence was consistent, irrespective of type of school attended. If we infer that urban children had the poorest opportunity for learning, we cannot conclude that this disadvantage was equally influential on all the factors involved in acquisition of written language. This result is in contrast with the findings for handicapped children (see Part Two). Accordingly, despite the important detrimental effects of inadequate schooling, this disadvantage should not be equated with such disabilities as mental retardation, speech defects, or other conditions that require special educational programming.

Syntax

The correctness of the language written also was equivalent for the three subgroups composing the standardization sample. According to the factor-analysis results (Table 17), this means that the urban and rural children differed from the suburban on only one of the factors measured on the PSLT; they were equal on the other two factors. These results have importance for educators in that they show differing growth patterns by type of school attended, but do not reveal the kinds of developmental disabilities found in exceptional children. By implication, if the circumstances of the three groups were equivalent, all three would manifest equivalent patterns in acquisition of written language.

Abstract-Concrete

Level of abstract meaning is so intimately related to story and sentence length that these constitute a single factor. It was expected, therefore, that the groups would vary on this aspect of written language. The variation was similar to that for total words and total sentences. The significance of this result should not be overlooked. At early school age, urban and rural children were limited in use of abstract meaning. Since this limitation suggests concomitant psychological effects, one feels an urgency about the total implications and circumstances. For many children, facilitation of language learning in early school life seems imperative if pervasive ill effects are to be avoided.

RELATION BETWEEN AUDITORY AND WRITTEN LANGUAGE

Auditory language is the first and most basic verbal system acquired by man. The read and written forms are learned initially by processing through the auditory, which has been established. The neurology of this learning is being clarified (Geschwind, 1972) and will undoubtedly be of vital importance to educators and psychologists. In Volume One, examples are presented of the written language of children with spelling disabilities (see also Boder, 1971). It is stressed that spelling in the written form entails simultaneous elicitation of auditory and visual images. Use of the expressive form (written) may be deficient even though the input form (reading) is intact (see Illustration 9 in Volume One).

Only in recent years have educators become aware that spelling disorders are indicative of learning disabilities. Neurologically, the angular gyrus plays a critical role in learning to spell correctly in the written form. The auditory form of the word is transmitted to this area, where it is then transduced into visual equivalents. In reading, this process is reversed. The visual patterns are transmitted to the angular gyrus and then to the auditory area, where they are transduced into auditory equivalents. To understand spelling and reading disabilities, it must be noted that one is a receptive process and the other is expressive; one may be dysfunctioning while the other is performing normally. Moreover, as seen often in children, the disorder may be in either the visual or the auditory processes.

Because of the importance of auditory language in learning the read and written forms, an investigation was made of the relations among these verbal systems. These studies included normal and exceptional children (see also Part Two). The model stressing the interrelations of the language forms evolved from studies of deaf children (Myklebust, 1964). That deafness from early life modifies the processes by which the child learns has been demonstrated (Neyhus and Myklebust, 1969; Hughes, 1971). Relatively less has been learned about the role of vision through studies of the blind. Moreover, the cognitive patterns that characterize groups of exceptional children, such as the mentally retarded, have been largely overlooked. Until the idiosyncratic effects of given handicaps on cognition have been determined, the most advantageous learning modes cannot be provided. To gain such information, an intercorrelation analysis was performed. First the findings for normal children are presented. Comparative results for exceptional children appear in Part Two.

Auditory Receptive and Written Language

Because of the intricate nature of these studies only a portion of the urban sample was included in this phase of the investigation. This sample was representative, selected to be comparable to the handicapped groups discussed in Part Two. The tests for appraising auditory language are presented in Chapter III.

From the data in Table 6, it can be seen that auditory receptive and written language are interrelated in normal children. Of the two measures of auditory receptive language, Test One (comprehension without visual matching) correlated most with the written word. The greatest association was at 7 years, the youngest age level studied. Except for syntax, which correlated through 11 years of age, auditory receptive and written language were closely associated at early school age, the period when the most basic cognitive processing occurs.

When the visual (read) and written forms are first introduced, these images are processed through the auditory. But after the auditory and visual equivalents have been learned, other factors become of equal or greater importance. This is not true of syntax, which continues to be related to auditory receptive language through 11 years of age. Syntax has been shown to be a function of auditory language (see the findings for deaf children in Myklebust, 1964; and VandenBerg, 1971). Hence, one aspect of auditory receptive language continues to show a relation with acquisition of written language well into elementary-school age.

Test Two was intended to measure facility in relating the auditory and visual verbal forms. For normal children this test was less successful than Test One. Only use of abstract meaning correlated with the scores for auditory receptive language, and these correlations appeared at 9, 11, and 13 years. Because this test necessitated that equivalents between the auditory and visual language forms be determined, communication of abstract meaning was more successful when such cognitive processing was achieved. Nevertheless, for auditory comprehension (Test One), there was a negative correlation with abstract meaning at the age of 15 years. Perhaps, unless the auditory and visual forms become equivalent and these cognitive processes are established, use of abstract meaning is reduced. As tests and procedures become more available, associations among auditory receptive, read, and written language forms can be more fruitfully investigated.

Auditory Expressive and Written Language

More significant interrelations appeared between auditory expressive and written language than between auditory receptive and written language; there were 10 for auditory receptive and 20 for auditory expressive (see Table 7). Inasmuch as auditory expressive is dependent on auditory receptive, these findings are indicative of the total interaction of the auditory and written language forms. The child acquires written language to the extent that the auditory has been learned and is available for processing of the read and written.

Again, most of the significant correlations appeared at the age of 7 years. The association between auditory and written language in early life was striking. Of the five scores on the PSLT, syntax and abstract-concrete were most closely related with output of the spoken word. The tests of auditory expressive language were consistent in this regard.

The findings for syntax were anticipated because of the auditory components of this factor. The results for abstract meaning, however, were unexpected. Both the auditory receptive and expressive tests manifested relations between use of abstract meaning in the written form and in auditory language; this association becomes more revealing through the studies of exceptional children, discussed in Part Two. But the correlation between the auditory and written language systems were age-dependent. In early life the associations were close; by 15 years of age there was no significant interaction. As developmental maturation is achieved and cognitive processes become established, the interdependence of auditory and written language undergoes a change. Though the normal individual continues to have facility in transducing from auditory to visual and from visual to auditory, he can use each separately. In reading, and to some extent in writing, he can bypass the auditory until there is again need to process through the auditory. This need arises when the read or written passages are difficult and the auditory must be activated for clarity and meaning.

Summary

The intercorrelation results for auditory receptive and auditory expressive language show that the greatest relations with the written word appeared in early life, precisely at the age when the child is learning the visual equivalents of the auditory form. These relations continued beyond 7 years of age for syntax and abstract-concrete. All five scores on the PSLT showed at least one significant correlation with written language; total sentences was least associated. These results for normal children are indicative of the cognitive processes involved in learning to use read and written language. That handicaps modify these processes is shown by the comparative results for exceptional children presented in Part Two.

DIFFERENCES BY AGE

To study the maturational patterns for acquisition of written language in greater detail, age-group differences were analyzed; these results are given in Tables 8 through 12.

Total Words

There were consistent increments in story length for both sexes up through 13 years of age. But as seen previously, most rapid growth was made by the females, and they showed no further significant increase in the number of words written per story after the age of 13 years. In comparison, the males showed a decrease in story length from 13 to 15 years, then made a significant gain between the ages of 15 and 17 years. In the pattern of maturation by age the most uniform gains in number of words written were made before 13 years of age. Thereafter, the pattern of age variation was related to sex, the females maturing earlier.

Total Sentences

The age-group variations for number of sentences written differed substantially from the results for story length. Obvious age-related increments occurred only between 7 and 9 years. Both sexes attained the level of 10 to 11 sentences per story and remained essentially at this level, though the pattern by sex was not identical. The data on words per sentence (Table 10) show that children mature in facility to write longer and more complex sentences as they become older, and therefore they do not write an increasing number of sentences; however, this configuration pertains only to normal children (see Part Two).

Words per Sentence

Growth in sentence length revealed marked linearity with age. Both sexes wrote sentences of greater length year by year, reaching a level of 15 to 16 words per sentence. But this level was attained at approximately 13 years by the females and at 15 years by the males.

Syntax

As noted previously, facility in use of syntax was attained early in life, with the greatest increment at 7 to 9 years of age. Moreover, there were no sex differences by age. Of the five scores derived from the PSLT, the least change after 9 years of age was in syntax.

Abstract-Concrete

The developmental configuration for use of abstract meaning varied by age and sex. Both males and females manifested gains between 7 and 9 years. Thereafter, sex was influential. The males made no growth from 9 to 11 years, then made gains from 11 to 13, showed no increment from 13 to 15, but achieved a substantial increase from 15 to 17 years. There was a consistent pattern of growth for the females from 7 through 11 years, with a plateau from 11 to 13, then a marked increment between the ages of 13 and 15 years; they showed no further gain after 15 years of age. The pattern for the males included two plateaus (9 to 11 and 13 to 15), with growth continuing through the age of 17 years. For the females there was only one plateau (11 to 13) with no further gain after 15 years.

DIFFERENCES BY SEX

Sex differences have been found in acquisition of language for both normal and exceptional children (McCarthy, 1954; Templin, 1957; Money, 1962; Myklebust, 1964), females acquiring language at an earlier age than males. The incidence of language disorders also appears higher in males. These trends, shown in Table 13, have implications for educational programs.

Total Words

The females exceeded the males in story length, and the differences at 7 and 15 years were highly significant. Both sexes made growth through 17 years of age; there was no maturational plateau. Because the difference at 17 years did not reach statistical significance, it may be that males do not attain a level of output equivalent to that of females. The findings for total sentences were similar.

Total Sentences

Differences appeared in the number of sentences written at 7, 9, and 15 years, all favoring the females, apparently explained by earlier maturation. The variation at 15 years, like the variation in total words at this age, may be due to the decrement in the productivity of the males. In general, the number of sentences written revealed differences more often than total words, and these differences favored the females.

Words per Sentence

The number of words written per sentence was similar by sex. The only significant difference was at 17 years of age, and this variation favored the males, the only instance in which they were superior. Though the males showed decrements in total words and total sentences at 15 years, they showed no such decrement in words per sentence. Their growth in words written per sentence was uniform from one age level to the next (see the growth curves in Volume One). They exceeded the females at 17 years because the females began to plateau at 13 years. The males manifested steady growth up to and including the age of 17 years. These results indicate that the growth patterns for written language by sex are not identical.

Syntax

Early maturation of syntactical ability was shown by both sexes. Differences appeared only at 11 and 15 years of age. Though a trend can be seen for the females to mature earlier, the sexes were equivalent in acquisition of syntax.

Abstract-Concrete

The sexes varied at one age level, 15 years, in conveyance of abstract meaning. This difference serves as a clue to the variations in maturational pattern by sex. The females made substantial gain from 13 to 15 years but little growth thereafter. In comparison, the males made slight gain from 13 to 15 years, with greater increment from 15 to 17 years. Like the other findings, these results indicate that the girls achieved maturity earlier than the boys. Despite this variation, both sexes made progress in expression of meaning throughout the entire age range. The difference, which was minor, was not in ability to express ideas but in the age at which this facet of written language reached its highest level. Neither sex was superior in communication of abstract meaning.

Summary

Of the nine statistically significant differences by sex, all but one favored the females, and four out of the nine (44 percent) were at the age of 15 years. The distribution of the differences was as follows: two at 7, one at 9, one at 11, none at 13, four at 15, and one at 17 years. At 7 and 15 years these differences reached the .01 level of significance; at 9, 11, and 17 years the level of significance was .05. These sex differences can be explained by the earlier maturation of females, being most obvious at 7 and 15 years.

The age-level analysis also showed this trend (see Tables 8 through 12); the females made no significant growth between the ages of 15 and 17 years. The 17-year-old males were superior to the 15-year-olds on total words, total sentences, and abstract-concrete. The males and females essentially were equal in facility with the written word by 17 years of age, but the females attained this level of function at approximately 15 years of age. The males made gains up to 17 years, not having attained a plateau even at this age for total words and total sentences or for abstract meaning. These differences by sex in growth patterns for written language should be recognized in educational programs.

INTERCORRELATIONS FOR WRITTEN LANGUAGE

There are a number of reasons for studying the interrelations among the scores derived from the PSLT. A scientific-clinical interest concerns clarification of the extent to which each of the five scores is independent. The interdependence of length of the product, syntactical correctness, and communication of meaning have not been studied previously.

There are other questions. Children often score high on one factor and low on others. Hence, the diagnostic usefulness, with implications for remedial instruction, might be enhanced by study of the interrelations of the scores. Such application of the PSLT is indicated by the results for exceptional children, as shown in the chapters that follow.

The relation of the five scores, one with the other, was evaluated in two ways. The first included the total sample as a group ($N=747$). In the second analysis age and sex were controlled to ascertain the influence of these variables.

Analysis of the Total Sample

Age

Chronological age, a critical indicator of developmental maturity, was studied in relation to the written language scores for the total sample. Ability to use the written word, age by age from early school life, has not been studied extensively. That age relations exist is apparent from the results given in Table 14. There were significant correlations between chronological age and all five of the scores on the PSLT. The order of magnitude from highest to lowest was words per sentence, abstract-concrete, total words, syntax, and total sentences. These findings are in agreement with those presented in Volume One, as well as with those discussed below. All the statistical analyses showed a high correlation between chronological age and words per sentence. Sentence length increased largely on the basis of increasing maturity as reflected by life age. But as found in the studies of exceptional children, when disabilities are present, irrespective of their nature, length of the sentence is reduced (see Part Two).

Length of the story and ability to convey depth of meaning also correlated with chronological age. As the child became older he not only wrote stories of greater length but he expressed more and more complex meaning. The two scores showing least relation with age were number of sentences and syntactical correctness. These results support earlier findings to the effect that after 9 to 11 years of age both these factors plateau; the child does not continue to write more and more sentences throughout all age levels. After he has acquired facility with complex language forms, he writes longer sentences, therefore fewer sentences per story. As revealed by our previous studies, facility with syntactical structure is accomplished early in life, largely by the age of 9 years. Because of minimal growth after 11 years of age, syntax is less associated with chronological age. Nevertheless, this varies greatly for exceptional children.

Total Words

Number of words written was significantly related with all four of the other scores. But the order of magnitude varied; the highest association was with total sentences, followed by abstract-concrete, words per sentence, and syntax. These findings suggest that the longer the story, the more sentences are required. A less obvious finding is that the more words used, the higher is the level of abstract meaning in the story. Language fluency (as indicated by total words), abstract ideas, and meaning were interrelated. Number of words correlated with abstraction to a higher degree than any of the other four measures. This implies that word fluency is related to imagination, use of abstract thought, and expression of meaning (see discussion of factor analysis). Total words was also correlated with words per sentence and syntax, but these relations were not as firm.

Total Sentences

As stated above, number of sentences and number of words were closely interrelated for normal children. This was not true for certain types of exceptional children. For example, the deaf, who are severely limited in language and who find it difficult to write long sentences, do not follow this pattern (Myklebust, 1964). Total sentences too was related to abstract-concrete and syntax, but not to words per sentence. Next to total words, the primary association was with depth of meaning (use of abstract thought). Again, abstraction and amount of language were closely interrelated.

Words per Sentence

A close association was found between chronological age and number of words written per sentence, as noted previously. To a high degree, words per sentence appears to be a function of the organismic integrity of the child. This factor was related to total words, abstract-concrete, and, to a lesser extent, to syntax; it did not correlate with total sentences. As shown by the studies of exceptional children, the number of words written per sentence is affected by various disabilities (see Part Two).

Syntax

Of the five scores, syntax showed least interrelation with other scores; the highest correlation was with abstract-concrete (.38). Language correctness, though a factor of importance, was not closely associated with number of words or sentences written, or with sentence length. But as shown below, these results varied with chronological age.

Abstract-Concrete

This scale was developed as a measure of meaning: the more abstract the ideas, the greater the depth of the meaning expressed. Use of abstraction was correlated with all the other scores, the order of magnitude being total words, total sentences, words per sentence, and syntax. The correlation with productivity, however, was much greater than that with syntactical accuracy. For normal children, language fluency and depth of meaning were closely interrelated. The greater the number of words they wrote, the more sentences they wrote, and the longer the sentence, the more abstract were the ideas conveyed in the story. For both normal and exceptional children, if verbal fluency and productivity can be fostered, expression of meaning will be enhanced. On the other hand, the stimulation of abstract ideas may bring about greater language fluency.

Analysis by Age and Sex

Because acquisition of written language varied by sex, an analysis was made to explore further the intercorrelation patterns among the PSLT scores by age and sex, including all the males (N=373) and females (N=374); the samples by age varied from a total of 61 to 64 for each sex. These results are presented in Table 15.

Total Words

The interrelations among number of words written and the other scores varied by age and sex. This might be expected inasmuch as the various factors of written language matured at different rates for each of the sexes. Nevertheless, although girls showed earlier maturation and greater language facility, the associations among these aspects of language and story length remained equivalent. Children who wrote the longest stories also wrote the most sentences and communicated the highest degree of abstract meaning, irrespective of age and sex.

Differences appeared in other comparisons: total words and words per sentence were unrelated for the females but were correlated at 7 and 9 years of age for the males. Syntax and story length were significantly associated for the males at 7, 9, and 11 years, but only at 7 years for the females. These variations by age and sex seem to reflect differences in rate of maturation. Story length was correlated mainly with number of sentences and abstract meaning for both sexes. Otherwise, this factor was slightly associated with sentence length for the males at the lower age level. It was also correlated with syntax for both sexes but again the relation was greater for the males.

Total Sentences

The number of sentences written and story length were closely related. Nevertheless, total sentences was negatively associated with words per sentence for both sexes from 11 through 17 years. Beginning at 11 years of age, the more sentences written, the shorter they tended to be. As shown previously (see Volume One), there was little increase in number of sentences after 11 years of age. Though number of words continued to increase, the child was capable of writing longer sentences and so had no need for more and more sentences; thus the relation between number of sentences and sentence length was negative after 11 years. That the child who cannot write longer and longer sentences must write more and more short ones is shown by the studies of exceptional children.

Total sentences, like total words, correlated with meaning, but the pattern varied by age and sex. For the females this correlation was significant at all age levels except at 15 years. For the males this relation was not significant at either 15 or 17 years. Number of sentences and abstract meaning were related for the males at 9, 11, and 13 years. These scores correlated for the females too, but only at 11 and 13 years. To some extent use of sentences and facility with abstract meaning varied by age and sex.

Number of sentences and syntax were interrelated for both sexes, but only at the lower age levels. These findings are consistent with previous results showing that syntax is acquired early in life; there is only slight improvement in syntax after 11 years. Therefore, as demonstrated by this correlation analysis, when syntax was being acquired, there was a relation with number of sentences written.

Words per Sentence

Except for total sentences, number of words per sentence was correlated with the other scores without regard for age and sex (see Table 14). When this analysis was made by age and sex, the results differed (see Table 15). For example, after 11 years there was a negative correlation with number of sentences; there was little increment in total sentences, but the number of words written per sentence continued to increase. The negative correlation confirms other findings in showing that at 11 years of age children shift from writing more and more sentences to writing longer ones. This was true of both sexes.

Otherwise, when analyzed by age and sex, words per sentence was correlated only with a few of the other scores. There was a correlation with syntax for both sexes at 7 years of age, and with abstract-concrete for the males at 7 years and for the females at 11 years. It is unusual that at 11 years all the correlations were negative, presumably because at this age level a plateau occurred for the other factors, whereas words per sentence showed marked linearity throughout the entire age range.

Syntax

Correctness of the language written correlated with the other scores at the lower age levels. For example, at 7 years of age there were significant relations for both sexes with all four of the other measures. This interrelation continued through 11 years for the males but appeared mainly at 7 years for the females. In early life syntax is a critical indicator of general facility in use of the written word. When development is normal, syntax ceases to be a major influence in females at 9 years and in males at 13 years.

Abstract-Concrete

The factors showing closest relation with abstract meaning were total words and total sentences, both measures of amount of language produced. The more the child described only that which was portrayed in the picture, the more he was stimulus-bound, and the shorter was his story. When imagination was used, giving the story a setting, plot, and purpose, the product was longer.

The interrelations between depth of meaning and the more technical aspects of language usage, such as words per sentence and syntax, were minimal, occurring at 7 and 9 years for the males and only at 7 years for the females. Level of meaning was associated much more with amount of language used than with its complexity (see Table 17).

A STUDY OF THIRD- AND FOURTH-GRADE PUBLIC-SCHOOL CHILDREN

Since completion of the initial standardization study, other investigations have been undertaken. One involved comparison of learning-disability and normal third- and fourth-grade public-school children. Because of their importance the results for normal children are presented below (see also Chapter VIII). For comparison with the standardization data it must be noted that these third- and fourth-graders were attending suburban schools.

The mean chronological age for the sample was 9.2 years. As a control group these children had been given an individual test of intelligence (Wechsler Intelligence Scale for Children, WISC) and their IQ's had been found to fall above 90. They also had been screened for ability to hear and see, and had been shown to have no gross disturbance of motor ability or of emotional adjustment. In other words, this sample was shown by examination to fall within normal limits on several variables.

The results for this selected sample, compared with the 9-year age group in the original standardization sample, are shown in Table 16. Except for ability to convey abstract meaning, the two samples were equivalent; however, the third- and fourth-graders scored below the suburban children originally studied (see Tables 1 through 5).

When reviewing the findings for a given child, group, or school it is necessary to consider the total circumstances because the results may vary on the basis of the type of school attended. Nevertheless, the results for the third- and fourth-graders are in close agreement with the original findings; therefore, the norms as established can be used for interpretation of test scores for most school children.

The Factors Measured

When the studies of written language were initiated, the PSLT was evolved to include three primary facets of verbal functioning:

productivity (amount of language produced) ; syntax (correctness) ; and abstract-concrete (meaning). After more data had been gathered, it was feasible to ascertain what factors were involved—the factors measured by the PSLT. To do this, a factor analysis was made of the scores for the 238 third- and fourth-graders. The results are presented in Table 17.

These data reveal three factors that must be considered when interpreting results for the PSLT, as shown also by the intercorrelation analysis (see Table 15). Though five scores are obtained from the test, only three basic factors are involved for normal children. Factor 1 comprises the number of words and sentences written and use of abstract meaning; number of words and sentences and use of abstract ideas are related. The precise nature of this relation is not clearly understood.

Factor 2 is syntax. The initial postulation—that a person may be verbally productive and yet syntactically incorrect—is supported by these results. Fluency, measured by the number of words and sentences written, does not assure successful learning of syntax. Further evidence of this is found in the studies of exceptional children, who sometimes have good ability in producing the expected story length but are deficient in syntax. The opposite also occurs. These factor-analysis results assist in formulation of a construct of written language and indicate the areas in need of remediation.

Factor 3 is words per sentence. Though scored as a measure of productivity, sentence length is relatively independent of the other scores. As indicated previously, words per sentence is developmentally stable and linear. As a factor, however, it is elusive and difficult to define. Presumably, facility with long sentences entails ability to formulate thoughts and to convert complex ideas into appropriate word forms so that intricate meanings can be expressed. This factor is in need of more investigation (McNeill, 1970).

Since only approximately 60 percent of the variance is accounted for by these three factors, other variables must be involved in success with written language. The data for exceptional children suggest that vision, hearing, mental ability, emotional disturbance, learning disabilities, and opportunity for schooling play an important role in learning to use the written word. In this study of third- and fourth-graders, these factors were controlled. It is significant that even 60 percent of the variance was accounted for by scores on the PSLT.

WORD USAGE IN WRITTEN LANGUAGE

Language development can be studied in a number of ways (Leopold, 1961; McNeill, 1966; Chomsky, 1967; Lenneberg, 1967). The design varies according to its purpose, but rarely have investigators focused on the relation of type of word acquired and developmental growth. Normal children do not acquire all words with equal facility, and chronological age is influential in determining when a given type of word will be incorporated into the vocabulary. Moreover, various types of disabilities affect the types of words acquired.

The question of the specific vocabulary attained year by year is important to understanding cognitive development and has connotations for the needs of exceptional children. For example, adverb usage by normal children varies by sex, and children with profound deafness from early life attain almost no use of this word form (Myklebust, 1964; VandenBerg, 1971). It appears, therefore, that there is a psychology of "word-type" development, not only a psychology of language development. Continuing with the example of the adverb, usage of this word form is attained by normal children mainly after 9 years of age (see Figure 7), and some handicapped children achieve only rudimentary proficiency with this word type. A possible explanation is that adverbs are used principally to qualify verbs and to express "some relation of place, time, manner, attendant circumstance, degree, cause, inference, result, condition, exception, concession, purpose, or means" (Barnhart, 1952). Compared with nouns, adverbial meanings are more complex and abstract. Moreover, if usage of this word type is not attained, cognitive functions, as well as learning mode, may be modified substantially.

In view of the importance of the relation of word type to developmental processes, the pattern of word usage in normal children was investigated. Using random selection, 200 stories were chosen, 40 at each of the age levels (20 for each sex) of 7, 9, 11, 13 and 15 years; the 17-year level was not included. The children who wrote the 200 stories were equated by age, intelligence, and sex. All the words written per story were tabulated on the basis of the part of speech into which the word typically would be classified (Perrin, 1942). The parts of speech were nouns, pronouns, verbs (present, past, future), adjectives, adverbs, infinitives, articles, prepositions, conjunctions, and interjections. The results are presented below.

Word-Type Comparison by Sex on Basis of All Words Written per Story

The findings from this analysis are shown in Table 18. The scores are the median percents of each part of speech represented in the story. The primary differences in word type appeared at 9 and 15 years. At 9 years the females used more pronouns, past-tense verbs, adverbs, prepositions, and conjunctions. At 15 years they exceeded the males in use of nouns, pronouns, adjectives, infinitives, adverbs, articles, prepositions, conjunctions, and interjections; the males and females were equivalent only in the use of verbs.

It seems that the females not only were more fluent than the males, as shown by their greater language output, but that the quality of their product also was superior. The implication for the psychology of language development is that the compositions written by children should be expected to vary by sex. Moreover, productions by boys should be appraised in comparison with those by other boys; those written by girls should be appraised in comparison with the work of other girls. But the role of educational procedures and methods must not be overlooked. Possibly, if proficiency in written language were stressed, keeping in mind the differences by sex, boys might develop greater facility and attain levels of usage equivalent to those of girls. Nevertheless, because of obvious variations by sex, psychologists and educators cannot view acquisition of the written word as an equal task for boys and girls. Recognition of this fact points out the need for variations in school programs.

Word-Type Comparison by Sex on Basis of Number of Different Words Written per Story

In the study of language development it is necessary to investigate both quantity and quality. Here the concern is with the richness of the vocabulary. This analysis disclosed the number of different words occurring within each category, not the incidence by word type. The quality of the child's vocabulary was put to test. As in the case of word-type incidence, the greatest variations were at 9 and 15 years, favoring the females (Table 19). At 9 years the girls used a greater variety of pronouns, past-tense verbs, and adverbs. The use of different adverbs by the girls was remarkable in comparison with the boys' productions; the girls' variety of usage was between three and four times greater.

There were almost no significant variations at the ages of 11 and 13 years. At this age interval the sexes were equal in their vocabularies; they were "talking the same language." This uniformity may be accounted for by the plateau experienced by the females, which allowed the males to reach a comparable level in quality of vocabulary. But at 15 years many differences appeared. More different words were written by the females in 7 out of the 12 comparisons. The males were equivalent only in the use of verbs, articles, and conjunctions. The girls attained greater richness of language earlier than the boys, entered into a plateau between 11 and 13 years, but by 15 years developed a variety of word usage that far exceeded the boys'.

The significance of these findings to learning, psychological adjustment, and creativity remains to be explored. Nevertheless, because educational and school achievement generally is judged in verbal terms, females either innately or experientially have a distinct advantage. Through earlier and superior use of pronouns, they are more capable of expressing personal reference without fixed meaning. But it is because of their more fluid use of adverbs that they are in position to convey relations and subtleties that are advantageous to psychological adjustment. It would be of considerable interest to ascertain whether males and females vary in nonverbal faculties. Is the nonverbal area the forte of males? Moreover, handicaps often preclude use of certain word types, especially adverbs. These language disabilities are critical to learning and to general psychological well-being, Though yet unexplored, analogical and metaphorical reasoning seems closely associated with facility in use of word forms that specify qualitative, relational, and fluid facets of experience. Handicaps that limit such language usage may be the most disabling of all.

Growth Curves by Word Type

The word-type usage patterns also were compared graphically. The data plotted were identical to those presented in the tables. The growth curves for the various word types on the basis of all the words written per story are presented first.

Nouns

The graphic pattern for noun usage is shown in Figure 1. A greater number of nouns was employed per story by both males and females as they became older. However, the patterns of increment by sex were not identical. The males made moderate, consistent gains from

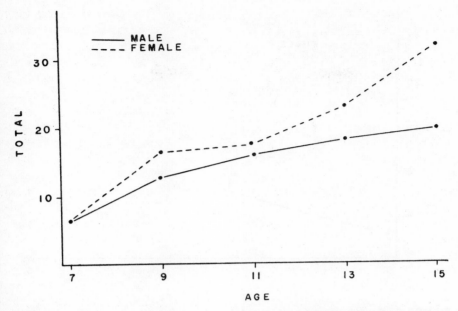

FIGURE 1. Comparison of males and females on number of nouns used in the story.

one age level to the next. Conversely, the females increased rapidly in noun usage from 7 to 9 years, then manifested no gain from 9 to 11 years—a characteristic of their growth pattern. From 11 to 15 years they demonstrated another rapid rise in use of nouns, gradually exceeding the males to a greater and greater extent.

Pronouns

The growth curves for pronouns also varied by sex (see Figure 2). The males typically made slow consistent gains throughout the age range from 7 to 15 years. Though gradual, their configuration was highly linear, with an increase per story of slightly less than two pronouns at each 2-year interval, approximately one per year. The females made greater gains per age interval in early life but declined in pronoun usage at 11 years. Hence, the growth curves are equivalent from 11 to 13 years. Then, typically, from 13 to 15 years the females made an unusually rapid gain in use of this part of speech.

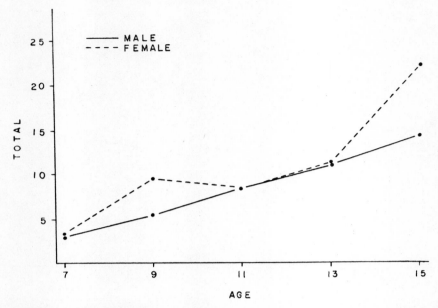

FIGURE 2. Comparison of males and females on number of pronouns used in the story.

Verbs

To obtain more complete information on acquisition of verb usage, the past, present, and future forms were treated separately. The results for present-tense verbs are shown in Figure 3. The sexes performed similarly from 7 to 11 years, increasing from two to four present verbs per story during this span of 4 years. Beyond 11 years the males continued to make slow, consistent gains, but the females achieved a dramatic increment, especially from 13 to 15 years of age. As shown in Figure 4, the pattern of growth for past-tense verbs was more similar by sex. The females exceeded the males, especially at 9 and 15 years, but the patterns were not highly divergent.

The use of future-tense verbs was revealing if not surprising. Very slight reference to the future was made by either sex until 13 years of age. In the written form, this part of speech was unusually late in developing (see Figure 5). Nevertheless, with the females leading, both sexes made rapid progress in use of this verb tense after 13 years. The significance of this finding is not clear, but reference to the future in written form may not be consequential to children until early adolescence. Whatever the true meaning in terms of maturation and

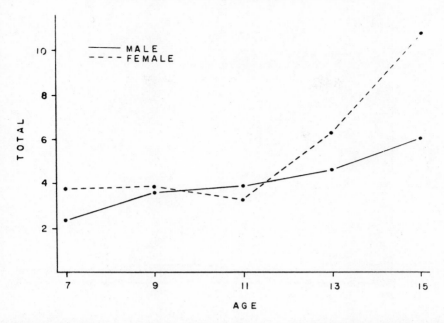

FIGURE 3. Comparison of males and females on number of present verbs used in the story.

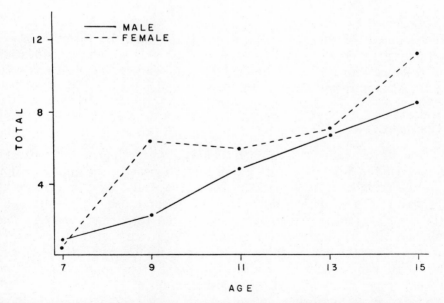

FIGURE 4. Comparison of males and females on number of past verbs used in the story.

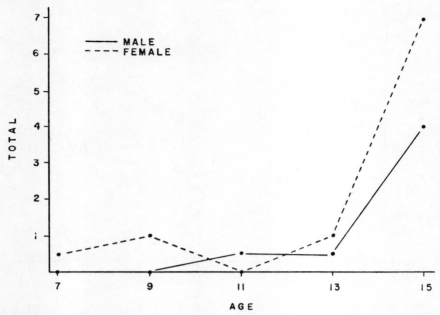

FIGURE 5. Comparison of males and females on number of future verbs used in the story.

development of time concepts, even at 15 years the future tense is employed far less frequently than the past and present. Clarification of these results and their importance to other psychological and educational factors must await further investigation.

Adjectives

One of the most linear and congruous developmental patterns appeared for adjectives (see Figure 6). Moreover, the configuration for the females was not typical; adjective usage did not plateau at 11 years. The statistical data disclosed greater use of adjectives by the females, and this is apparent also from the growth curves. The females increased from two adjectives per story at 7 years to 17 adjectives at the age of 15 years, a gain of almost two adjectives per year. By comparison the males progressed from approximately one adjective per story at 7 years to a maximum of 11 at the age of 15, a rate of little more than one adjective per year. Girls seem to have an advantage over boys in expression of qualitative meanings. But

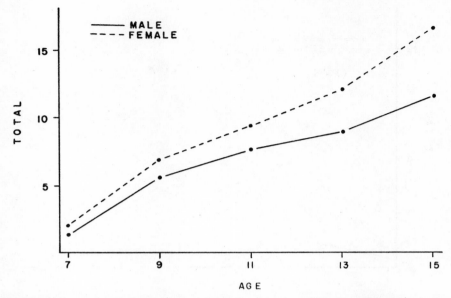

FIGURE 6. Comparison of males and females on number of adjectives used in the story.

additional study of these variations by sex is needed. Such information is critical to further understanding of the associations between language, learning, and cognition.

Adverbs

Another wide variation by sex occurred in the development of adverb usage (see Figure 7). The females characteristically made rapid gains from 7 to 9 years of age, followed by a decrement at 11 years. Thereafter, they again manifested rapid growth, exceeding the males by nearly six adverbs per story at the age of 15 years. The males also performed in a typical manner, making uniform gains from one age level to the next, their greatest increment occurring between 11 and 15 years. Acquisition of adverb usage varied widely by sex.

Though the psychological significance of these findings is not yet fully realized, a number of questions come to mind. It has been shown that males and females differ in acquisition and use of language. But psychologists and educators have been reluctant to take such find-

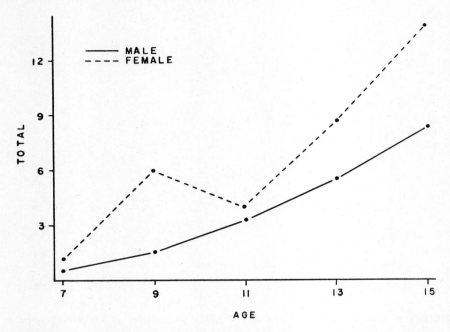

FIGURE 7. Comparison of males and females on number of adverbs used in the story.

ings seriously. If we are to provide maximum advantage for learning, in and out of school, the significance of these findings must be explored. The specific effects of handicapping conditions, all types of disabilities, should be ascertained.

Perhaps the most vital question concerns the implications for interpersonal relations, for perception and expression of feelings and of subtle meanings. Some of the most apparent sex differences concern acquisition and use of adjectives and adverbs, and it is precisely these word forms that are especially relevant to communication of emotional, qualitative meanings experienced in daily life. An obvious need, therefore, is for educators to initiate programs that focus on raising the level of such language usage in males. In addition, behavioral scientists should conduct investigations aimed at further clarifying the consequences of these variations by sex. Only then can the next step be accomplished: expansion of knowledge about the extent to which males and females can become equivalent in this sphere of learning.

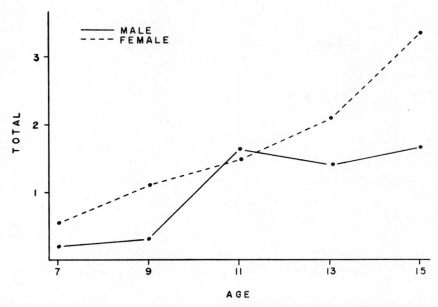

FIGURE 8. Comparison of males and females on number of infinitives used in the story.

Infinitives

Meager use was made of infinitives. Moreover, the growth curves were not typical for either of the sexes, as shown in Figure 8. The males made unusual gains at 9 years, peaked at 11 years, then declined moderately at 13 years, and remained on a plateau to 15 years. The females showed uniform increments by age from 7 to 13 years, then attained a sharp upward trend between the years of 13 and 15. The variation by sex was substantial.

Articles

The sexes were more equal in use of articles than in use of most of the other word types. The primary difference was that the females manifested gains at the age of 13, whereas the males declined slightly between 13 and 15 years. At the age of 15 the females used approximately 12 articles per story, while the males used this word form only about 9 times per story (see Figure 9).

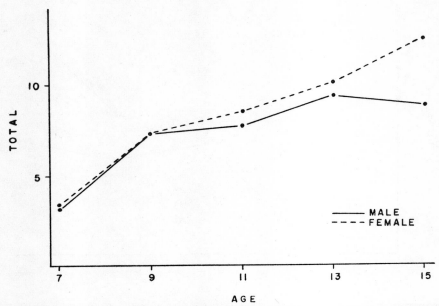

FIGURE 9. Comparison of males and females on number of articles used in the story.

Prepositions

As with articles, the primary differences in use of prepositions occurred between 13 and 15 years. The females made a sharp rise in use of this word type at 13, but the males showed no gain from 13 to 15 years. As a result, at the higher age level the females exceeded the males at a rate of more than five prepositions per story (see Figure 10).

Conjunctions

The developmental configuration for conjunctions was characteristic by sex. The males made uniform gains and showed considerable linearity from 7 to 15 years, as shown in Figure 11. The females too followed their typical pattern of rapid increments from 7 to 9 years and rapid gains thereafter, especially between 13 and 15 years.

Interjections

The growth pattern for interjections also varied by sex. The males made very slight use of this word type, as did the females until the

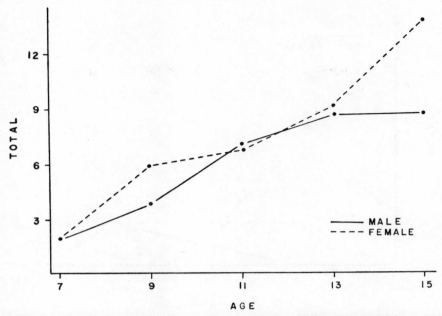

FIGURE 10. Comparison of males and females on number of prepositions used in the story.

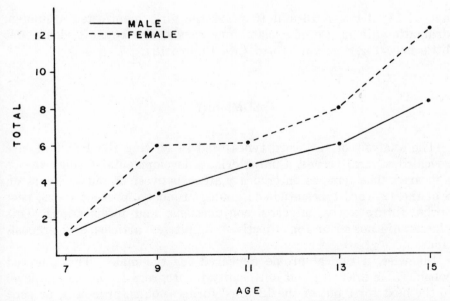

FIGURE 11. Comparison of males and females on number of conjunctions used in the story.

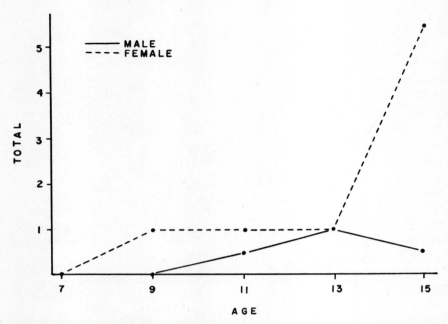

FIGURE 12. Comparison of males and females on number of interjections used in the story.

age of 13. Between 13 and 15 years the girls manifested a sudden, dramatic gain in use of exclamatory words. The boys, it seems, felt little need for this word form (see Figure 12).

SUMMARY

The analysis of the word types used in writing the PSLT stories revealed several trends. Characteristic developmental configurations appeared. The females entered a plateau between 9 and 11 years on 8 of the 12 word types studied: nouns, pronouns, present verbs, past verbs, future verbs, adverbs, conjunctions, and interjections. This plateau did not occur for adjectives, infinitives, articles, and prepositions.

Likewise, a typical profile appeared for the males. They showed considerable linearity and uniformity in progress from one age level to the next for 9 out of the 12 word forms: nouns, pronouns, present verbs, past verbs, adverbs, adjectives, articles, prepositions, and conjunctions. This characteristic pattern did not appear for infinitives, future verbs, and interjections.

These results indicate that acquisition of written language developmentally varies systematically by sex. Moreover, these differences are specific to certain types of words. Also, in general, males showed little growth by word type after 13 years, whereas females often exhibited wide gains from 13 to 15 years of age. A ready explanation for these differences is not at hand, but an immediate question concerns the effectiveness of school programs for each of the sexes. To illustrate, one of the most significant variations occurred in use of adjectives and adverbs. Because of the importance of these word forms in expression of relations and quality of meaning, it is incumbent on educators to attempt to teach these facets of language, with special emphasis on the needs of boys. The limitations in language usage indicated by these studies are not necessarily irremediable if appropriate educational programs and excellent teaching are provided. On the other hand, recognition of sex differences has broad implications for study of the psychology of language. These variations urgently need investigation inasmuch as they may be related to the learning styles and cognitive processes underlying many facets of school failure, especially in males.

Word-Type Intercorrelations for Males and Females Combined

Frequency of word-type use has been studied in the past, but the extent to which use of a certain word form is related to use of others has rarely been investigated. Such developmental relations in written language were explored through an intercorrelation analysis of the word types for the sexes combined; the results are presented in Tables 20 through 24. The following discussion is based on an interpretation in which a correlation of .50 or greater was used as a cutoff point.

At 7 years the intercorrelation of word classes was not well established; nouns were associated with articles and prepositions, pronouns with past-tense verbs and prepositions. There was a greater number of correlations above .50 at 9 years; nouns were related with six other word forms, pronouns with five, adjectives with two, past-tense verbs with three, future-tense verbs with one, infinitives with one, and adverbs with one. At 11 years there was only a moderate change, but articles and conjunctions now showed relations with other word types. At 13 years there were many changes. For example, nouns correlated (above .50) with 9 out of the 11 possibilities; total words and total verbs were omitted. Moreover, all but one of the word types (prepositions) showed a high relation with the other word classes.

Using the incidence of intercorrelations as a criterion, a high degree of flexibility in usage was not established in written language until at least 13 years of age. After this age there was a plateau; the number of correlations remained the same from 13 to 15 years. Totaling the number of correlations by age (Tables 20 through 24) shows that there were 22 at 7 years, 41 at 9 years, 29 at 11 years, 53 at 13 years, and 53 at 15 years; total verbs and total words were omitted. The typical decline from 9 to 11 years was observed in these results, with a gain from 11 to 13 years but no gain thereafter. The interrelations among the word classes were established by 13 years of age. Unless these word relations are achieved, fluency and complexity of language cannot be attained. This may be the basis for many of the cognitive limitations in exceptional children.

There were significant sidelights to this analysis. Using .50 as the cutoff point (omitting total verbs), there were 5 correlations with number of words written at 7 years, 9 at 9 years, 7 at 11 years, 11 at 13, and 8 at 15. With typical exceptions, the pattern was that the more interrelations among the word types, the longer the story, but only up to 13 years of age. Again, there was a plateau between 13 and 15 years.

Another such sidelight was the negative correlation for past and present verbs. At 7 years the figure was $-.29$, at 9 years this negative relation increased to $-.49$, and at 11 years it was $-.63$. At the ages of 13 and 15 the correlation was $-.41$ and $-.40$, respectively. These results suggest a developmental pattern for use of past and present tense. The more present tense was used, the less reference to the past. This interaction increased steadily up to 11 years. Thereafter, usage of these time sequences stabilized, but the future tense was interrelated only rarely with the other word types. As noted previously, this time reference appeared late in the developmental pattern.

Summary

The word-type relations with the sexes combined followed a pattern of growth from one age to the next. But if these interrelations are taken as a criterion, this configuration does not go beyond 13 years of age. Facility in use of word classes in written language may be fully established by the age of 13. These findings are in agreement with the results for syntax, in which there was slight growth after 13 years.

Intercorrelation of Word Type by Age and Sex

Certain qualitative aspects of language development cannot be ascertained without determining the interdependence of one word with another. The first words acquired by children are nouns, referred to in Volume One as *naming level*. Later nouns are combined with verbs to form short, descriptive sentences such as *Boy run*. But there is little information available concerning the more complex relations among the primary word forms as the child gains greater facility with language. Using the intercorrelation technique, the interdependence of each of the word types by age and sex was investigated. Hence, it was possible to analyze further the developmental characteristics of written language. The same random sample of 200 stories used in the other word-type studies formed the basis of this evaluation (see Tables 25 through 29).

7 Years

The number of significant intercorrelations by word type for the 7-year-olds is shown in Table 30. There was a total of 38 relations among the word classes for the girls and 74 among those written by the boys, almost twice as many for the males. This wide variation occurred mainly because of the greater association of six of the word types for the males: nouns, pronouns, adjectives, future-tense verbs, articles, and prepositions. The relation of adjectives to other word forms serves as an illustration; no such correlations were found for females but for males there were six.

There was a critical difference in the way words were combined to form sentences in early school life, the age at which children begin to acquire facility with the written word. The psychodynamics of these variations in learning styles are not clear. Nevertheless, it seems that females are less dependent on global facets of language; they acquire each word form more independently. Conversely, males are more dependent on acquiring use of the various word forms simultaneously. Possibly this difference is due to greater (or earlier) verbal facility in females. Further study may reveal the importance of these differences to cognition and learning.

9 Years

At 7 years of age many more significant correlations appeared for the males. At 9 years this pattern was reversed. For the females there was a total of 106 relations among the word types, but only 61 for the males, a difference of 45. The major variation, favoring the girls, derived from the correlations for nouns, pronouns, past-tense verbs, adjectives, infinitives, articles, and conjunctions. These results contradict the supposition that females have greater verbal facility than males, as suggested by the discussion of the 7-year-olds. If a global learning style is assumed to be advantageous, the males attained this style earlier than the females. Though the exact meaning of these variations by sex must await further study, at 7 years the pattern of learning was more inclusive for males. This pattern did not appear for females until 9 years.

11 Years

The intercorrelation by sex at 11 years was substantially less variable. There were 96 relations for the males and 84 for the females; only two wide differences appeared and these involved nouns and interjections. These findings are in agreement with the incidence studies of word type on the basis of all of the words written (see Table 18). Though widely different at 7 and 9 years, characteristically the sexes performed similarly at 11 years.

13 Years

Also typical, following the uniformity at 11 years, was the difference at 13 years. This pattern was manifested again in this intercorrelation analysis. There were 151 significant intercorrelations for the females and only 74 for the males; 77 more for the females. Of the 13 comparisons, 9 were more interrelated with other word forms for the females. Moreover, the females showed a maximum number of associations (12) 8 times, and only 1 less than maximum (11) was exhibited twice. A given word type, such as a verb, was closely related to all the other word forms when used by the females. This pattern was much less apparent for the males.

15 Years

At 15 years the number of word-type relations again favored the females but the difference was less marked than at 13 years: 123 for the females and 90 for the males. No wide variations occurred for a single word class. The pattern was for the males to gain between 13 and 15 years but for the females to decline.

Summary

A pattern of variation by age and sex was disclosed by this inter-correlation analysis. In early life (7 years) male usage showed greater interdependence among the various word types. At 9 years this trend was reversed, females having a greater global learning pattern. No major difference was found at 11 years, but thereafter the females again took the lead, the greatest variation by sex occurring at 13 years. Another notable difference, as shown in Table 30, was the configuration for males and females. The pattern of relations among the word types for the males showed a decline from 7 to 9 years, an increment from 9 to 11, a decline from 11 to 13, and another increment from 13 to 15 years. In comparison, the pattern for the females showed a marked rise from 7 to 9 years, a decline from 9 to 11, another marked gain from 11 to 13 years, with a moderate decline from 13 to 15 years.

Though these findings are difficult to interpret, consistent with a number of other findings, the females achieved maturation at an earlier age than the males. Also, comparatively, males did not attain the same level of language usage. If we assume that close correlation among the word classes is indicative of richness and fluidity in use of the written word, then the females were superior. Further research might reveal the consequences of these variations in acquisition of written language, especially with regard to the cognitive-verbal learning styles that characterize the sexes.

THE WRITTEN LANGUAGE OF URUGUAYAN AND AMERICAN CHILDREN: A CROSS-CULTURAL STUDY

Workers in various countries are pursuing studies of language development. Fortunately, it is possible to compare the acquisition of written language by normal and exceptional children in different countries (Tuana, 1971; VandenBerg, 1971). Such investigations are critical to constructs concerning the psychoneurology of learning. For example, the left hemisphere of the brain carries major responsibility for verbal language learning when the verbal system is phonetic, as in the Western world (Mountcastle, 1962). When the system is ideographic, however, differences in the psychoneurology of learning are predicted. Because ideograms are pictographic and nonverbal, it appears that the right hemisphere has major responsibility for acquisition of this form of written expression. Evidence is forthcoming which supports this construct (Millikan and Darley, 1967).

There are also critical psychological considerations. For example, languages such as French, Spanish, and English may present varying levels of difficulty in learning. If so, comparative developmental growth curves would vary. Another factor is the extent to which opportunities for written language learning differ from one country to another. Such considerations must encompass the laws pertaining to school entrance, methods of teaching, and availability of schools.

Because translations are not involved, and because the PSLT can be given to small groups, cross-cultural studies are not difficult to accomplish. The child writes his story in his native tongue. The standardized scoring procedures can be used (except for ideographic writing when exceptions must be made).

The Written Language of Uruguayan Children

A major step forward in the study of written language has been accomplished through the work of Tuana and her associates in Uruguay (1971). This is the most extensive investigation made outside of the United States. This contribution made possible definitive comparisons between Uruguayan and American children in acquisition of written language and provided information on learning Spanish as compared with learning English.

Tuana administered the PSLT to 413 boys and 368 girls, a total sample of 781 children. The children were distributed throughout the elementary-school age as follows:

Grade	Males	Females	Total
2nd	94	58	152
3rd	77	75	152
4th	94	77	171
5th	61	80	141
6th	87	78	165
Total	413	368	781

Mental ages were derived by grade through administration of the Kuhlmann-Anderson Test. Using these scores as a basis, the grade scores were converted into age-level scores, making them comparable to those used in standardizing the PSLT on American children. Data are given only for 7-, 9-, and 11-year-olds because 13- and 15-year-olds were not included in the Uruguayan investigation.

Total Words

Calculation of number of words written is a convenient way to secure information on facility with the written word. Initially it was not predicted that total words would be valuable as an indicator of progress in language acquisition; data to this effect also were presented in Volume One. The comparative statistics for Uruguayan and American children shown in Table 31 reveal that the Uruguayan group wrote more words per story than the American at 7 years, but at 9 and 11 years they were equivalent. There was progressive maturation for both groups, with the females producing more words than the males (see Figure 13). Even though they were learning different languages, and there were wide geographical and cultural differences, the written language form was acquired at a given rate, presumably determined by developmental factors.

Total Sentences

In the standardization studies (on American children) close association was found between number of words and number of sentences written per story, but the pattern was for number of sentences to

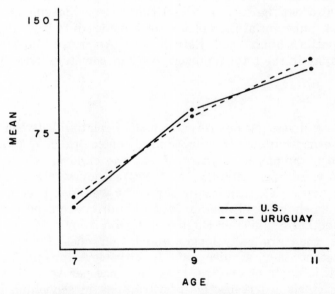

FIGURE 13. Comparison of U.S. and Uruguayan children on total words.

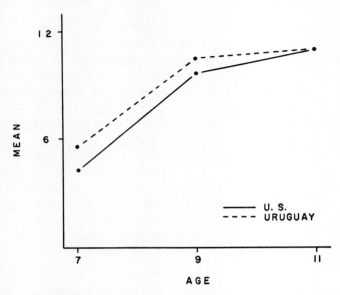

FIGURE 14. Comparison of U.S. and Uruguayan children on total sentences.

diminish as the child became older. This trend began at 11 years of age, apparently because the child then was ready to write longer and longer sentences so he did not write more and more of them. This pattern also can be seen in the Uruguayan children, as shown in Figure 14. Substantial increments were made up to 9 years, then the growth pattern diminished. Both groups, American and Uruguayan, were similar in the total sentences written per story (see Table 32).

Words per Sentence

The early investigations revealed a close relation between the number of words written per story and chronological age (see Volume One). For example, at 7 years of age the children wrote approximately 7 words per sentence, at 9 years they wrote 9, and at 11 years they wrote 11. A dramatic similarity was found for Uruguayan children, as shown in Table 33. When children acquired written language, whether Spanish or English, they did so by first writing short sentences, then gradually longer and longer ones. Present evidence suggests that they acquire this facility developmentally through growth increments of one word per sentence per year. This pattern was characteristic irrespective of variations in schooling, language, geographical location, and even in sex (see Figure 15).

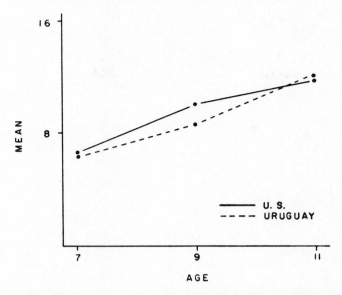

FIGURE 15. Comparison of U.S. and Uruguayan children on words per sentence.

Syntax

Syntactical accuracy was achieved early in life, with only slight growth after 9 years of age (see Volume One). The syntax of a language is determined by the auditory form, the way it is spoken. Accordingly, because mastery of the auditory form is achieved early in life as soon as the child was capable of expressing himself in the written form, he showed no further growth in syntax.

Results comparing Uruguayan and American children in use of syntax are presented in Table 34. The growth patterns and syntax quotients were remarkably similar. Both groups attained essentially adult levels of accuracy by the age of 9 years, an unusual finding considering the many variables involved. Apparently, children learning the syntax of Spanish do so with the same ease, or difficulty, as those learning English (see Figure 16).

Abstract-Concrete

The abstract-concrete scale was developed to obtain information on communication of meaning. The abstract-concrete score represents the level of abstraction expressed in the story, the imagination and depth of meaning. American children had a minor advantage at 7

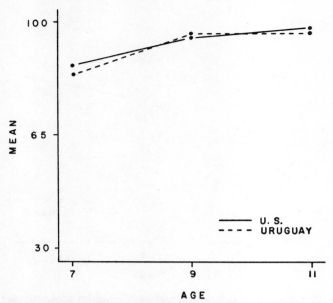

FIGURE 16. Comparison of U.S. and Uruguayan children on syntax.

and 9 years, but again, the similarity of the results is striking (see Table 35). Whether his native tongue was Spanish or English, the child gradually learned to express abstract ideas at a given rate, with certain increments year by year. As shown by the initial studies, this growth continued through 17 years in males but plateaued at 15 years for females. The pattern for the Uruguayan and American children was not identical, however, as can be seen in Figure 17. The level of abstract meaning expressed by the English-speaking group nearly doubled from 7 to 9 years of age, whereas only slight increments occurred between 9 and 11 years. The Spanish-speaking children made more gradual progress from one age level to the next. Nevertheless, at 11 years the groups obtained almost identical scores.

Other Comparisons

As shown in Volume One, 8- and 10-year-olds were not included in the original sample; scores for these age levels were provided through interpolation. Tuana's investigation provides standardization data for these age groups. Her results were compared with those obtained through interpolation and are presented in Table 36. With few exceptions there was little difference between the scores from

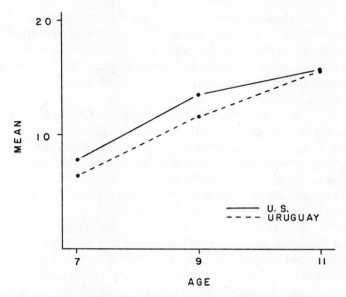

FIGURE 17. Comparison of U.S. and Uruguayan children on abstract-concrete.

the standardization data for Uruguayan children and the scores for American children derived by interpolation.

The agreement of these findings lends confidence to the accuracy with which written language can be measured. Moreover, the significance of developmental factors in language learning is heightened. The native language, schooling, and cultural surroundings may vary without critical impact on acquisition of the written word.

Summary

There has been much interest in the effects of culture on learning, especially in regard to language acquisition. Investigations relating to this question include work in linguistics (Carroll, 1953), anthropology (Ferguson, 1964), and psychology (Slobin, 1971). Nevertheless, research evidence has been slow in developing, perhaps because objective techniques have not been available. The cross-cultural results described above indicate that the PSLT provides a reliable and valid means whereby such investigations can be accomplished.

Psychologists and educators are concerned with the relative impact on learning of culture as compared with a handicap. Because of the collaboration of colleagues and former students, evidence is forthcoming from various countries. One such investigation on deaf children in New Zealand (VandenBerg, 1971) discloses that the handicap, not the culture per se, is the important factor in school learning. These results, like those from Uruguay, indicate that developmental integrity and the handicap in question demand attention, irrespective of the culture involved.

But there are other considerations. Sex differences appear consistently, regardless of cultural influences. Though premature as a conclusion, it may be that innate variations in language learning are characteristic by sex. Whatever the etiology or explanation, educators cannot ignore these variations. Substantially different scales are indicated when successful achievement is determined for boys in comparison with girls.

Indirectly, this cross-cultural study has implications for the psychology of learning in regard to both read and written language. The child does not write until he reads; reading is input and writing is output. Because of this psychoneurological reciprocity of language learning, we can assume that Uruguayan and American children are equivalent in reading achievement, as well as in written language. The task of learning Spanish or English appears comparable; the level of difficulty of the input, output, integrative, and transducing processes does not vary. These languages represent equal complexity in phonetic components, syntax, punctuation, and linguistic structure. These findings enhance constructs of language acquisition and should expedite development of curricula to enhance learning in all children.

Part Two

DISORDERS
OF WRITTEN LANGUAGE

Chapter III

Studies of Exceptional Children

As an area of investigation in relation to learning and cognition written language has not been emphasized. The pioneering work of Orton (1937) is an exception. Nevertheless, some workers refer to the clinical and educational significance of disorders in writing (Kinsbourne and Warrington, 1966). Boder (1971) especially has noted ways in which spelling disorders can be utilized in diagnosing learning disabilities. These are encouraging indications that written language is being recognized as an avenue that offers promise for deeper understanding of the needs of children, particularly those who have disorders associated with handicaps. On the other hand, it is distressing that a recent symposium of scientists concerned with perceptual and reading disorders gave no attention to disorders of written language (Young and Lindsley, 1970). Investigators have not yet fully recognized that the disorders of read and written language can be conceptualized, diagnosed, and remediated most effectively when studied on a continuum, as receptive and expressive forms of the same verbal system.

Those interested in language are not alone in largely overlooking the significance of written language. Except in relation to early-life deafness (Myklebust, 1964), study of the development and disorders of the written word in handicapped children has been neglected in special education. Even new and innovative programs incorporate little or no material on this facet of cognition and academic learning. Yet not only are such specialized programs essential to meeting the needs of exceptional children, they broaden and deepen our understanding of the psychoneurology of learning in all children. This has been shown by the work of Sperry (1970) and Geschwind (1968, 1972). Through their research the role of the hemispheres of the brain in the acquisition of facility with read and written language has been extended. Pribram (1969) and other scientists involved with psychoneurological learning disabilities also highlight the initiation of a new era for special education. Psychologists, educators, psychiatrists, language pathologists, and other clinicians and scientists are beginning to conceptualize reading and writing disorders more opportunely. Studies of handicapped children are unusually revealing in this regard. Through them new insights are gained into the essence of all language learning, and thereby the challenging task of educational remediation can be approached with greater assurance.

PLAN OF THE STUDIES

An extensive research project was undertaken to investigate the effects of handicaps on the development and disorders of written language. This study included groups of children classified as having reading disability, mental retardation, speech defects, and social-emotional disturbance, as well as a control group of normal children. The population was selected from six public schools in a large metropolitan area. These schools were representative of a wide range of racial, ethnic, and cultural groups. Moreover, the four populations of exceptional children included those so classified in these schools, that is, those receiving special education. The control group was selected from the same schools. The results by group are presented in the following four chapters. (The learning-disability study described in Chapter VIII was not a part of this initial investigation.)

Rationale

Though some educators emphasize the ill effects of categorizing a child on the basis of his major disability, there is a growing awareness of the need to learn more about learning, including the impact of handicaps. Moreover, awareness of the disadvantages of such categorization does not preclude determination of the characteristic deficiencies that result from given disabilities. These characteristic deficiencies are relevant to understanding the psychology by which a given child learns. It seems, therefore, obligatory to ascertain the characteristic differences that exist on the basis of what has happened to the child.

One way of proceeding is to compare the learning profiles, deficits, and integrities of those having a certain disability with the normal and with those having other types of disabilities. This plan was followed in these investigations covering four types of exceptional children. The primary purpose was to gain insight concerning the ways that children classified for special education in the public schools varied from each other, especially in facility with written language. It was presupposed that these insights are essential for initiating effective educational remediation. For example, it was hypothesized that if children having articulation defects were deficient in auditory language, and if those having reading disabilities had similar deficiencies, then both groups might be limited in written language, albeit their symptomatic manifestations were different. Similar postulations were made for the other groups. Several investigative procedures were applied to gather data on these questions.

Investigative Procedures

The plan and design of the study emphasized psychoneurological facets of learning (Myklebust, 1968, 1971). Hence, the semiautonomous systems concept (Hebb, 1963) served as a background for selection of the tests to be administered, with emphasis on the development and disorders of written language. But written language was not considered in isolation. It was assumed that more knowledge concerning acquisition of the written word would be gained if this language form was studied in relation to the read. Moreover, as stressed in Volume One,* auditory language was viewed as the foundation for both the read and written forms. Since this rationale necessitated inclusion of both auditory and visual language processes, receptively and expressively, a test battery was evolved to determine comprehension of the spoken word, ability to use spoken language expressively, visual receptive language ability, (reading) and visual expressive language (writing) ability.

Hearing and Vision

To preclude the results being confounded with sensory impairment, individual screening tests of hearing and vision were administered to all the children. Hearing acuity was determined by a puretone test and visual acuity by the Snellen Chart. Children with a hearing loss of 35 decibels (ISO) or greater in both ears, or a visual impairment of more than 20/40 with refraction, were excluded.

---

* *Development and Disorders of Written Language*, Volume One, *Picture Story Language Test* (Myklebust, 1965).

Cognitive Ability

An indication of the cognitive level of function by group was considered a significant controlling factor in the study of language development, though it was presupposed that language facility may be limited even in the intellectually gifted. The Primary Mental Abilities (PMA) Test (Thurstone and Thurstone, 1962) was chosen as the principal measure of cognitive ability because it covers both verbal and nonverbal functions and has the advantage of providing quotients for each of the factors. It was administered as a group test. Because of its common use with exceptional children, and to supply a second indication of cognitive levels, the Draw-A-Man Test (Goodenough, 1926) was also administered.

Psychomotor Functions

There is an impressive body of information in child development, special education, and psychology on the significance of motor abilities in the appraisal of children (Oseretsky, 1931; Gesell and Amatruda, 1947; Myklebust, 1954; Sloan, 1955; Goetzinger, 1961; Goldfarb, 1961). Moreover, handedness has been found to be of importance in relation to aphasia and dyslexia (Zangwill, 1960; Hécaen and Ajuriaguerra, 1964; Eisenson, 1971). Motor tests also are of value in distinguishing between children whose deficiencies are principally organic and those whose deficits are primarily nonorganic (Myklebust, 1946, 1954, 1964). Therefore, the Heath Railwalking Test (Heath, 1942) was individually administered to the entire sample, exceptional children and the controls.

Auditory Language: Receptive

The purpose was to study receptive and expressive language processes. Because the sample was large, group techniques were used whenever possible. A complicating factor was the unavailability of standardized procedures for measuring facility with auditory language. Objective tests for appraisal of comprehension of the spoken word continue to be a neglected area of research in child development, linguistics, and language pathology. Inasmuch as it was necessary to use a group technique, the child was required to give his responses in writing. This approach has limitations because it assumes competence in utilizing this expressive language form. On the other hand, if tests of comprehension are given individually, with few exceptions the child is required to respond by speaking. Therefore, the reader is cautioned to be alert to the methods applied and to make interpretations accordingly. Precise procedures that permit objective scoring of nonverbal expressive responses to tests of auditory comprehension have not yet been evolved.

Two tests of auditory processing were administered; each was given and scored separately. The instructions were given only once; the children were told to listen carefully because the instructions would not be repeated. Spelling and legibility were not scored, and ample time was given for completion of one task before the next was presented. The first four items represented simple auditory processing: the child was requested to write *your name,* then *the name of something you throw, eat, and ride.* Though simple, these items required the child to comprehend the task and recollect the names of such objects. Items 5 and 6 were more complex, testing comprehension of increasingly difficult auditory language as well as perception of time in relation to daily routines.

The next three items were heavily dependent on auditory sequencing: each item involved a span of five words, but the items differed substantially. Item 7 entailed comprehension of the difficult phrase, *every other word;* thus, more than span was involved. To accomplish the task it was necessary to manipulate the word sequence in a precise, selective manner. Item 8 was also a measure of ability to visualize words letter by letter, without viewing the visual equivalents. It was hypothesized that this task might be useful in ascertaining relation among the auditory, read, and written language forms. Item 9 was included to determine whether the child could *group* or *categorize* words that pertained to given concepts. Again, retention of the sequence was imperative if the problem were to be solved, but judgment of each of the word meanings in association with the others also was necessary. Though the psychoneurology of mathematical processes may be different from that of word processes (Cohn, 1971), Item 10 was included to evaluate this function. This was the only item in Test One that was directly dependent on ability to read, as well as on comprehension of the instructions given auditorially.

Test Two of auditory receptive language consisted of items that required relating what was heard with what appeared visually before the child; this test was directly concerned with interneurosensory processing of auditory information into visual equivalents. The first two items included comprehension of the simple instruction to perform a task given auditorially. But solution necessitated visual recognition of letters of the alphabet. The third item was similar but the auditory comprehension task was much more complex; three separate instructions (a line through the e's, a cross on the o's and a line under the t's) must be comprehended and related to a specific letter. Items 4 and 5 required yet a higher level of processing because of the need to understand the meaning of *every other and every third,* and *around all the o's that are followed by e's.* In these items, too, what was heard had to be related precisely to what appeared before the child visually.

Auditory Language: Expressive

In evaluation of expressive processes the objective was to obtain information on use of auditory language for purposes of communication with others. The primary factor was *meaning.* Hence, articulation, rate of utterance, syntax, and related aspects were not scored. It was necessary to administer the tests of expressive ability individually.

Again, two tests were used. The first was the opposites test from the Detroit Tests of Learning Aptitude (Baker and Leland, 1959). This measure was chosen because of experience with it when examining children and adults with expressive aphasia. When asked to give an opposite, the individual must scan his pool of known words and retrieve one, the only one that meets the requirement of being an opposite of the word presented. Children having deficits in word-finding often cannot perform this task; a child may score low for other reasons, such as expressive aphasia of the apraxic type (Myklebust, 1971a). But this was consonant with our purpose, that is, to identify as many children as possible with deficiencies in auditory expressive language.

For the second measure the Binet Vocabulary Test was chosen (Terman and Merrill, 1960). Like the Detroit opposites, this test was based on norms and standardized procedures for administration. As a measure of auditory expressive language it required the child to be precise about the meaning of what he said. If he knew the meaning but could not express it, he failed.

A limitation of these tests of expressive language is that they correlate highly with intelligence, though they were not chosen as mental tests. For research purposes it is unfortunate that measures of verbal facility also, to an extent, are measures of intelligence. This does not preclude their use for study of language behavior. As a control, the PMA and the Draw-A-Man tests were administered as indicators of cognitive abilities, verbal and nonverbal. Therefore, the results from the tests designated as language tests could be interpreted in relation to the indicators of mental ability.

Read and Written Language

Visual language was studied receptively and expressively, but because of the large sample only a screening test of reading could be given. Previous experience with the Columbia Vocabulary Test (Myklebust, 1964) prompted its being chosen again. Its reliability was demonstrated by the results for the normal control group. These findings were in close agreement with the original standardization, although Gansl and Garrett (1939) did their research on this test approximately 40 years prior to this investigation.

Behind all these techniques was the goal of obtaining data on the development and disorders of written language. A necessary step, therefore, was to evolve a test for measuring this unique expressive verbal process. Out of this need came the Picture Story Language Test (PSLT). The normative, standardization results are presented in Volume One. The original investigation, as well as the studies described below, suggest that the PSLT is a reliable and valid test for appraisal of written language. It was administered to all the children in groups of 10.

The auditory language tests, with instructions for administration, are given below.

TESTS OF AUDITORY LANGUAGE

A. The test is to be given to groups of *five* children. Space the children so that they cannot see each others' papers. Give each child the form he is to use for his responses.
B. Give the instructions clearly, being certain that every child hears them. Before testing begins say: "Listen carefully because the directions will be given only once."

Test One: Auditory Comprehension

1. Write your name on the line after the number one. (If the child asks whether he should write his full name, say: "Yes, if you can.")
2. Write the name of a toy that you throw.
3. Write the name of something you eat.
4. Write the name of something you ride.
5. Write a word that tells what you should do if you might be late for school.
6. Write the day it was yesterday.

7. I am going to say five words. You write the first word and every other word: *toy, ball, boy, see, little*.
8. I am going to say five words. You write the first letter of each word: *shoe, pencil, match, chair, gum*.
9. I am going to say five words. One of these words does not belong with the others. Write the word that does not belong with the others: *plate, saucer, bread, bowl, pitcher*.
10. You see the three rows of numbers on the paper before you? If the numbers in each line are arranged in order from the smallest to the largest, what will the middle number be? Find it and draw a line under it.

Test Two: Auditory to Visual

Now you see five rows of letters. Listen carefully and do just what I say. Remember, I will tell you what to do only once.
1. Draw a line through all the e's.
2. Draw a cross on the a's and circle the t's.
3. Draw a line through the e's, put a cross on the o's, and put a line under all the t's.
4. Draw a line through every other o and every third e.
5. Draw a circle around all the o's that are followed by e's.

TESTS OF AUDITORY LANGUAGE: STUDENT RESPONSE FORM

Test One

1. _____
2. _____
3. _____
4. _____
5. _____
6. _____
7. _____ _____ _____ _____ _____
8. _____ _____ _____ _____ _____
9. _____
10.
    1) 1 6 2 4 5
    2) 3 4 9 8 2
    3) 8 3 7 1 2

Test Two

1. a e e d f a e o c t e a b o
2. a o e t b a t o e o c b d t a o e
3. b o c e t a o b r e a o e r t l s o e
4. o e o t a o b e o a b o c a o e e t o s r o
5. o a b o e c t r o s o e r l s a o e a b o d l m

Chapter IV

Written Language and Reading Disabilities

There is much interest in the processes involved in learning to read (Young and Lindsley, 1970). But curiously, this interest has been concerned only with the input side; attention has been devoted to receptive functions (reading) without consideration of the concomitant interacting expressive aspects (writing). As in study of spoken language, more is learned about reading when receptive and expressive functions are investigated simultaneously.

In Volume One* a hierarchical relation for the language systems was suggested: auditory is acquired first, reading (visual receptive) next, and written (visual expressive) last. Using this frame of reference, it seemed propitious to include a group of reading-disability children in the studies of development and disorders of written language. Practical considerations involved implications for remedial reading, but on a theoretical basis these children might provide vital clues concerning the interrelations between auditory and visual language.

Neurologists have demonstrated that brain dysfunctions may cause dyslexia. This psychoneurological condition has been known since approximately 1865 (Ingram, 1970). Subsequently, Hinshelwood (1917), Orton (1925), and Money (1966), among others, have extended knowledge of the ways in which brain disturbances are associated with reading disabilities. Nevertheless, only in recent years has it been recognized that dyslexia is a common cause of deficiencies that affect learning to read (Hermann, 1959; Rabinovitch, 1959; Quiros, 1964; Boder, 1971).

There is an underlying assumption in the United States that reading disabilities in children are attributable to emotional disturbances. Emotional factors should not be overlooked, but the work of Connolly (1971) and of Killen (1972) clearly indicate that emotional distur-

* *Development and Disorders of Written Language,* Volume One, *Picture Story Language Test* (Myklebust, 1965).

63

bance as an etiological factor has been stressed unduly. There are four primary causes of reading disabilities: emotional disturbance, lack of adequate schooling, visual impairment, and brain dysfunction. The incidence of each of these disturbances in school children has not been ascertained, but it is apparent that dyslexia contributes more than has been generally recognized. When the syndrome commonly associated with dyslexia is observed in a child, intensive diagnostic studies should be made (Myklebust and Johnson, 1962).

A STUDY OF READING-DISABILITY CHILDREN

To secure information on the possible relations between deficits in read and written language, a study was undertaken of a group of reading-disability children enrolled in a metropolitan public-school system. These children had been educationally diagnosed as requiring remedial reading. A control group of normal children was selected from the same schools. In this way racial, ethnic, and socioeconomic factors were minimized. For inclusion in the experimental group, the child had to be classified as having a reading disability and be enrolled in a remedial-reading program. All children so categorized at the ages of 7, 9, 11, 13, and 15 years in six schools composed the reading-disability population.

The distribution by age was revealing; there were no children so classified at the age of 7 years. Presumably, those having difficulty in learning to read were identified by teachers and psychologists before reaching the age of 8 or 9 years, but were not included in the program of remedial reading. Most of the children identified by the criteria were between 11 and 13 years; comparatively, there were fewer at the ages of 9 and 15. Those aged 15 years may have been inferior to the remainder of the sample because in some ways they seemed to constitute a portion of the total group in whom other factors, such as lower cognitive ability, were influential. To broaden the scope of the investigation, in addition to written language the following functions were appraised: mental ability, spoken language (receptive and expressive), reading, and locomotor coordination. Cognitive ability was evaluated by means of the Primary Mental Abilities (PMA) Test and the Goodenough Draw-A-Man Test.

Cognitive Abilities

In the study of children with reading disabilities, there was special concern with the question of homogeneity: how these children differed from a normal group selected from the same schools. The consideration was whether the group was homogeneous in other ways besides the common problem of inability to learn to read: Did the children have other learning disabilities, verbal or nonverbal? Did they vary on measures of cognitive ability? In other words, were reading-disability children characterized by a single trait or a complex of conditions?

Primary Mental Abilities

To obtain an indication of the level of cognitive ability the PMA Test and the Draw-A-Man Test were administered; both were given in small groups. The entire PMA Test was administered, including portions that require reading, so success on the verbal and nonverbal subtests could be compared. The results are shown in Table 37.

The children who had reading disabilities scored lowest on the subtests that required verbal facility, but they scored above 90 IQ on several of the nonverbal tasks: verbal pictures, reasoning (figures), perception, space, and number. As compared with the normal, however, the reading-disability children tended to score lower as they became older. With some exceptions, the highest scores were attained by the 9- and 11-year-olds, and the lowest by the 15-year age group. The specific reason for this trend is not clear but warrants attention. Often, in working with reading-disability children, it can be observed that they perform more and more below average as they become older; if they are one grade below the norm at 10 years of age they may be two grades below at the age of 14 years. It is not their learning potential that diminishes; rather, they are unable to achieve at the normal rate, and frequently this is reflected as a negative correlation between reading scores and age.

There were other considerations. As the reading-disability children became older, they scored lower on both verbal and nonverbal tests. Thus the question of cognitive ability cannot be overlooked. Children with the greatest capacity for learning may have been more successful in reading achievement and, gradually, as they became older, no longer required remedial reading. Nevertheless, because of the results for language learning (see below), it would be fallacious to assume that deficit in potential was a primary cause of the reading disabilities in this group of children.

Draw-A-Man

The Draw-A-Man Test has been used by many workers as an indication of developmental maturation (Ilg and Ames, 1964) and as evidence for dysfunctions in the brain (Cohn, 1971). It has proved of value in the study of deaf children (Myklebust, 1964) and for evaluation of learning-disability children (Johnson and Myklebust, 1967) when included in a diagnostic battery. Typically, when reading-disability children begin to read, competence in drawing the human figure improves. Also, learning-disability children often score higher on the performance part of the Wechsler Intelligence Scale for Children (WISC) than on the Draw-A-Man Test. The reason for the association between learning disabilities and ability to draw a man has not been fully determined. Some investigators attribute virtually all distortions in such drawings to emotional disturbance, and others view them as an indication of deficiencies in body image related to neurogenic involvements. Presumably both influences may be operative.

The results for the reading-disability group in comparison with the normal are presented in Table 38. The children with deficits in reading scored below the normal at all age levels. The poor readers were less able to draw the human figure, showing the same trend by age that appeared for the PMA Test scores. Whether interpreted as indicative of psychogenic or neurogenic limitations, there can be little question that the reading-disability children were deficient in body-image perception. This may be indicative of generalized developmental immaturity. The implications of these findings are considered further below.

Auditory Language

Written language was a primary concern in these studies but it was assumed that inclusion of other aspects of language might enhance understanding of the needs of reading-disability children. Disturbances in any one of the language forms (spoken, read, written) can be perceived most beneficially when appraised in relation to the others. The reading-disability children were severely limited in facility with written language (see Table 42). This deficiency might be due to disabilities in reading, in auditory language, or in both. Thus, the investigation was planned so data would be available on auditory and read language as well as on the written.

Auditory Receptive Language

Comparative findings for the normal and reading-disability children are presented in Table 39. As stated previously, success on Test One required ability to comprehend the instructions, to bring an appropriate word to mind, and to write that word in readable form. Failure on this test might be due to deficits in any one or more of these processes. The developmental patterns for the normal and reading-disability children were similar, both groups reaching a plateau at 13 years of age. But the poor readers were markedly inferior to the normal; not until 13 years of age did they achieve a level of function equal to that of the normal 9-year-old child.

The developmental patterns elicited by Test Two also were equivalent in that neither group reached a plateau by 15 years of age; success required matching what was heard (instructions) with what appeared on the page. The developmental configuration varied in that those with reading disabilities, though inferior, made greater gains at each of the 2-year intervals; their rate of gain exceeded that of the controls, so their performance at the age of 15 corresponded to the normal.

Previously, we noted that the 15-year-old poor readers were inferior on tests of cognitive ability. Such inadequacy did not appear on the tests of auditory receptive language, indicating that they were not inferior intellectually. Nevertheless, even at 15 years their level of ability to comprehend instructions auditorially and to relate them to the read form of language was equivalent only to that of an 11-year-old normal child. Therefore, both tests of auditory receptive language showed the reading-disability group to be from 3 to 4 years below average in this type of learning. Although the tests required both written responses (Test One) and recognition of letters in the read form (Test Two), these results show that the reading-disability group was deficient in ability to comprehend the spoken word. The data presented below support these results.

Auditory Expressive Language

When auditory receptive language is limited, auditory expressive language is modified; output is dependent on input. It is evident that the poor readers were inferior in use of spoken language (see Table 40). The tests of auditory expressive language did not require reading or writing because the children responded only by speaking. It is significant, therefore, that the reading-disability group was most inferior on Test One, ability to give opposites. They performed at a level 3 to 4 years below normal on this test.

The children with reading disabilities had other limitations: they could not give the opposite of the word that was heard. Perhaps they were unable to comprehend the task or to produce the specific single-word response required. In the first instance the deficit lies in recognizing a concept, such as temperature; *one* of the extremes is given and the task is to provide the other—*hot* for *cold*. In the second instance the limitation is more precisely verbal; the problem is recognized but the children cannot provide the exact word indicated. They may be unable to recall it or to utter it.

From the point of view of language pathology these conditions differ widely and involve different neurodynamic processes. If the limitation is in ability to assimilate, intellectual inferiority would be likely. But the tests of cognitive ability do not suggest such inferiority. If the deficit is in comprehending the word spoken by the examiner, the problem is one of input—*receptive aphasia*—and the results of tests of auditory receptive language suggest that some of the children may have been affected by this limitation. Reading-disability children probably are also limited in auditory recall; they understand the task and comprehend the word given by the examiner, but are unable to bring to mind the specific word required. This condition, frequently encountered in language pathology, is designated *amnestic aphasia;* it may account for the reading disability of some of the children studied. Or some may have been able to comprehend the task, understand the word provided, and recall the required word, but unable to utter it. This condition, *expressive aphasia,* is a type of apraxia (Myklebust, 1971a).

The level of inferiority on Test One should be noted. At the age of 15 years the reading-disability children had attained a level of auditory expressive language equivalent to that of the average 9-year-old, a deficit of 6 years. In addition, they showed no growth after 13 years, whereas the normal children continued to mabe gains through 15 years of age. This variation at the age of 15 may be due to selective factors. The poor readers at this age were especially inferior on the opposites test. But they did not show this limitation on the other tests of language, including the tests of reading. Moreover, they were homogeneous, suggesting the same type of overall involvement in this age group.

The differences by group were evident also on Test Two, a test requiring definition of words; the level of inferiority again ranged from 3 to 4 years. Moreover, the developmental pattern was similar to that demonstrated by Test One. The normal group showed progression from 9 through 15 years, but the reading-disability children reached a plateau at 13 years.

The findings for auditory expressive language did not indicate that the deficit in output was directly reciprocal to deficiency in input. Rather, these children had language deficits separate and distinct from their limitations in auditory receptive language. Therefore, this population of reading-disability children did not present a unitary problem—a deficiency only in reading—but were limited in auditory language, receptively and expressively. These limitations were more substantial than would be expected on the basis of differences in cognitive ability. If remedial reading is to be effective, this broader scope of learning disabilities must be considered and auditory language deficiencies must be stressed, rather than only the visual as is commonly done.

Read Language

The children in the reading-disability group were classified as needing remedial reading, and hence, were considered homogeneous in that they were unable to learn to read normally. To determine their level of achievement the Columbia Vocabulary Test was administered. The results are shown in Table 41; scores for the 9-year-olds were so low as to preclude statistical analysis.

The reading-disability children were severely inferior in vocabulary. At the 11- and 13-year age levels their achievement was approximately one-half of average, and at 15 years approximately one-third; variability was less than for the normal. Their inferiority is revealed further in that at 15 years of age their capability was at the third- to fourth-grade level. Characteristic of children with reading disabilities, they did not make the expected gains as they became older. It is not uncommon to find poor readers who evidence greater retardation year by year. Nevertheless, this group showed advancement from 11 to 13 years, but at a rate below that of the control group. They made no gains from 13 to 15 years, whereas the normals advanced rapidly during this age interval.

The hypothesis was that auditory language develops first, followed by the read and written. Accordingly, the spoken word is most readily achieved; but if speaking is not acquired normally, reading and writing are impeded. These findings for read language support this presumption. Though significantly below average in auditory language, the reading-disability children were even more inferior in read language. Furthermore, as shown by the results below, their retardation in written language exceeded their retardation in reading.

Programs of remedial reading might be of greater benefit if this configuration were recognized. This does not mean that identical programs would meet individual needs. Though homogeneous in having reading disabilities, this population is viewed as heterogeneous in regard to the types of reading disabilities involved. Yet it appears that a first concern of the remedial-reading teacher might be the ways in which auditory language deficits are primary, with the further realization that only when heard and spoken language is firmly established can read language be achieved in a normal manner. On the other hand, the principle of simultaneity should not be ignored. As auditory language is developed, the read and written forms can be embraced. The significant consideration, therefore, is that remediation should not begin with reading and writing. Facility with auditory language is basic, serving as the foundation for remediation at the levels of read and written language. Only when these reciprocities are recognized can remedial reading be most beneficial. Nature has provided a psychoneurological system that operates according to certain laws or principles. Gradually these principles of operation, of learning, are being clarified. The more remediation approaches are based on these principles of learning, the more successful they will be.

Written Language

A facet of consequence to the theoretical model pertained to the cognitive relations between learning to read and learning to write. Even though interactions of read and written language are complex, deficits in reading reciprocally reduce facility with the written word; this basic principle concerns the interdependence of input and output. In other words, reading and writing are facets of the same language system, reading constituting the input process and writing the output. It follows that output processes might be disturbed, even severely, without concomitant imposition on input. The reverse does not appear as a natural sequence; when impositions on input occur, modifications of output follow. Investigation of such theoretical constructs requires long-time research effort. But clinicians and educators often are impressed with the progress made when these principles guide the educational remediation procedures.

The findings for written language support the frame of reference outlined here and discussed in Volume One. But there were other reasons for studying facility with the written word in reading-disability children. For example, there was the possibility that the Picture Story Language Test (PSLT) could be used as a screening test for reading disabilities, somewhat as suggested by the work of Boder (1971). Moreover, through comparison of the findings for other handicapped children, the nature of reading disabilities might be further clarified.

The PSLT was administered to groups of from 5 to 10 children. The results for the reading-disability sample compared with the total standardization group are presented in Table 42.

Total Words

The reading-disability children wrote much shorter stories. At no age level did the number of words written per story by this group reach one-half the number written by the control children; in most instances the ratio was closer to one-third of average. But the developmental pattern for the groups was similar, both showing growth from 9 to 13 years, with a decline or plateau at 15 years (see Figure 18). Nevertheless, the reading-disability children were markedly

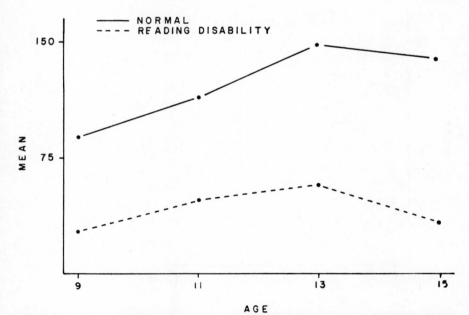

FIGURE 18. Comparison of normal and reading-disability children on total words.

deficient in output of written language, suggesting a lack of fluency, a laboriousness, in use of the written word.

Total Sentences

The high correlation between total words and total sentences for the normal also appeared for the reading-disability group. They wrote shorter stories as measured both by total words and total sentences. Nevertheless, they made gains from 9 through 13 years, and this growth (essentially one sentence per age interval) was at a rate commensurate with the normal. At 9 years of age they performed at a level substantially below average and, although making gains, remained at the same ratio of inferiority. They never caught up (see Figure 19).

Words per Sentence

The reading-disability children were inferior also on number of words written per sentence, but they were more equal to the controls on this factor of written language. Even with marked deficits in

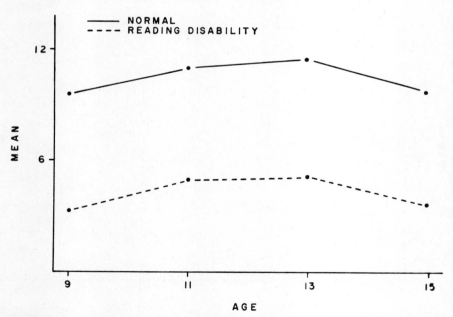

FIGURE 19. Comparison of normal and reading-disability children on total sentences.

syntax at 9 years, they were not significantly different from average in sentence length at this age level. Moreover, at 13 years they wrote sentences slightly above average in length for normal 11-year-olds, a deficit of about 2 years. At 15 years they achieved a level of two-thirds of average. The factor-analysis data (see Table 17) indicate that words per sentence is largely independent of productivity and correctness (syntax). The reading-disability children were not equally inferior on all factors of written language, a result that has implications for programs of remediation. The deficit in reading was specific to language aspects, not mainly to an inability to formulate and organize ideas into units that represent sentences. But because of the poor performance of the 15-year-old group, the significance of the data at the upper age level is obscure. In contrast to the normal, those with reading disabilities did not evince the developmental linearity for words per sentence, as can be seen in Figure 20.

Syntax

The results for syntax show the reading-disability children to be seriously deficient in language structure. They lacked facility in

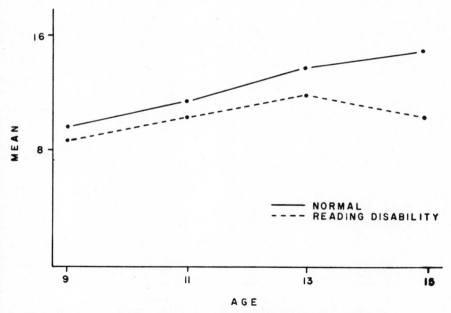

FIGURE 20. Comparison of normal and reading-disability children on words per sentence.

correct use of tense, punctuation, word order, and other aspects of syntax. At 9 years of age their syntax quotient was 17 points below average, but at 11, 13, and 15 years it was only 6 to 8 points lower. Also, at 9 years the standard deviation was more than four times greater than for normal children. When a child has a reading disability, he is seriously delayed in acquiring basic knowledge of the syntactical relations among words. That this significant handicap is overcome to a degree is shown by the findings at 11 years of age. But like the normals, the reading-disability children reached a plateau at 11 years, making no gains in use of syntax after this age (see Figure 21). These results provide another focus for understanding the nature of reading disabilities. Syntax learning is auditory, deriving from the spoken language form. At 9 years of age the children with reading disabilities were struggling along with syntactical facility below that of the average 7-year-old—clear evidence of a marked deficiency in auditory receptive language. Hence, as a factor of written language, syntax is in urgent need of remediation and growth must be fostered beyond the age of 11 years.

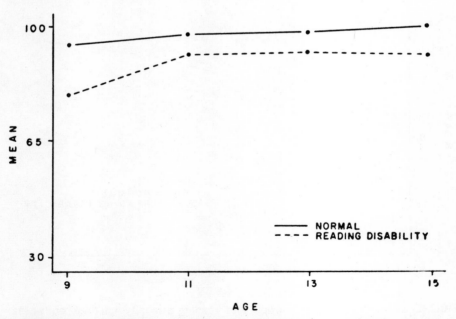

FIGURE 21. Comparison of normal and reading-disability children on syntax.

Abstract-Concrete

The reading-disability children were limited in use of abstract meaning. Except for the 15-year-olds, they made gains from one age level to the next, but their rate of progress was slower than that of the controls (see Figure 22). As shown by the factor analysis, use of abstract meaning is closely related to language fluency, to the magnitude of the pool of words available to the child. The deficit in conveying abstract meaning must be considered in relation to the inferiority in story length. This factor (total words, total sentences, and use of abstract meaning) is critical to successful achievement in written language. In reading-disability children it must be considered of utmost importance. Remedial-reading programs might define this limitation as being of first concern.

Summary

The written language of reading-disability children was inferior on all the measures. But of the three factors measured on the PSLT, those most deficient were productivity (including abstract-concrete)

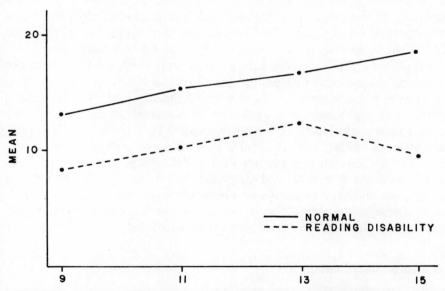

FIGURE 22. Comparison of normal and reading-disability children on abstract-concrete.

and syntax; least affected was words per sentence. In general, compared with spoken and read language, written language was the most seriously deficient.

Intercorrelation of Auditory and Written Language

The intercorrelation of auditory and written language in normal children is discussed in Chapter II. Significant relations appeared with all of the PSLT scores, but the association occurred primarily in early life, before 9 years of age. An intercorrelation analysis also was made for the reading-disability population. These results are presented in Tables 43 and 44. Compared with the normal, there were fewer significant relations. For auditory receptive language the only significant relations were with syntax. The reading-disability children, like the normals, evidenced the auditory basis of this language factor. In contrast to the normal, this association was not consistent, appearing at 9 and 13 years but not at 11 years. In addition, at 15 years the correlation was negative. Though the sample was small at this age level, this finding may reflect the clinical observation that, as they become older, some reading-disability children become rigid and fixed in cognitive functioning. A given process, such as the auditory, because it is more dependable, becomes the only one on which they rely—it runs away with them. Transducing from one modality to the other becomes less and less workable, thus the negative correlation. The negative correlation for syntax at 9 years on Test Two of expressive language may occur on this same basis.

Because of the few correlations that appeared, except in minor respects, cross-modal processing (auditory to visual—visual to auditory) was not achieved by the reading-disability children. In normal children this processing is apparent at early school age, when they learn to associate heard and read language. To a considerable extent, this was not achieved by the children with reading disabilities. These data again focus on the essence of the deficiency. The reading-disability child has a generalized language deficit, the predominant base being poor auditory receptive and auditory expressive language. This basic disturbance persists and precludes normal cross-modal learning so that the visual equivalents remain isolated and detached.

Locomotor Coordination

These studies of exceptional children have concerned the question of homogeneity, the extent to which those in a given category resemble each other and the manner in which the groups differ from normal. As a part of the plan, appraisal of motor abilities was included. As shown by Heath (1942), exogenous and endogenous mentally retarded children vary in locomotor coordination; they also differ from the normal. Because etiology of retardation and motor ability are correlated (Myklebust, 1954, 1964), study of motor coordination in the reading-disability group was deemed important. Deficits in motor functioning are especially prevalent in children with neurogenic disturbances. The motor deficiencies related to disorders of the central nervous system differ from those caused by damage to the peripheral nervous system (Myklebust, 1964).

To evaluate the motor abilities of the reading-disability children, the Heath Railwalking Test was administered (Myklebust, 1954). As defined by Heath, this is a measure of locomotor coordination. The results for the poor readers compared with the normal control group are presented in Table 45. The reading-disability children were markedly inferior to the normal, performing below average by approximately 20 percent at each of the age levels. The rate of growth for the normals and for the poor readers was similar, indicating that those with deficits in reading were disturbed in locomotor coordination in early life (before 9 years) and remained deficient essentially to the same degree through the age of 15 years.

Again, reading disability was not a unitary factor but was associated with disturbances of locomotor coordination. Thus, it is difficult to rationalize the prevalent opinion that reading disabilities are attributable to emotional disturbance alone. The type of motor dysfunction that appeared in this study is not commonly associated with psychogenic factors. The results, both for language and motor abilities, point to broad organismic involvements, reflected in maturational imbalance and delays. These imbalances are revealed in cognitive disturbances, affecting auditory and visual learning, and can also be observed in disturbed motor processes. Perhaps this disability can be best described as a psychoneurological disorder. This designation emphasizes both psychological and neurological impositions and implies that a broad perspective to educational remediation would be most advantageous. But as indicated throughout this chapter, there are many specifics to be considered. Unfortunately, some educators choose to focus on only one of these facets, such as the auditory, visual, or motor. A more beneficial approach would be to include all these in the remediation program, but in the manner in which nature has determined the sequences for learning. The teacher would then not emphasize visual (read) language learning without awareness of the status and role of the auditory. In other words, greatest benefits in learning are achieved when all facets interact properly, one with the other.

A STUDY OF DYSLEXIC CHILDREN

It is important to understand more fully the complex problem of dyslexia in children. Some workers have suggested that the Gerstmann syndrome (Gerstmann, 1940) is associated with poor reading achievement in children (Myklebust and Boshes, 1960; Myklebust and Johnson, 1962; Boshes and Myklebust, 1964; Johnson and Myklebust, 1965; Kinsbourne and Warrington, 1966). Nevertheless, research evidence specific to childhood dyslexia remains meager. To gain further knowledge concerning this condition, a group of children was studied for whom this diagnostic classification seemed most warranted. The focus of the investigation was on written language and the results are presented here.

The Sample

The dyslexic population consisted of 66 children seen at a non-medical clinic specializing in language disabilities; there were 59 males and 7 females. These children had been referred by the public schools and other agencies. The ratio of males to females, in general, was consistent with the findings of other investigators (Hermann, 1959; Money, 1966). The children included in the sample met the following criteria: IQ level of 90 or above on the performance scale of the WISC, normal hearing and vision, no crippling condition. They also scored at the twenty-fifth percentile or lower on at least one standardized test of reading achievement. Depending on the age of the child, the following reading tests were administered: Gates Test (oral reading, word recognition, paragraph meaning, general significance, precise directions, noting details, level of comprehension) and the Columbia Vocabulary Test. The minimum chronological age was 7 years and the maximum age was 18 years and 5 months.

These children were evaluated neurologically and electroencephalographically; a total of 83.8 percent had positive neurological findings. Though not conclusive, these results support the classification of dyslexia; neurological disturbances were detected in many of the children. The normal control group was selected from urban public schools and was composed of children from the original standardization sample. As can be seen from the data in Chapter II, the mean scores for this control group were equivalent to those of the urban children on whom the PSLT was standardized.

Written Language

The findings for the dyslexic children in comparison with the normal control group are presented in Table 46. Because of the small number of dyslexics, these results must be interpreted with caution. But it is apparent (together with the further analysis given below) that the dyslexic children experienced major difficulty with the written word. The differences between the scores for the dyslexic and normal children reached statistical significance mainly in early life, but variations were evident. Except for the results for the 9-year-olds, the most obvious limitation was in story length. At all ages, except for the 17-year-olds, those with dyslexia wrote shorter stories. But at 9 years the dyslexics were inferior on all scores except use of abstract meaning.

There was other evidence of the difficulties in acquiring written language. At 9, 11, and 13 years the variability of the syntax scores was much greater than for the normals; therefore, a number of the dyslexics were deficient in acquisition of syntactical forms. That correct usage was an obstacle is shown also by the significantly lower syntax quotients at 9 and 11 years of age. Normal children acquired an adult level of syntax facility by 11 years but the dyslexics did not achieve this degree of success until 15 years of age. These findings reveal that the dyslexic children were deficient in auditory language learning and thus could not normally learn to read and achieve success with written language.

The performance of the dyslexics did not conform to the factor-analysis findings for normal children. Factor 1 for the normal consisted of total words, total sentences, and use of abstract meaning. The dyslexic children were deficient in total words and total sentences but not in abstract-concrete. Although they showed marked limitations in productivity, they were capable of expressing themselves in abstract terms. These results are provocative because they suggest equivalent use of abstract ideas and a cognitive learning style that varied from the normal. The factors composing written language for normal children may not be identical to those for the dyslexic.

Intercorrelation of PSLT Scores

The intercorrelation of the five scores for written language for normal children is discussed in Chapter II. These findings for the dyslexic group are shown in Table 47. The patterns of relation for the dyslexic and normal children did not vary widely, but differences appeared. Words per sentence and the number of sentences written were correlated for the dyslexics but not for the normals. For normal children, the more words written per sentence, the fewer sentences required. The dyslexics, being limited in syntax ability, wrote more sentences as they acquired facility in writing longer sentences. This relation is complicated further in that dyslexic children were highly deficient in output. They achieved a level of productivity (as indicated by number of sentences) equivalent to approximately two-thirds of average. The reading disability modified the natural association between number of sentences and sentence length found for normal children: the more words written per sentence, the fewer sentences needed.

A similar circumstance is evident for the syntax findings. In normal children the correlation between syntax and the other scores diminished after 7 years of age and was not significant after 11 years. For the dyslexic, syntax ability was associated with the other scores and remained interrelated until 15 years of age; this relation was positive (see Table 48). Dyslexia apparently disturbed the maturational process relating to acquisition of correct language usage. Facility with the written word seems to have been impeded so that all the factors involved were more interdependent; this is indicated also by the greater magnitude of the intercorrelations for the dyslexics in comparison with the normal.

Intercorrelation of Written Language and Auditory Abilities

Psychologists and educators responsible for planning remediation programs for children with reading disabilities often find it difficult to predict the most successful approaches. Many agree that general IQ scores are of only slight value in suggesting the cognitive disturbances present in the child.

In evaluating dyslexic children it is advantageous to secure examinations by an ophthalmologist, a neurologist, an electroencephalographist, a psychologist, and a reading specialist; general health also should be considered. In planning the educational remediation program all these diagnostic studies are of value, but the information derived from the educational and psychological studies is most directly applicable to cognitive learning factors. Some of the ways such information can be utilized are illustrated by the intercorrelation data presented here.

Three tests of cognitive abilities were administered: WISC, Detroit Learning Aptitute Test, and Draw-A-Man Test. A priori, the subtests from this battery were classified according to the predominant sensory modality required for their administration, auditory or visual. This classification resulted in 11 tests of auditory cognitive functioning and 6 of visual functioning. The intercorrelations among the five written language scores and each of the subtests (visual and auditory) then were ascertained. The findings for auditory learning processes are shown in Table 49.

There were significant intercorrelations between achievement in written language and all but two of the auditory cognitive tests: oral commissions was unrelated to syntax and total sentences. There can be little question that for the dyslexics auditory processes and success with written language were closely associated. Nevertheless, because of the common practice of using the WISC in study of reading-disability children, it is notable that except for syntax, the verbal (auditory) portion of this test was not closely correlated with success in learning to use the written word. The function most related to acquisition of written language was verbal opposites. Orientation and likenesses and differences also showed marked associations with written language learning.

An immediate implication of these results is the danger of undue reliance on a given test, such as the WISC, when making diagnostic studies of reading-disability children. Other instruments may be more advantageous in defining the type of cognitive function critical to academic learning. Moreover, tests such as the Detroit may provide more critical information for planning specific remediation.

Intercorrelation of Written Language and Visual Abilities

The tests classified as visual are not directly comparable with the auditory because they were essentially nonverbal, whereas those designated as auditory were essentially verbal. Nevertheless, it was anticipated that an analysis of the relation between visual nonverbal functions and facility with the written word would be useful. The results for the six subtests classified as visual are shown in Table 50. Of the 30 possibilities, only 6 did not show a statistically significant correlation with acquisition of written language, and 5 of these occurred because there were no relations between written language and ability to draw a man; the only other nonsignificant finding was for total words and visual span for letters.

On the basis of the rankings of the correlations, picture absurdities showed the closest correlation, followed by visual span for letters and the designs test. The lowest relations appeared for the Draw-A-Man Test followed by the WISC performance; the results for the Draw-A-Man were entirely negative. The magnitude of the intercorrelations for the visual cognitive functions was lower than for the auditory; the highest correlation for the visual functions was .68 (picture absurdities and total words), and for auditory functions the highest was .82 (verbal opposites and total words).

Perhaps the most consequential aspects of this analysis pertain to the commonly used mental tests, the WISC and the Draw-A-Man tests. Neither the verbal nor the performance IQ's on the WISC, except in rare instances, were closely associated with facility in use of the written word. The Draw-A-Man showed no significant relations. Psychologists should be cautious when interpreting the results from these tests for reading-disability children. The Detroit Test is more revealing of critical learning processes and is more indicative of the cognitive disturbances that must be considered when planning educational remediation.

Other inferences concern the specific cognitive processes, auditory and visual, of greatest consequence to acquisition of written language by dyslexics. Opposites, orientation, and likeness-differences ranked highest in the battery of auditory tests. Picture absurdities, designs, and letter span ranked as most critical in the battery of visual tests. The processes of greatest importance to acquisition of written language involved generalization and integration, rather than recognition or recall of letters. These findings support the results obtained by Blank and Bridger (1967). In addition to other aspects, educators need to initiate remediation programs that emphasize integrative learning.

Chapter V

Written Language and Mental Retardation

A vital question before educators and psychologists is how mental retardation and language deficiencies interact or are interrelated. The history of special education is replete with illustrations of the need to further delineate this complex issue. Marked language disorders occur in otherwise mentally competent children, and some who rank far below average in intelligence do not exhibit language deficiencies. Yet that there are intricate, perhaps close, relations between mental retardation and at least some aspects of language learning has been shown by many workers (Schiefelbusch *et al.*, 1967).

The definition of mental retardation as well as the definition of language must be considered a part of this predominant issue. In this discussion the language deficits in question are not those associated with sensory impairment or with obvious motor disturbances. Rather, they are of the type associated with central nervous system deficiencies, usually referred to as limitations in intelligence. As shown by the data, the language facility of mentally retarded children varies according to whether the language form is spoken, read, or written.

Unfortunately, the language of the retarded has been studied mainly in the spoken form; rarely have the read and written forms been included. Moreover, present knowledge essentially is in global terms—extent of the delay in acquisition of language (Mathews, 1971). There has been little emphasis on what is meant by language or whether the delay is primarily in acquisition of meaning or in receptive or expressive aspects.

Factor analysis demonstrates that exceptional children may be deficient in acquiring certain, but not all, facets of language. Accordingly, the data presented below suggest that educable mentally retarded school children are more successful in achieving facility with some factors of language than with others. Perhaps more concern should be given to the precise manner in which they learn to use language, as well as to the specific facets that appear most difficult.

This approach may be more accurate and provide a means whereby their pattern of language learning can be analyzed according to the cognitive processes characterizing each child or group of educable mentally handicapped (EMH) children.

A STUDY OF LANGUAGE

When the language study of EMH children was inaugurated, it was hoped that information would be gained on the interaction or interdependence of verbal facility and classification as educable mentally handicapped. There was a concern for accurate diagnosis, for definition of the problem. It seemed possible that some children classed as mentally retarded actually had childhood aphasia or dyslexia or dysgraphia (Myklebust, 1971a). It seemed urgent to study these children in such a way as to differentiate aphasia, dyslexia, dysgraphia, and other reading and orthographic involvements, from the deficits commonly designated mental retardation. A subsidiary concern was to gather information on the extent to which any language disorder (spoken, read, or written) characterized this group of exceptional children, and on the ways these disorders may contribute to limitations in cognitive functioning. Accordingly, the investigation included auditory as well as read and written language.

The Sample

The samples, normal and retarded, were selected from the same schools in a large urban school system. The EMH children were enrolled in special education classes at the time of the investigation. As discussed in Chapter III, they had normal hearing and vision, their motor functioning was not impaired, and they were not otherwise deviate. In the school system from which this population was selected children were classified as needing special education if their IQ was below 80 and above 50. All the children so classified, who did not have other handicaps, were included, but participation was dependent on ability to respond. The number of males exceeded the number of females at all age levels, the largest number of children occurring at the age levels of 13 and 15 years. Because of varying limitations by age, the entire test battery could not be administered to all the children. Thus, depending on the nature of the task, the number of children varied.

Cognitive Abilities

To secure information on cognitive levels of function, the Primary Mental Abilities (PMA) Test and the Draw-A-Man Test were administered. The comparative results on the PMA for the normal and the retarded are shown in Table 51. The normal group scored within the average range, the lowest score being 104 and the highest 111. The scores for the retarded were remarkably uniform, the lowest being 60 and the highest 71, a range of 11 points. The retarded children were functioning at a level close to two-thirds of average, with little variation from one factor to the other, verbal or nonverbal. It may be of some importance, nevertheless, that the lowest scores were for reasoning and the highest for number and verbal pictures. The findings for the Draw-A-Man Test are given in Table 52; the sample included substantially fewer children. The highest scores were obtained by the 9-year-olds. At the other age levels the results are in close agreement with the scores on the PMA Test.

These results on the cognitive levels of function suggest that the EMH children were characteristic of those classified as mentally retarded and in need of special education. The children so designated were defined as having IQ's below 80 and above 50, a range of 30 points. Thus the projected median IQ is 65, the score that represents the mean level of function on the measures of cognitive ability. However, as indicated by the data presented below, this generalization cannot be used as the only basis for program planning for this group of children. Though research continues to be limited, it must be recognized that any one of these children might be an underachiever and in need of remediation for specific disabilities. The range of 30 points (from IQ 50 to IQ 80) is substantial, and therefore, the needs vary according to the level of cognitive functioning.

Typically, special education programming is based on the assumption that there is no variation in the learning patterns of the mentally retarded, that they learn in the same way as normal children but at a reduced level. According to this concept a retarded child 12 years of age (whose functional ability is two-thirds of average) would achieve educationally as the normal 9-year-old. This approach, in common practice for some decades, adheres to the "degree of involvement" construct of intelligence and mental retardation. There is need for redefinition in terms of a more dynamic construct that includes the cognitive abilities frame of reference. Such a dynamic approach would permit development of a learning model that recognizes variations within the population of the mentally retarded and adheres to the principle that many of these children require specialized programs that stress language or nonverbal learning or both. Further discussion of these issues is reserved until after presentation of the results for language acquisition: spoken, read, and written.

Auditory Language

Auditory Receptive Language

Language development was appraised in four ways: auditory receptive, auditory expressive, read, and written. Two measures of auditory receptive language were obtained. Test One necessitated understanding the instructions, following the directions, and writing the responses. Test Two required comprehending directions and relating this auditory language form to the visual form that appeared before the child. The results for the mentally retarded compared with the normal are given in Table 53.

The retarded were inferior at all age levels. Moreover, the ratio between the groups remained unusually stable from age to age. The difference between the scores for Test One was 8 points at 9, 13, and 15 years, and 10 points at 11 years. For Test Two the difference at 11 and 13 years was 11 points, and at 15 years it was 8 points. The normal children reached a plateau on Test One at 11 years, whereas the retarded made developmental gains throughout the age range of 9 to 15 years. Thus, at the upper age level they were less inferior than at the early ages. These results suggest that the retarded, though functionally below average, achieved greater success in comprehending the spoken word as they became older. This pattern appeared also for Test Two. The retarded made a gain of 3.5 points from 13 to 15 years but the gain made by the normal children was 1.2 points. The retarded scored at approximately 50 percent of normal in early life and around 70% of normal at the upper age levels.

These findings suggest that the retarded were capable of substantial gains in learning through the age of 15 years, even with marked deficits in auditory language in early life. The extent to which these gains may continue beyond the age of 15 is not evident from this study; the upper limits for this learning should be established. The retarded achieved below their cognitive levels in early life but were more successful in reaching this level as they became older. There was some indication that they might exceed the levels indicated by the PMA Test because they continued to show growth after 15 years of age. Moreover, these children were not receiving specialized assistance in development of auditory receptive language. If such remediation were given, it is conceivable that they would have scored higher on the language tests and perhaps on the PMA Test.

Auditory Expressive Language

Facility with auditory expressive language also was evaluated in two ways. Test One required that the child give the opposite of the word given by the examiner. Test Two was a measure of the child's ability to define words. The results are presented in Table 54. The retarded were inferior on both tests at all age levels. Their performance on these measures, in ratio to the normal, was lower than for receptive language. On the opposites test they progressed from approximately one-fourth of average at 11 years to one-half at 15 years. On definition of words their achievement was one-third of average at 11 and 13 years, and approximately 40% at 15 years.

This pattern varied from the findings for auditory receptive language because the retarded children's inferiority in expressive language was greater. In receptive language their scores were more equivalent to the cognitive levels disclosed by the PMA Test, but in expressive language they fell substantially below these levels. These children showed disturbances in conversion of input data into equivalent output form, designated as a conversion loss.

The exact feature of conversion loss remains to be determined in mentally retarded children; greater familiarity with this condition has been gained in relation to children with language disorders who are not retarded (Myklebust, 1971a). In terms of cognitive processes and the psychology of learning for the mentally retarded, it is essential that psychologists and educators recognize that retarded children face specific disturbances that require specialized remediation; they do not necessarily learn as the average child does, only at a reduced level. The retarded must have the advantage of intensive analysis of their patterns of learning and clear description of the deficits for which remediation is necessary. In addition, there is great need to continue to amass information on the specific nature of the conversion loss phenomenon so that better learning opportunities can be made available to this group of children.

Read Language

A primary distinction between educable and trainable children, as determined educationally, is that the trainable are not expected to learn to read. In the studies described here, in addition to the question of relations among the forms of language, there was a desire to explore the extent to which the educable were successful in learning to read.

The results comparing the normal and retarded children are presented in Table 55; the test of reading was a measure of vocabulary. A significant finding was that at 9 and 11 years the retarded children scored so low that the data could not be included for statistical analysis. Even at the ages of 13 and 15 years, ability to read was limited. At the 13-year age level their competence was at approximately one-third of average. At the age of 15 they were successful only at one-ninth of the average level; this decline at 15 years was not present for auditory language.

Several implications emerge. As suggested by the hypothesis (see Volume One),* auditory language was achieved more successfully than the read; more integrity and potential for learning are required for the second form of language acquired. But it cannot be assumed that the EMH children had achieved their maximum success in learning to read. What they might have achieved with the advantage of specialized reading programs is unknown.

It is in this connection that the implications should be of most value. There were deficits in auditory language and there is evidence that if the level of function in auditory language were raised, there would be reciprocal benefits in read language. Moreover, there was a conversion loss from input to output in auditory language, and the results for reading suggest another type of conversion loss. The retarded were markedly deficient in the cognitive processes of going from the auditory to the visual form of language. Initially, in learning to read, visual information must be superimposed on the auditory. As a cognitive function, this emerges as an unusually difficult learning task for EMH children. Precisely for this reason it may be of critical importance to develop educational remediation procedures aimed at alleviating this disturbance. More inclusively, educational programs that stress comprehension of auditory language, transducing of this form into spoken language, and conversion of auditory into the read (visual) form of language are essential. This approach signifies the advantages of redefining the educational and learning needs of retarded children. Teachers then would not follow the principle of simply reducing level of difficulty and teaching the retarded like the normal. They would evolve techniques aimed at the specific

* *Development and Disorders of Written Language*, Volume One, Picture Story Language Test (Myklebust, 1965).

deficits and learning modes of the child, irrespective of his level of overall cognitive functioning. They would assume that the extent of the limitation is only one aspect of his total circumstances; it may not be a highly useful indicator in determining the psychology by which he learns most effectively. Though more evidence must be collected, the mentally retarded vary from average in their manner of learning and present a complex challenge for all concerned with their learning and adjustment.

Written Language

Studies of the development of written language in exceptional children, including in the mentally retarded, are rare. Variation in the learning patterns in acquiring this language form was a focus of the studies described here, though there was interest in gaining information relative to all the language systems. The presupposition was that a higher level of cognitive function is required to achieve facility with written than with read language and that reading requires a higher developmental level than spoken language. Accordingly, it was anticipated that comparing normal and EMH children would provide insights into all facets of language learning and indicate areas of deficit that would enhance understanding of retarded children. The findings for written language are presented in Table 56.

Total Words

The EMH children were inferior on all aspects of written language; they were not equivalent to the normal on any one of the five scores or on any one of the three factors derived from the Picture Story Language Test (PSLT). Theirs was the most generalized deficit of any of the groups of exceptional children studied. They varied from approximately one-tenth of average at 9 years of age to one-fifth at 13 and 15 years. The length of their stories was about 80 words less at 9 years, 100 words less at 11 years, 111 words less at 13 years, and 106 words less at 15 years. The extent of their limitation in productivity remained stable throughout the age range, as shown by Figure 23. A further indication of differences developmentally is that the normal group's stories increased in length from 90 words at 9 years to a maximum of approximately 150 words at 13 years, an increment of almost 60 words and an average of 15 words per age level. In contrast, the EMH wrote only 9 words at 9 years and increased

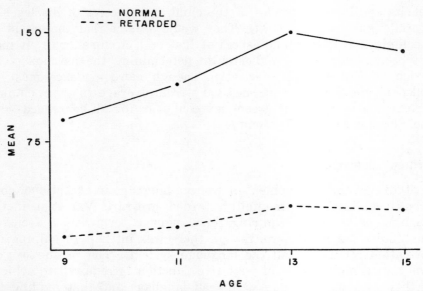

FIGURE 23. Comparison of normal and mentally retarded children on total words.

to a maximum of 32 words, an average gain of 8 words per age level. The retarded achieved approximately one-half the rate of growth in story length compared with the control group. In terms of the factors of written language measured by the PSLT, Factor I (total words, total sentences, and abstract-concrete) proved most difficult for the EMH children.

In view of the cognitive levels of the retarded, as reflected by the PMA Test scores, the marked limitation in written language productivity is difficult to explain. On the other hand, the extent of the deficiency is consistent with the hypothesis that the written language form requires greater psychoneurological integrity than the auditory or read forms. Nevertheless, we cannot overlook the implication that the retarded children were underachieving. This is in contrast to auditory receptive language because in this type of verbal learning they were more successful in reaching expected levels of proficiency.

Total Sentences

The pattern of development in number of sentences written was similar to the normal. Gains were made up to 13 years, after which the retarded children reached a plateau (see Figure 24). Though

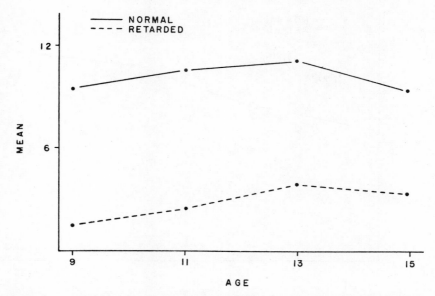

FIGURE 24. Comparison of normal and mentally retarded children on total sentences.

they wrote increasingly longer stories up to 15 years, like the normals, after 13 years they wrote longer, not more, sentences. The extent of the deficit remained constant; the EMH children wrote approximately eight sentences less at each of the age levels. The limitation in productivity, as measured by the number of sentences written, was severe in early life and, though growth occurred, remained markedly deficient throughout the greater portion of the school years.

Words per Sentence

Sentence length proved an unusually stable measure of written language and revealed a highly linear growth pattern for normal children. As one of the factors composing the PSLT, it was distinctly independent of the other factors. The configuration for the developmental pattern for the retarded also was remarkably uniform from one age to the other (see Figure 25). The EMH children gained approximately two words per sentence at each 2-year interval (one word per year), a rate of growth equal to the normal. But initially (at 9 years), they wrote approximately seven words less per sentence, and this ratio of inferiority compared with the control group remained throughout the age range. More specifically, the retarded

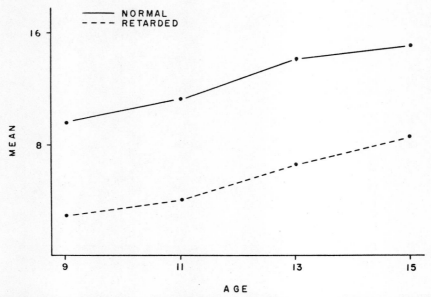

FIGURE 25. Comparison of normal and mentally retarded children on words per sentence.

wrote sentences of about one-third average length at 9 and 11 years and about one-half average length at 13 and 15 years.

These results are in close agreement with those for total words and total sentences; the EMH children showed equivalent deficits on two of the three factors of written language measured by the PSLT. Again, a primary question is the extent to which this inferiority can be attributed to underachievement. At 15 years of age the EMH children wrote shorter sentences than the average 9-year-old. It seems unlikely that this degree of retardation can be explained on the basis of generalized intellectual subnormality. Even in terms of our estimates of cognitive ability, achievement might be predicted at a level of two-thirds of average, not one-half of average as indicated by these findings. For special education the implication is that programs should be developed and designed to focus specifically on raising the level of output of written language. Such programs might include remedial instruction for the related language forms, the spoken and read.

Syntax

The findings for the correctness of the language written disclose the significance of considering the specific effects of the handicap

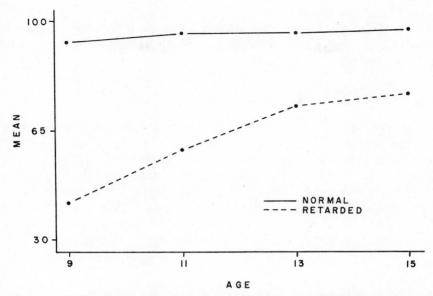

FIGURE 26. Comparison of normal and mentally retarded children on syntax.

on language acquisition. The EMH children were not equally inferior on all aspects of written language. Their level of success on the third factor measured on the PSLT (syntax) was substantially greater than on the other two factors (discussed above). The syntax quotients were approximately three-fourths of average; the other scores were about one-half of average. In contrast to their performance on total words, total sentences, and words per sentence, the retarded showed considerable growth from 9 through 15 years of age. At 9 years their syntax quotient was 55 points below average, at 11 years 38 points lower, at 13 years 24 points, and at 15 years only 22 points below average (see Figure 26).

These results are intriguing. The EMH children were severely delayed in acquisition of syntax, but continued to develop this aspect of language long after the age at which it is fully established in normal children. Their upper level of success may be even higher than shown by the data because a plateau had not been reached at 15 years. Though their success was greater with syntax, at the upper age level they performed less well than the average 9-year-old child.

In terms of the psychology of language learning, EMH children were delayed in acquisition of auditory language; thus, they could not achieve the higher forms, the read and written. Syntax, which is a facet of spoken language, was not fully established even at 15 years of age. These are implications that must be pursued by special education if the EMH are to be more successful with the read and written language forms. But, even so, the need for remediation of syntax is less urgent than development of output, as demonstrated by story and sentence length.

Abstract-Concrete

The abstract-concrete scale was developed as a measure of meaning; in normal children this aspect fell into the same factor as total words and total sentences. The EMH children made gains in use of abstract meaning but at a level of only about one-half of average. In contrast with the control group, they reached a plateau at 13 years (see Figure 27), as they did on certain of the other measures of language. This lack of gain after 13 years is of serious consequence and warrants attention from psychologists and educators.

Summary

The findings for the retarded suggest the precise nature of their inferiority in written language; they attained their highest level of

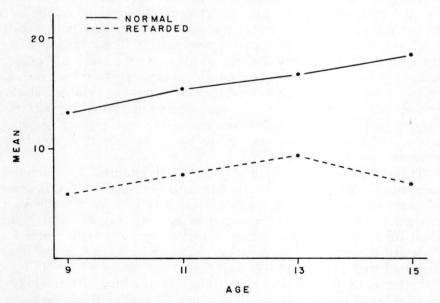

FIGURE 27. Comparison of normal and mentally retarded children on abstract-concrete.

function in correct usage. They were most effective when converting auditory receptive language into syntactically correct written language. They were most deficient when converting the spoken and read forms into written expressions of adequate length; they were unable to acquire an output level commensurate with expectations. The limitation in productivity is associated with their poor performance in use of abstract meaning. Presumably, if output could be fostered through remediation, communication of meaning also would be enhanced. These are complex educational problems, but educators cannot avoid them.

Intercorrelation of Auditory and Written Language

The mentally retarded were deficient in all aspects of language learning: spoken, read, and written. In some respects their limitations reflected a cognitive disturbance of the interneurosensory type (Myklebust *et al.*, 1971). Auditory information was not readily converted into visual equivalents, nor was input adequately converted into output. Perhaps, to a degree greater than previously anticipated, EMH children are encumbered by cognitive dysfunctions that require specific educational approaches.

This possibility was explored further through an intercorrelation analysis of the relations between auditory and written language (see Tables 57 and 58). There were significant associations with auditory receptive language only at the age of 15 years; for auditory expressive language there was one significant correlation, at 13 years. This limited association between auditory and written language was not observed for the normal or for the other groups of exceptional children. The correlations with auditory receptive language appeared only at 15 years, and only for sentence length, syntax, and use of abstract meaning; there were no correlations with story length and number of sentences.

Diagnostically, and in terms of cognitive functioning, the EMH children found it difficult to convert one form of language (auditory) into its visual equivalent. Because this cognitive function emerged by 15 years of age, it can be concluded that it was acquired, but at a severely retarded rate and only to a moderate extent; in certain respects reciprocal processing of auditory and visual information was not attained. Greatest success with this type of learning in normal children was seen between 7 to 9 years of age. The EMH had less success in interneurosensory learning and achieved it at a much later age.

On the basis of the PMA Test results, the average cognitive level of function for the EMH group was approximately 10 years. Inasmuch as normal children achieved success in learning the visual equivalents of auditory language primarily between 7 and 9 years of age, the EMH children should have accomplished similar learning, unless cognitive disturbances were present. Why they did not is the principal question before the psychologist and educator. The advantages that would derive from highly programmed remedial education are not known, but there is a need for such an emphasis in special education.

Locomotor Coordination

A number of investigators have been interested in the relations between motor development and mental retardation (Sloan, 1955). Heath (1942), who devised the Railwalking Test used in these studies, found an association between locomotor coordination and etiological type (endogenous or exogenous) of mental retardation. Other data show a similar association between locomotor coordination and etiological type of deafness in children (Myklebust, 1964). Because of these associations, a study was undertaken of the locomotor abilities of the EMH children. Motor ability offers an opportunity for evaluating relations between the psychodynamic (cognitive) and neurodynamic aspects of behavior, a question of concern to investigators. One aspect of the question is whether psychological or neuromotor factors show the more normal progression developmentally.

The Railwalking Test was administered individually to both EMH and control groups. The results are shown in Table 59. The retarded were significantly inferior to the controls at all age levels. The developmental configuration also varied by group in that the EMH children reached a plateau at 13 years, whereas the normals made wide gains in locomotor ability between 13 and 15 years. Except at the age of 15, the retarded remained at a stable level of growth compared with the controls, their score being 35 points below average at 9 years, 33 points below at 11 years, and 36 points below at 13 years.

These differences in locomotor coordination are of consequence to the total developmental complex of EMH children; even at 15 years their performance was below the norm for 9-year-olds. The precise relations between neuromotor deficits and language learning are unknown, but this area of study is in urgent need of scientific investigation. These findings demonstrate both cognitive and motor deficiencies in EMH children, but whether one can be improved through remediation of the other remains to be ascertained. The results also emphasize that an inclusive psychoneurological model is necessary when programs for these children are developed.

SUMMARY

The EMH children manifested a complex of limitations in language learning. Their greatest facility was with the spoken word. But even at this level cognitive malfunctioning was evident in their inability to adequately convert receptive into expressive equivalents. A favorable sign was their continuing gain in comprehension of the spoken word even at 15 years of age, an indication that they would achieve a level of function beyond that shown by these data.

Deficits existed in transducing from auditory to visual language, from the spoken to the read. And as predicted by the model, the greatest inferiority was in written language. But this deficit varied by factor, with most normal achievement in the area of syntax. Educational programs must be introduced that focus on the specific cognitive disability. Only then can maximum learning be expected.

More broadly, the problem of mental retardation in children should be redefined, especially in relation to language learning and instruction. Educators in the past have been influenced largely, if not exclusively, by the *degree* of involvement; hence, the designations trainable and educable. In view of present knowledge, *type* of involvement should be given equal consideration. When the type of deficit is considered, the limitations in learning can be analyzed in terms of a cognitive model. This has many advantages for the child.

A psychoneurological model also enhances understanding of the mentally retarded, and teachers might profit from studies on brain function that clarify the different roles served by each of the hemispheres (Mountcastle, 1962; Millikan and Darley, 1967; Geschwind, 1972). Evidence is gradually accruing that the left hemisphere has major responsibility for language learning, and thus has been designated the dominant hemisphere. The right hemisphere is thought to be mainly responsible for nonverbal learning.

Using this psychoneurological model, an investigation was made of the degree of handedness demonstrated by mentally retarded children; more than 1000 children were examined. Results of the study, based on the original work of Doll (1916), revealed that degree of handedness (laterality) and level of functional intelligence are related (Myklebust *et al.*, 1973). These findings provide a clue to the ways in which mental retardation and language learning may be associated. Unless the left hemisphere develops, the necessary specialized function which permits acquisition of language is impeded. If this imposition is fundamental, effective means and methods for circumventing or alleviating it must be explored. This is possible on the basis of the cognitive model. The necessary psychoneurological functions may be enhanced if appropriate remediation is provided. For example, the teacher may stress interneurosensory learning through techniques that emphasize converting input to output, auditory to visual, and read to written language. These are challenging possibilities, but their inclusion in educational programs assumes a change in perspective, a change from perceiving the child only in terms of degree of involvement to perceiving him in terms of cognitive function. Such a change would lead to a new educational definition of mental retardation.

Chapter VI

Written Language and Disorders of Articulation

Speech and language are not synonymous. A person may have normal language but be limited in ability to speak. Conversely, one may have a disorder of language but be normal in ability to enunciate. In this chapter data are presented on the language abilities of children with disorders of articulation. Conflicting opinions have been expressed concerning possible relations between articulation defects and deficiencies in language (Powers, 1971).

Though ability to speak and ability to use language are not necessarily associated, many disorders of articulation are caused by dysarthria, a condition that results from minimal brain dysfunction. With a base in neurology, dysarthria (partial) and anarthria (total) refer to paralytic involvements of the tongue and other facets of the speech mechanism. When dysarthria is present, inferences may be made concerning the presence of other brain disturbances that impede acquisition of language. For example, aphasia and dyslexia are language disorders that derive from dysfunctions in the brain. A question for research, therefore, is to determine the association of deficits that are causally related. Nevertheless, ascertaining etiological relations was not the primary objective of this study. Rather, the aim was to clarify the learning disabilities that occur in children who have articulation defects, with special reference to written language.

LANGUAGE ABILITY OF CHILDREN WITH DISORDERS OF ARTICULATION

The Sample

The sample consisted of children, taken from six schools in a metropolitan setting, who were receiving speech therapy. Excluded were stutterers and children with cleft palate or cerebral palsy. Those included were representative of children characteristically classified as having disorders of articulation. Through the choice of schools, socioeconomic, ethnic, and racial differences were minimized. The control group of normal children was selected from the same schools. The incidence of children receiving speech therapy was highest at 7 years, with fewer at each succeeding age level. Most were not continued in speech therapy after 11 years of age.

Cognitive Abilities

The Primary Mental Abilities (PMA) Test was used to evaluate the cognitive levels of function. The scores revealed that the children with disorders of articulation were not inferior intellectually to the normals, though significant differences appeared (see Table 60). Compared with the controls, the group with articulation disorders was limited mainly on factors requiring language facility, reading or use of words in solving the cognitive task. This is exemplified by the scores on the reasoning tests. With one exception the children with articulation disorders scored lowest on word grouping, a test that depends on ability to read as well as on acquisition of vocabulary. In contrast, figure grouping, perceptual speed, and number are largely nonverbal. As revealed also by the language test results presented below, their cognitive functioning appears to have been impeded by deficiencies in language. These data support the findings of McGrady (1964) that language disabilities and articulation defects are associated.

The Draw-A-Man Test also was administered; the results are presented in Table 61. Again, the major finding was the similarity of the populations, experimental and control, albeit a significant difference appeared at 11 years in favor of the controls. These data suggest that the children with articulation disorders were not disturbed in body-image perception, self-perception, or person perception. These findings imply that children with articulation disorders differ from those designated as having learning disabilities. Previous studies have shown that children presenting marked deficits in learning, but without speech defects, often are disturbed in ability to draw a man (Johnson and Myklebust, 1967).

Auditory Language

A primary objective of this investigation was to study interactions of the language forms: spoken, read, and written. Though there is interest in the associations between articulation deficits and language disorders, definitive research continues to lag, particularly with respect to written language (Powers, 1971).

Auditory Receptive Language

Two tests of ability to comprehend the spoken word were given (see discussion of techniques in Chapter III). Only minor differences appeared (see Table 62). At 9 and 11 years of age the speech-handicapped performed below the levels of the control group. Both groups showed developmental maturation by age, but children with articulation deficits made little progress from 9 to 11 years. Thus, though there was evidence that the children with articulation disorders were disturbed in facility with auditory language, they did not differ widely from the normal.

Auditory Expressive Language

Because input and output are reciprocally related, a deficiency in receptive language should be reflected in expressive functions. The findings given in Table 63 reveal this trend. Children with disturbances in articulation showed moderate deficits in auditory receptive functioning, but substantial deficits in facility with auditory expressive language. Again, these variations occurred at the ages of 9 and 11 years, suggesting direct interaction of input and output. Such inferences, however, must be made with caution.

The configuration of the maturational pattern varied by group. On the opposites test the normals made wide gains from 7 to 9 years (18 points), and from 9 to 11 years (10 points), with a slight increment from 11 to 13 years. The speech-handicapped showed a gain of 9 points from 7 to 9 years, only 2 points from 9 to 11, and a marked rise (20 points) from 11 to 13 years. Though equivalent to normal at 7 years, their growth pattern was much slower between 9 and 11 years. In addition to an articulation defect, these children were delayed in attaining normal levels of auditory expressive language. This trend appeared also for the results on definition of words.

Read Language

Monroe (1932) in an early study, and more recently McGrady (1968), found evidence of reading disabilities in children with speech defects. The present investigation concerned possible relations among all the language systems: spoken, read, and written. As in the other groups of exceptional children, the Columbia Vocabulary Test was administered to secure data on reading levels; the results are shown in Table 64. The children with disorders of articulation were much less proficient in reading at 9 and 11 years of age. Moreover, as with auditory expressive language, there was considerable variation in the developmental patterns by group. The controls gained 12 points from 9 to 11 years, and 10 points from 11 to 13 years. In contrast, the children with articulation defects showed an increment of 8 points between 9 and 11 years and 20 points from 11 to 13 years.

These findings indicate that articulation disorders are likely to be accompanied by language disorders. To some extent the deficits in language appear to be explained by delays in maturational development, because the children with articulation defects tended to attain normal levels as they became older. Nevertheless, deficits in articulation did not occur on a unitary basis. Children having such deficits need remediation for language disorders.

Written Language

Only meager attention has been given to the possibility that children with articulation defects may also have disorders of written language. In view of their deficiencies in spoken and read language, special concern was devoted to this question in this investigation. As discussed in Volume One,* a primary hypothesis was that deficiencies at the level of auditory language would impede acquisition of visual language, both read and written. The data below support this postulation; children with disorders of articulation had moderate limitations in auditory language, significant deficiencies in read language, and severe disturbances in written language. The results for the last-mentioned are given in Table 65.

Total Words

The Picture Story Language Test (PSLT) results disclosed that the children with articulation disorders were unusually deficient in the number of words written. Moreover, this limitation in productivity increased with age. At 7 years of age they wrote approximately 10 words less per story than the normal. At 9 years this discrepancy increased to 50 words, at 11 years to 65 words, and at 13 years to

---

* *Development and Disorders of Written Language*, Volume One, *Picture Story Language Test* (Myklebust, 1965).

90 words. These were severe limitations in acquisition and use of written language. The greater deficiency at the upper age levels occurred mainly because of poor progress in written language development as age increased. The speech-handicapped children were highly retarded in facility with the written word and, contrary to their performance on auditory and read language, they became more inadequate as they reached the later elementary-school years (see Figure 28).

Complex problems in learning were presented by this group of children. In addition to disorders of articulation they were markedly deficient in output of the written word. The factor-analysis results for normal children (see Table 17) revealed that total words and sentences and abstract-concrete (meaning) formed a major component of written language as measured by the PSLT. This factor presented unusual difficulties for children with disorders of articulation; they were more equivalent to normal on the other factors. The implication is that remediation by speech pathologists and special education teachers should focus on development of vocabulary and output. But there is a significant correlation between story length (output) and communication of abstract meaning. Therefore, word

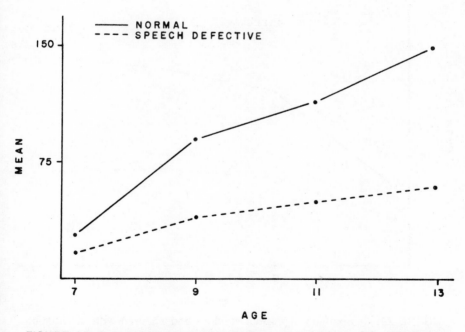

FIGURE 28. Comparison of normal children and children with articulation disorders on total words.

meaning—read and written—should also be emphasized. It may be that school failure in speech-handicapped children is more directly related to their poor facility with visual language than to their deficiencies in auditory language. The primary emphasis, therefore, should be on interneurosensory learning, on conversion of the auditory form into the read and written form. In view of these children's normal level of cognitive functioning and their moderate deficits in auditory language, the outlook for improved facility with the read and written word seems good. On the other hand, more than speech therapy must be offered if this improvement is to be achieved.

Total Sentences

The limitation in productivity was shown also by the number of sentences written per story. Children with deficits in articulation were inferior to normals at all age levels, and the differences were highly significant. But the pattern of performance was unlike that for number of words. The articulation-deficient group reached a plateau at 11 years of age, and in terms of difference scores, their deficiencies did not increase with age (see Figure 29). Compared

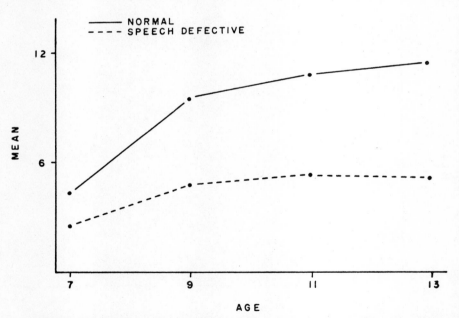

FIGURE 29. Comparison of normal children and children with articulation disorders on total sentences.

with the control group, at 7 years they wrote approximately two sentences less per story, at 9 years this discrepancy increased to five sentences, at 11 years it remained at five, and at 13 years it was six. Like the normals, as the speech-handicapped became older they wrote longer sentences, not more and more sentences; this is confirmed by the data for words per sentence. But as an indicator of output of language the findings for total sentences disclose a significant limitation.

Words per Sentence

The performance of the speech-handicapped group was more nearly normal on sentence length (see Figure 30). Marked differences occurred only at 7 and 9 years of age. This is in contrast to number of words written because as the children became older their facility with words per sentence improved; they were not equally deficient on all facets of written language. For example, at 13 years of age they were only 2 years retarded in sentence length, but approximately 5 years in story length. Inasmuch as words per sentence is independent of total words, as shown by the factor analysis, these children

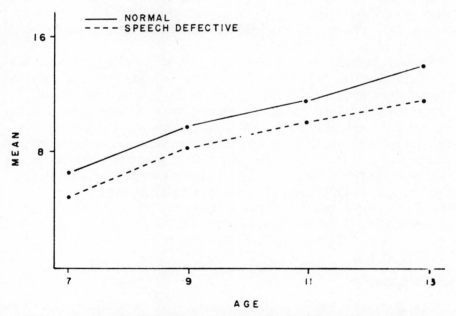

FIGURE 30. Comparison of normal children and children with articulation disorders on words per sentence.

were more limited in generalized output and fluency than in facility to produce a sentence of normal length; this conclusion is supported by the data on syntax.

These data indicate the type of language deficit experienced by the child who has an articulation disorder. His limitation is mainly inability to produce a story with a setting and a plot, one which entails richness of meaning. This deficiency may be due to a lack of vocabulary or to an inability to formulate ideas in a manner that permits such use of written language. It is in this respect that these findings may be useful in planning remediation. Children with articulation disorders need more assistance in acquiring vocabulary and general fluency of output than in the technical aspects of sentence structure and syntax. This finding may be one of the most significant outcomes of the present investigation.

Syntax

The articulation-deficient children were markedly inadequate in use of syntax in early life but achieved more normal function by the age of 13 years. At 7 years they were 21 points below average, but by 9 years much of this limitation had been overcome, the syntax quotient at this age being only 12 points below the mean for the control group. This gain in correct usage continued at 11, reaching normal levels at 13 years, as shown by Figure 31.

These data, together with the findings for total words, total sentences, and words per sentence, indicate in a striking manner that the children with articulation defects in early school age had a generalized deficiency in use of the written word. However, as they became older, certain aspects of this limitation were overcome. Gradually, they attained facility in producing sentences of more normal length and in correct use of syntax. Their greatest need, therefore, is for educational programs that emphasize output: vocabulary, fluency, and story organization. They require less stress on producing sentences of normal length and correct syntax. They urgently need remediation for one of the factors of written language measured by the PSLT; less urgently they need help with the other two.

Abstract-Concrete

The abstract-concrete scale was developed to measure meaning; this score represents proficiency in use of abstract ideas. The measure is correlated with total words and sentences, being one of the three

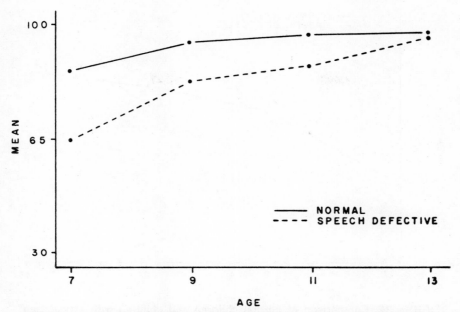

FIGURE 31. Comparison of normal children and children with articulation disorders on syntax.

components of Factor 1. The children with deficits in articulation were unusually inferior in communication of abstract meaning. This limitation persisted at all levels. They were most equivalent to the controls at 7 years of age, when their score was only a little more than two points below average. At the upper age levels this difference was slightly less than six points. The developmental pattern also varied (see Figure 32). The normals made a substantial gain in use of abstract meaning between 7 and 9 years, with progressively less increment at 11 and 13 years. The speech-handicapped, like the controls, made their greatest advance between 7 and 9 years, but thereafter made little gain.

The reason for this inability to maintain growth in communication of meaning is not clear, but when an articulatory disorder was present the child was unusually concrete in writing a story; he was more limited to the observable. He did not usually include plot, setting, or role-playing; nor did he employ interpersonal relations, metaphor, allegory, or moral values. This may be caused by disturbances of inner language. Because story length and use of abstraction are closely associated, if greater fluency could be developed,

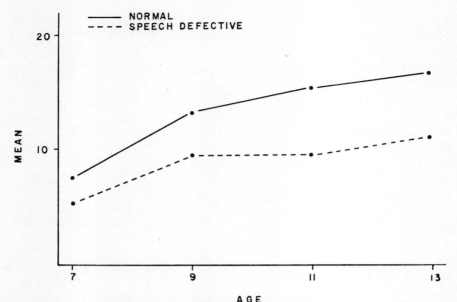

FIGURE 32. Comparison of normal children and children with articulation disorders on abstract-concrete.

presumably depth of meaning also would be enhanced. Perhaps the converse also would apply. With development of inner language, output might be fostered. Nevertheless, because of the limitations of our knowledge at this time, it would be advantageous for educators and speech pathologists to use both approaches—instruction in word usage as well as in abstract meaning. Children having disorders of articulation are not deficient only in ability to enunciate. They experience severe deficits in language, particularly in written form.

Intercorrelation of Auditory and Written Language

The speech-handicapped children were deficient in all aspects of language: spoken, read, and written. To explore these verbal cognitive disturbances more fully, an intercorrelation analysis was made of the results for the spoken and written forms (see Tables 66 and 67). Auditory comprehension and use of the written word were more closely associated than for the controls. This difference occurred for total words and sentences, the facet of written language on which the speech-handicapped group was most inferior, and it appeared at 9 years of age. Apparently, the children with deficits in articulation were disturbed in auditory receptive language, requiring more years of maturation before visual language could be processed through the auditory. This possibility is indicated also by the results for syntax, inasmuch as correct usage did not parallel the developmental pattern of normal children.

As there were differences in the patterns for auditory receptive language, so there were differences in the relations for auditory expressive language. Auditory expressive language was unduly associated with the written in early life, indicating a rigid interaction between the spoken and written forms. This disturbance seems to have persisted, because normal associations between these language systems did not develop at the upper age levels.

The children with articulation disorders had disturbances in cognition involving relations among the spoken, read, and written language forms. They were deficient in acquiring certain facets of auditory language—a primary disability—but in addition were unable to acquire the visual equivalents of the auditory form; there were both intraneurosensory and interneurosensory cognitive dysfunctions. Hence, an inclusive approach to remediation is indicated, with attention to the specific characteristics of their deficiencies. Emphasis might well be placed on auditory language, especially expressive, but the program also should stress conversion of auditory information visual equivalents.

Locomotor Coordination

The Health Railwalking Test, a measure of locomotor coordination, was administered to all the groups of exceptional children. The results for the speech-handicapped children are given in Table 68. These children were markedly inferior to the controls, but these differences were mainly at 7 and 9 years of age; the sample was small at the upper ages. The pattern of development for the controls showed a major gain between 7 and 9 years (24 points), a modest gain between 9 and 11 years (about 6 points), and, again, considerable gain between 11 and 13 years (15 points). In comparison, the configuration for the articulation-deficient group varied substantially. There was modest growth from 7 to 9 years (7 points), a greater increment from 9 to 11 years (14 points), and almost no change thereafter.

The speech-handicapped not only were inferior to the controls, but their growth pattern also varied, with the major advancement occurring between 9 and 11 years, instead of between 7 and 9 years. These differences suggest that some of the variation is attributable to maturational delay rather than to disorder. The deficits in generalized locomotor coordination were obvious prior to 11 years of age, after which motor function became equivalent to normal; neurodynamic factors were influential in early life, the deficits being developmental, not a permanent disability. Nevertheless, it is unlikely that this explanation pertains to all the children in this population. There is need for further study, especially at the upper school ages. In the meantime, the language-learning problems of children with articulation disorders should be regarded as inclusive, demanding special education programming in various ways.

Chapter VII

Written Language and Social-Emotional Disturbances

Children with social-emotional disturbances need assistance from educators, psychologists, and other professional workers. They constitute a significant portion of those included under the regimen of special education. Yet their definition as a group has presented difficulties. Currently, so far as delivery of services is concerned, they are often combined with the mentally retarded and those with learning disabilities. This plan is advantageous only if the cognitive learning styles of these groups are similar; unfortunately, scientific evidence to this effect is lacking. Precisely for this reason a group of socially-emotionally disturbed children was included in these studies of language acquisition and learning.

Research evidence must be accumulated about the impact of social-emotional disturbances on cognition. If such disturbances do not modify the pattern or style of learning, the most logical remediation approach would be one of educational management rather than one that stresses modes of learning. The basic question is whether the psychology by which the child learns most effectively has been altered. To explore this question a group of socially-emotionally disturbed children was compared with a control group and with other groups of exceptional children.

LANGUAGE ABILITY OF SOCIALLY-EMOTIONALLY DISTURBED CHILDREN

The Sample

As with all types of exceptional children, the sample or population depends on the selective criteria applied. In this investigation the socially-emotionally disturbed group was chosen in the same way as the other groups of exceptional children. The sample thus consisted of all the children at the specified ages who were enrolled in special education programs, hence, selection had been made on an operational basis by school personnel. A wide range of behavior problems was represented, from moderate to severe. Some children were in such serious conflict with society that they required detention; others presented disturbances primarily in the classroom. It is appropriate to view these children as characteristic of those unable to conform to a variety of the requirements prescribed by public schools in a large metropolitan setting, as well as to the regulations imposed by society as a whole. Many were attending school because they were required to do so. They were described as academic failures, delinquent, and urgently in need of special services. The control group was selected from the same schools.

Cognitive Abilities

Cognitive abilities were appraised through administration of the Primary Mental Abilities (PMA) Test and the Draw-A-Man Test. These data are presented as a perspective from which to evaluate the results of language-learning investigations. However, since the sample was not large, the results must be interpreted with caution.

Primary Mental Abilities

PMA Test scores for the disturbed children compared with the controls are shown in Table 69. There were a number of significant differences, the disturbed group performing below the controls. Statistically, the two groups were most alike on spatial relations, but their performances varied in several respects. Almost without exception the youngest disturbed group (9 years) scored higher than the disturbed children at the other age levels, and the 11-year-olds usually scored lowest. When an average is taken of all age groups combined, the highest to lowest IQ's among the disturbed children were: verbal pictures, 93; number, 90; space, 87; perceptual speed, 86; verbal ability, 85; word fluency, 82; reasoning (nonreading), 80; verbal words, 79; reasoning (words and figures), 76; and reasoning (reading), 68. Of the 10 IQ scores, 5 were above 85 and only 1 below 75. Of the 5 scores above 85, 4 were for nonverbal processes, and of the 5 scores below 85, 4 were for verbal processes.

According to these results the socially-emotionally disturbed had limitations in language that were influential in determining their level of cognitive functioning; this deficit seemed seriously to impede their performance. On the basis of their nonverbal scores, they were within normal limits in cognitive functions, and on the basis of their scores on the total battery, they were within the limits of low normal. Considering their emotional involvement and verbal limitations, it is unusual that their demonstrated cognitive functions were so adequate.

Draw-A-Man

The socially-emotionally disturbed were inferior to the controls in their performance on the Draw-A-Man Test (see Table 70). Their ratio to the normal was at three-fourths at 9 and 11 years, essentially equivalent to the controls at 13 years, and approximately seven-tenths of average at 15 years. The behavior problems sustained by these children apparently were influential in limiting their function on this test, albeit this influence varied by age. The Draw-A-Man Test may be sensitive to disturbance of feelings and attitudes that serve as a basis for interpersonal relations. The data do not indicate whether this possibility explains the below-average function of the disturbed group or whether cognitive factors are involved. Whatever the basic cause, these children with behavior disorders might profit from remediation that includes emphasis on development of body image, as well as on self-perception and person perception. Assistance with feelings of identification should be especially advantageous. Moreover, as shown by previous study (Johnson and Myklebust, 1967), children with deficits in learning often show improvement in human figure drawing as they progress in academic learning. Therefore, the inferiority of the disturbed group may be overcome by indirect remediation, by an inclusive program that stresses both verbal and nonverbal learning.

Auditory Language

The socially-emotionally disturbed children had been classified for special education because of their inability to conform to classroom routines. They were not regarded principally as varying from normal in cognitive functions; they were not considered analogous to the mentally retarded or to those with learning disabilities.

A major focus of the present investigation was to gather data that would assist educators to establish guidelines for this group of children. It was assumed that behavioral disturbances do not necessarily imply cognitive disabilities, though both deviations may be present in certain children. Other studies have verified that marked deficits in learning often appear without concomitant emotional disturbance (Myklebust et al., 1972). Presumably, the converse also is common. The questions then are: Why do a significant number of children find school and social adjustment difficult, and how can they be served most efficaciously. To investigate these questions, auditory, read, and written language were evaluated, together with a survey of their locomotor ability. It is necessary to bear in mind, however, that because it is difficult to obtain samples of children with this type of behavior disorder, the number at each age level was small.

Auditory Receptive Language

Differences between the groups in ability to comprehend the spoken word appeared for both tests of auditory receptive language (see Table 71). The children with behavior disturbances were markedly inferior to the controls, but mainly at the lower age levels. The controls made little gain on Test One throughout the age range studied because for them the level of difficulty was not great; the difference between their scores from 9 to 15 years was only two points. The socially-emotionally disturbed almost doubled their score during this age span, the range being approximately eight points. Because of this unusual growth (on this test), they were equal to the normal at 15 years of age, albeit not until 13 years were they equivalent to the average 9-year-old. They encountered considerable difficulty in acquiring normal facility in comprehension of the spoken word.

The pattern of their performance on Test Two (ability to process auditory information into visual equivalents) was similar. Again, they made no gain between 9 and 11 years. But from 11 to 13 years their gain far exceeded the normal; the controls showed an increment of 2 points and the disturbed gained 10 points. This remarkable development placed the disturbed children close to average by 13 and 15 years of age. These findings, in agreement with the results for Test One, suggest that the socially-emotionally disturbed children were severely delayed in acquisition of auditory receptive language. Though they attained essentially normal function, they did so at a much later age. This deviate developmental pattern must be assumed to have been influential in their adjustment and implies that cognitive factors were involved in their disturbed behavior. This possibility will be considered further after additional findings have been reviewed.

Auditory Expressive Language

The results for auditory expressive language paralleled those for auditory receptive (see Table 72). The socially-emotionally disturbed were inferior to the controls at all age levels, but this deviation was greatest at the early ages on Test One (opposites); the degree of deficit on Test Two (definitions) remained stable throughout the age range. Nevertheless, their facility with expressive language remained at a seriously low level. Their performance was consistent on both measures in that by 15 years of age their usage was equal to that of the average 11-year-old.

Because the disturbed children were deficient in auditory receptive language they would be expected to show inferiority on expressive functions. But whether this disability is directly reciprocal to input deficits remains to be determined. According to these findings both receptive and expressive limitations were present, and both must be considered in planning educational remediation. Because of the basic nature of auditory language, with implications for all learning and adjustment, such remediation is urgent. Classification only on the basis of disturbed behavior is inappropriate; attention must be given to the deficiencies in learning if programs are to be most advantageous. However, the precise nature of these deficiencies has not been ascertained. Unlike most learning-disability children, this disturbed group revealed a pattern more typical of maturational delay than of cognitive malfunctioning.

Read Language

Scores on the test of reading vocabulary could be evaluated statistically only for the 13- and 15-year-old children; scorable responses were not obtained from the 9- and 11-year-olds. The socially-emotionally disturbed children were severely limited in ability to read and their limitation increased with age (see Table 73). The mean difference at 13 years was 13 points and at 15 years it was 25 points. As they reached the age of 15 their reading proficiency was below that of the average child of 13 years.

Reading disabilities often have been attributed to emotional disturbance. On this presumption this group of children might be expected to have trouble learning to read. On the other hand, many emotionally disturbed children show no deficits in language acquisition. The children in the present sample were severely disturbed behaviorally, but they were also immature developmentally. The complex question, therefore, is whether regarding them only in terms of their emotional disturbance is sufficiently encompassing to be of maximum benefit. Though cognitive disabilities may not be primary, the children's developmental immaturity causes them to be unable to profit normally from programs based on a unitary aspect of their total involvement. Their mode of learning varied from that characteristic of the mentally retarded and from that of children with learning disabilities (see Chapters V and VIII). Therefore, remedial programs must be modified according to the children's developmental patterns. Such programs should stress language learning, specifically acquisition of auditory language and conversion of this form to the read. Further indication of these needs is shown by the performance on the Picture Story Language Test (PSLT).

WRITTEN LANGUAGE

The PSLT was administered to the socially-emotionally disturbed children to ascertain further their status in academic achievement and school learning. Because they were deficient in auditory and read language, it was anticipated they would be inferior in written language. According to the construct of hierarchical relations among these language systems, as discussed in Volume One,* their deficits would be least extensive for auditory and most extensive for written language. This postulation is supported by the results presented in Table 74; the disturbed children were unusually limited in all aspects of written language.

Total Words

Stories of normal length were few, and lack of productivity increased with age. At 9 years the disturbed children's output was below the norm for 7-year-olds, at 11 it was equal to that of the 7-year-olds, at 13 it was equivalent to that of 8-year-olds, and there were no gains thereafter. Another indication of their deficit in output was the actual number of words written per story. Compared with the controls they wrote 75 words less at 9 years, 94 less at 11 years, 95 less

---

* *Development and Disorders of Written Language*, Volume One, *Picture Story Language Test* (Myklebust, 1965).

at 13 years, and 85 words less at 15 years. An especially critical feature of this marked deficiency in story length was the plateau after 13 years of age. The developmental configuration, however, was similar to the normal after 11 years of age (see Figure 33) ; the disturbed children gained only 7 words between 9 and 11 years and the normal gained 26. From 11 to 13 years the disturbed and normal made an equivalent gain—32 and 33 words, respectively. But though the socially-emotionally disturbed were far below average in output of words at 13 years, they made no further growth, a factor of importance in terms of acquisition of facility with written language.

Inasmuch as story length, together with number of sentences and use of abstract meaning, is a major component of Factor 1 (as measured by the PSLT), this deficit in output seems of utmost concern in understanding the educational needs of this group of exceptional children. If they are to become more adequate academically and perhaps socially, they must be helped to attain greater proficiency in language. The program of educational remediation must stress receptive, expressive, and inner language functioning. This need is reinforced by the data presented below.

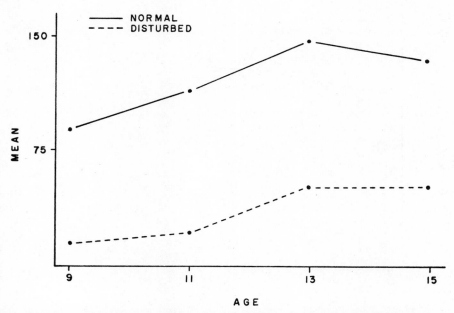

FIGURE 33. Comparison of normal and socially-emotionally disturbed children on total words.

Total Sentences

The normal children showed no increment in number of sentences written after 13 years of age. Because by this age they had mastered syntactical aspects, they wrote longer stories but not more sentences per story. From the growth curve shown in Figure 34, it is apparent that the socially-emotionally disturbed children followed an equivalent developmental pattern. At 9 and 11 years of age they wrote eight sentences less per story but at 13 years this dropped to six, and at 15 to five. Nevertheless, they attained a maximum level of only approximately one-half of average. They, too, wrote fewer sentences as they became older because the sentences were longer, but this plateau followed a marked deficiency. If they had not plateaued they might have attained more normal levels of output for sentences.

Words per Sentence

The number of words written per sentence has proved a stable and independent measure of acquisition of written language. The normal

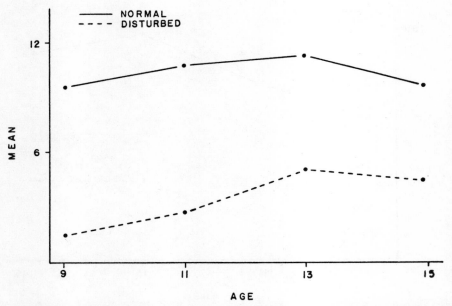

FIGURE 34. Comparison of normal and socially-emotionally disturbed children on total sentences.

children gained almost two words per sentence from 9 to 11 years and the disturbed gained less than one-half word per sentence. Between 11 and 13 years, however, the controls gained two and one-half words, and the socially-emotionally disturbed three and one-half. This is further evidence of their lag in early life, with a tendency to improve later (see Figure 35). This rate of gain was not maintained between 13 and 15 years, because their increment was slightly more than one word per sentence and the controls made a gain of almost three words. Therefore, at 15 years of age the level attained by the disturbed children was equal to that of a normal child of 11 years. This 4-year retardation in words per sentence is a severe indication of immaturity in written language. Moreover, the deficiency is in a different dimension than total words and total sentences. Sentence formulation, as well as output of words, is for these disturbed children a problem of considerable magnitude. In fact, as revealed further by the syntax results, the disturbed children presented a pattern of generalized deficiency in acquisition of the written word. They were seriously limited on all factors.

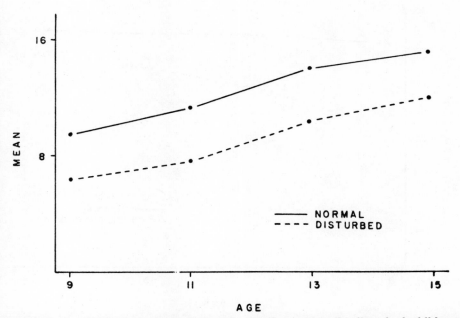

FIGURE 35. Comparison of normal and socially-emotionally disturbed children on words per sentence.

Syntax

The socially-emotionally disturbed were inferior in syntax usage at all age levels; nevertheless, their greatest proficiency with written language was on this factor. The developmental configuration also was unusual and in contrast to most of the other patterns. At 9 years the disturbed group had a syntax quotient of 67.8, a deficit of 28 points compared with the controls; at 11 years their quotient was 76, a deficit of 21 points. Their facility with correct usage by the age of 13 was represented by a quotient score of 86, a deficit of 11 points. By the age of 15 they attained a score of 90.4, a deficiency of only 8 points. As shown by Figure 36, the disturbed children continued to improve through the age of 15 years, in marked contrast to the normals, who achieved adult levels of syntax usage at about 9 years of age.

These results provide insights into the language deficits that occurred in the children with behavioral disturbances. Correct syntax is learned from the auditory language form and thus is acquired early in life by the average child. The disturbed children showed deficiencies in auditory receptive language, not attaining normal levels until about 15 years of age. This same pattern of growth appeared for

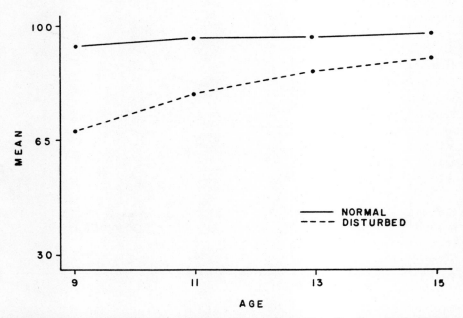

FIGURE 36. Comparison of normal and socially-emotionally disturbed children on syntax.

syntax; facility in correct usage was acquired slowly and gradually over a long period of time, as the children gained in ability to comprehend what the speaker said. This pattern may be a factor in their poor performance on number of words per sentence. Long sentences can be formulated and written only when syntactical structures have been mastered. In view of the delay in achieving facility in correct syntax usage, it is logical that the disturbed children were unable to execute long and complex sentences. Consideration must be given to these factors when educational remediation is initiated.

Abstract-Concrete

Communication of abstract meaning is closely related to productivity, as indicated by the number of words and sentences written. However, meaning also may be thought of as reflecting the level of attainment in inner language because thought processes are involved in use of a plot, characterization, setting, metaphor, allegory, and moral of the story. This scale is based on the concept that concreteness is reflected by limiting the story to what is observable in the picture. The normative data reveal that such use of imagination, such growth of inner language, is achieved gradually, year by year, by normal children.

The socially-emotionally disturbed ranked far below the controls in ability to engage in abstract meaning. But they too made gains throughout the age range, as shown in Figure 37. At 9 years their performance was at a level approximately one-half of average, with the same ratio of growth at 11 years. By 13 years they used abstractions at a level of 60 percent of the norm for the controls; this ratio at 15 years was 65 percent of average. According to the scale (see Volume One) this means that the maximum attainment was at Level III: Concrete-Imaginative, whereas the controls achieved Level V: Abstract-Imaginative.

Facility in expression of abstract meaning is closely associated with language proficiency. Because of the marked limitations in the language of the socially-emotionally disturbed, it was anticipated that they would not be able to use abstract meanings in a normal manner. Through enhancement of their language facility (spoken, read, and written), their ability to convey abstract meaning would be improved. An immediate approach would be to emphasize fluency—output as expressed in story length—because use of abstraction is a component of the same factor. But an intriguing possibility is that development of inner language can be fostered directly. The teacher should present

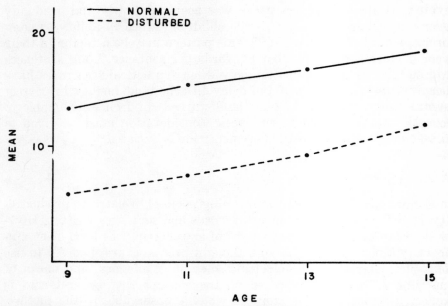

FIGURE 37. Comparison of normal and socially-emotionally disturbed children on abstract-concrete.

topics, pictures, objects, or even anecdotes relative to current happenings, and ask the children to engage in responses entailing abstract, imaginative sequences. Such directed and controlled remedial procedures might assist these children to use abstract ideas and meanings. Their needs are great and innovative programs will be required if socially-emotionally disturbed children are to have the advantages to which they are entitled.

Intercorrelation of Auditory and Written Language

Rarely have the cognitive functions of socially-emotionally disturbed children been investigated. The results of tests of spoken, read, and written language suggest that these children followed a developmental pattern similar to the normal but with a slower rate of growth. They did not show strength in some facets of learning, with marked deficits in others, as is often the case with learning-disability children. They adhered more to the pattern of the controls, with a substantial variation in maturational rate. The results from the intercorrelation analysis also show this trend.

Auditory receptive and written language were associated, especially at the age of 9 years (see Table 75). However, use of abstraction was an exception; acquisition of meaning showed no correlation with the written form except at 15 years on the test of ability to transduce auditory information into visual equivalents. This, too, may indicate delays in development of function. In other respects, facility in processing auditory language into the visual equivalent was more closely correlated in the disturbed than in the normal. Both sentence length and syntax were associated with use of the written word. It is precisely these facets on which the socially-emotionally disturbed showed most normal development.

The findings for auditory expressive language also provide insights into the nature of the language deficits of this group of children. Output of spoken language for the controls was correlated with use of the written word. Except for a minor exception (syntax), this was not true for the disturbed children. These data supply further evidence that the disturbed children were impeded in development of interneurosensory processing functions. Use of spoken language follows ability to comprehend. From the data in Table 76, it is evident that at 15 years of age the disturbed group had acquired facility in auditory expressive language at a level equal to that of the average 11-year-old. Moreover, at the age of 15 their written language was at approximately the 8-year level. In view of these marked variations, their ability to process from the spoken to the written word evidently had not yet been established.

Complex cognitive processes are involved in language learning; further study of these functions developmentally is necessary and perhaps imminent. Whether these processes were disturbed in the children with behavior disorders, or mainly impeded in development, remains to be established. Nevertheless, the children were deficient in acquiring all forms of language: spoken, read, and written. Their pattern suggests a delay in maturation rather than a disturbance in cognition of the type associated with learning disabilities. If these findings are confirmed by further research, the focus of educational remediation should be modification on the basis of developmental immaturity more than on the basis of strengths and weaknesses. Language learning should be emphasized, with intensive effort on development of auditory language. In contrast to many learning-disability children, disturbed children must concentrate on acquisition of meaning; inner language should be emphasized through inauguration of specialized curricula. Though the causes of their disturbed behavior are various, adjustment is difficult for these children because they do not understand much of the language used by those with whom they come in contact. Accordingly, instruction in word meaning may significantly assist them in becoming more amenable, in and out of school.

Locomotor Coordination

Motor functions are a significant facet of behavior and offer opportunities for appraisal of developmental disorders, often providing evidence that assists in distinguishing between psychogenic and neurogenic involvements. Because of their poor performance in the area of language acquisition, it seemed important to have information on the motor development of socially-emotionally disturbed children.

The Heath Railwalking Test was administered and the results are presented in Table 77. The pattern of motor development varied by group. Between the ages of 9 and 11 years the controls made a gain of 5 points but the disturbed had a loss of 8 points; the 11-year-olds deviated also in other respects. But from 11 to 13 years the disturbed gained at a rate twice that of the normals; they advanced 31 points compared with 15 for the controls. Nevertheless, because of their poor proficiency in early life their score at 13 years was 15 points below average, and at 15 it was 28 points below average. The degree of their retardation in motor development varied from 2 to 4 years. The disturbed group made limited gains after 13 years of age, whereas the controls continued to improve up to the age of 15.

SUMMARY

The total significance of these findings is not clear; additional research is necessary. The socially-emotionally disturbed children appeared developmentally immature; they presented a pervasive disorder of which the behavioral abnormality was but one aspect. These children were seriously deficient in types of learning and development expected at a certain age. Therefore, they were inferior but not unable to learn. With time they progressed and in limited respects achieved at a level approximating the normal. Their need for specialized remediation, in the area of motor learning as well as language, is obvious. To consider them only in terms of emotional disturbance is to minimize their disorder and to misjudge the pervasive nature of their requirements.

In general, the performance of the socially-emotionally disturbed children was not comparable to that of the mentally retarded or of those with learning disabilities (see Chapters V and VIII). These three types of exceptional children have certain deficits in common but the ways in which they are dissimilar are often more revealing of their patterns of learning and development and more suggestive of the manner in which their needs can be met most effectively. Therefore, irrespective of their school classification, socially-emotionally disturbed children have problems that are unique and that must form the basis of their remediation programs.

Chapter VIII

Written Language and Learning Disabilities

Children with learning disabilities are not inferior intellectually and are not characterized by social-emotional maladjustment. They are designated as having a learning disability because they have integrity of intelligence, motor ability, hearing, vision, and emotional adjustment, but cannot learn normally even when schooling is optimum. The cause of their disability may be endogenous, exogenous, or developmental (Myklebust, 1968, 1971). This group of exceptional children is one of the largest requiring special education.

Learning disabilities may be verbal or nonverbal. Deficiencies in verbal learning seem to be most prevalent, but this observation may reflect the fact that verbal learning is the most readily measured and closely related to school success. Nevertheless, language disorders are common and involve all the verbal systems: spoken, read, and written. Disorders of spoken language, the aphasias, constitute a major category of disabilities at preschool and early school ages (Myklebust, 1971b). Dyslexia is a disturbance of read language. This condition, influencing the lives of many children, has not been commonly recognized as a type of learning disability. It was first described in children in 1872 by Broadbent and has been widely accepted in many countries (Hermann, 1959; Tuana *et al.*, 1971).

Disorders of written language also constitute major learning disabilities. These take various forms, some of which can be identified by the Picture Story Language Test (PSLT). Boder (1971) has shown that written spelling patterns can be used in diagnosis of dyslexia. She emphasizes the interrelation of read and written language. If the reading level is at the expected age but writing is limited, the child's condition may be dysgraphia (see Volume One).*

---

* *Development and Disorders of Written Language*, Volume One, *Picture Story Language Test* (Myklebust, 1965).

However, as revealed by the studies reported in this volume, written language may be deficient for a variety of reasons. Only through careful evaluation can the precise disorder be determined. Study of the disorders of written language has only just begun and warrants attention from a number of disciplines.

READ AND WRITTEN LANGUAGE OF LEARNING-DISABILITY CHILDREN

With the collaboration of four metropolitan public schools, an investigation was made of the incidence and types of learning disabilities (Myklebust, 1972). Specialists involving five disciplines participated: education, psychology, electroencephalography, ophthalmology, and pediatric neurology. The findings for read and written language are considered here, but first the background of the study is reviewed.

The initial population consisted of 2767 children, all the third- and fourth-graders in the four participating schools. Screening tests were used to identify the underachievers. Using a learning quotient (LQ) to represent the ratio between learning potential and achievement (Myklebust, 1968), pass-fail criteria were established. The advantage of the LQ for objectively defining a learning disability has been demonstrated (Johnson and Myklebust, 1967; Myklebust, 1968, 1973). Children having sensory impairment, mental retardation, emotional disturbance, or obvious motor disorders were excluded from the study.

Two experimental groups were selected, differing on the basis of the severity of the learning disability. Group 1 consisted of children with a moderate deficit, represented by an LQ of 89 to 85; an LQ of 90 or above was defined as normal. Group 2 was made up of children with severe deficits, represented by an LQ of 84 or lower. Separate control groups were obtained for each of these populations. To serve as a control, the child passed all the selective test criteria and was of the same sex and from the same classroom as the experimental subject with whom he was paired. Consequently, the samples consisted of 116 children with moderate learning deficits paired with 116 normals, and 112 children with severe learning deficits paired with 112 normals. The findings for read and written language from this investigation are considered here.

Read Language

Poor reading achievement is one of the most common failures of learning-disability children. Many fail in reading because they have a form of dyslexia. Remedial-reading teachers and other educators are obligated to recognize this type of learning disability and to evolve remediation programs that focus specifically on this problem.

Seven reading-proficiency tests were used, covering a wide range of processes involved in learning to read. Without exception these tests differentiated between the children with deficiencies in learning and those who were learning normally. The differences were at high levels of significance for both the moderate and severe groups (see Table 78). The mean scores for the children with severe learning-disability were lower than those for children with moderate involvement. Reading ability not only distinguished the poor learners from the normal, but proved effective in designating the extent to which learning was impeded.

Both groups of children with deficits in learning were inferior to the controls on all seven tests of reading ability. The order of deficiency from greatest to least for the moderate-disability group was comprehension, vocabulary, accuracy, nonsense words, syllabication, oral reading, and word parts. For the severe-disability group this order was comprehension, vocabulary, accuracy, syllabication, nonsense words, oral reading, and word parts. These findings reveal that the order of the specific deficits in reading was almost identical for the learning-deficiency groups. The type of disturbance was highly similar irrespective of the extent of the disability in learning. The range of the reading scores for the experimental groups also was similar; the highest and lowest scores differed by approximately 1 year.

A discriminant analysis using 47 scores disclosed that ability to syllabicate ranked highest as a discriminator between good and poor learners (Myklebust, 1973). In this analysis of greatest to least deficiency in reading, this test ranked fifth (out of seven) for the moderate group and fourth for the severe group. Therefore, the best discriminator is not necessarily the measure that indicates the greatest disturbance in reading. For both groups of poor learners the most disturbed reading processes were comprehension, vocabulary, and accuracy. Though all seven of the reading processes measured were involved in the reading disability, the two most critical to learning-disability children appear to be comprehension and vocabulary. These might serve as the basis for remedial-reading programs for such children.

Written Language

The model evolved for these studies of development and disorders of written language stressed that input precedes output. Read and written language were defined as being dependent on the same language form, the visual. According to this construct, reading is the receptive and writing the expressive phase of this language system. If there are deficits in input (reading), these will be reflected as impositions on output (writing). This construct in no way negates the importance of determining the presence or absence of disturbances in both processes, receptive and expressive. But results that show expressive functions to exceed the receptive might well be questioned, though the opposite occurs frequently. Facility with written language was studied intensively in this investigation of learning disabilities in third- and fourth-grade public-school chldren. The results are presented by degree of involvement (moderate or severe).

Moderate-Learning-Disability Group

Children who had an LQ of 89 to 85 on 1 or more of 21 psycho-educational tests were classified as having a moderate learning disability (Myklebust and Boshes, 1969). This group was paired with a control group. The PSLT was administered to evaluate the ways in which written language might be involved in these moderate disturbances of learning. The results are shown in Table 79. Except for number of sentences, all the scores revealed significant differences in favor of the controls; children with moderate deficits in learning, as shown also by the other measures, were inferior in written language.

Furthermore, this deficiency was generalized, extending across the three factors measured by the PSLT (see results for factor analysis). On two of the scales, syntax and abstract-concrete, the moderate-learning-disability children were more than 1 year retarded, and on the other three scales they were from three-fourths to nine-tenths year behind the controls. The fact that the greatest limitations occurred for syntax and communication of abstract meaning is important diagnostically and in terms of educational remediation. Though all three factors of written language were affected by the learning disability, expression of meaning and correct use of syntax were most impaired.

These findings reflect the basic learning processes that have been disturbed. The syntax disorder directly implicates the auditory facets of the deficit in learning. Inasmuch as auditory language is the most fundamental of the language forms, there is a secondary imposition on acquisition of meaning, on inner language. The significance of these disturbances in understanding the learning disability is unequivocal. In addition, these results must be related to the findings for read language because comprehension and syllabication (converting from visual to auditory) were critical factors in the reading retardation. The data for written language, therefore, are in close agreement with those for reading. The deficiency in syntax is analogous to the syllabication disability in that both connote deficits in auditory receptive language. The retardation in use of abstract meaning is comparable to the disturbance of ability to comprehend as shown by the reading tests: both suggest a basic defect in development of inner language.

The role of read and written language in learning disabilities, even when the involvement is only moderate, is illustrated by these results and carries implications for remedial instruction. The most basic need is for emphasis on auditory language, mainly on word meaning and secondarily on the cognitive processes involved in converting auditory language into visual equivalents. The findings for the group with severe learning disabilities further indicate these needs.

Severe-Learning-Disability Group

The children classified as having a severe learning disability had an LQ of 84 or lower on 1 or more of 21 psychoeducational tests, other than on written language. As with the moderately involved group, the PSLT was given to study the ways in which written language might be influential in the learning disability. The results for the group with severe deficits and for the paired controls are shown in Table 80.

It is significant that the pattern of these findings is similar to the one for the children with moderate learning deficits, with a slight variation. In the severe group the greatest deficit was in syntax; the retardation was over 2.5 years. The second most extensive limitation was in communication of abstract meaning. These two facets, meaning and syntax, also were lowest for the moderate group.

Number of sentences written was not significantly different from the controls, as was true for the moderates. Because the children with deficits in learning wrote many fewer words per story (total words), but not fewer sentences, it is apparent that they wrote shorter sentences; this is confirmed by the results for words per sentence. Instead of writing longer sentences as they became older, because of their language disorder they wrote more and more short ones; they were unable simultaneously to write longer stories, as did the normal children.

Together with the other results, these findings for number of sentences show the marked disorders in this group of learning-disability children. They were unable to function normally at the level of auditory language, as shown by the extensive deficiency in use of syntax. Inner language was considerably impaired as disclosed by the abstract-concrete scale. More generally, all three factors of written language measured by the PSLT were deficient developmentally. Fluency was inferior, as shown by number of words, as was sentence length, correct usage, and communication of meaning.

Summary

These findings clarify the cognitive disturbances found in learning-disability children. They were inferior on all aspects of written language, irrespective of the extent of the deficit in learning. But in agreement with the original classification, those having severe involvements had substantially greater disability. The PSLT differentiated the learning-disability children from the normal and, in addition, revealed differences on the basis of the severity of the deficiency in learning.

The results also suggested the relation of language-learning processes to learning disabilities. Since both read and written language were evaluated, the groups could be compared on input and output levels of visual language. For the controls the age scores in reading were 2 to 3 years above the scores for written language. As predicted, input levels exceeded output levels, but the extent of this variation was not expected. Considerable redundancy seems necessary to attain normal levels of output; receptive (reading) functions must have developed extensively to provide the necessary basis for expressive functions (writing). These interactions between read and written language for normal children serve as a point of reference in differential diagnosis of visual language disorders.

In contrast to the normal, the children with deficiencies in learning had comparable age scores for read and written language; input and output were equivalent, so the redundancy phenomenon did not appear. Though further investigation must be made of these interactions, it appears that the learning-disability children were retarded in written language because of their limitations in reading, and that read language was deficient because of disorders in auditory language. Presumably, if reading ability were facilitated, written language would be improved. However, each child must be carefully evaluated because the relations of read to written language vary. The disturbance in learning may involve only input processes, only output, or a combination of both. Nevertheless, the results of this investigation may serve as a guide. In learning-disability children, as well as in other exceptional children, it is advantageous to regard read and written language as the input and output forms of one language system, the visual. Only when these forms, or processes, are seen in relation to each other can the child's needs be determined precisely and the learning disability adequately defined.

These findings for written language indicate the remediation needs of learning-disability children. Fluency, as represented by story length, must be enhanced. This may be approached by development of greater redundancy, by increasing facility in reading. The generation and formulation of sentences of normal length also must be fostered. Inasmuch as syntax is related to facility in producing sentences, this aspect may be incorporated into the program for development of adequate expression in sentence form. Using the PSLT norms, the number of words per sentence written by the child can be ascertained. Then the child may be given a topic about which he writes spontaneously. With this performance serving as a basis, he can be assisted in formulating other sentences, with the objective that the new sentences include one more word than those written previously. Simultaneously, it may be necessary to give assistance in correct use of syntax.

Fundamental to the total approach is the need to give instruction in word meaning. For learning-disability children this may be the most critical dimension of remediation in language. On the basis of the data at hand, it is logical to assume that such instruction is so essential as to require approximately one-half the time given to language remediation. Though it may take various forms (vocabulary building, development of word meaning), it seems essential if the child is to attain facility with the read and written language forms. Initiation of such programs of remediation in language is one of the greatest challenges in special education because the programs are critical for all exceptional children.

Correlation Between Read and Written Language

The correlations between auditory and written language for the other groups of exceptional children are discussed in the preceding chapters. Here the concern is with the interactions of read and written language in children having learning disabilities. Study of these interactions has presented complex problems, a major limitation being the inadequacy of available tests. More objective measures are being developed, and as research evidence is forthcoming, educators and psychologists have become occupied with the fundamental problem of how read and written language are interrelated

Seven tests of reading were given (see Table 78). They measured the following skills: oral reading, accuracy, comprehension, vocabulary, word parts, nonsense words, and syllabication. The scores on these reading tests and the PSLT scores were compared through an intercorrelation analysis. The findings from this analysis are presented separately for the moderate- and severe-learning-disability groups.

Moderate-Learning-Disability Group

The intercorrelations for those with moderate deficits in learning compared with the normal are shown in Table 81; the correlations fall at the .01 level of significance. The pattern of the relations between read and written language varied by group. For example, there were six correlations with syntax for children with learning deficiencies but only two for the normal. The normal third- and fourth-grade child, it seems, had achieved the level of facility in syntax necessary for learning to read so the written language processes could bypass this auditory phase and function independently. This was not true of those with disturbances in learning, even though the disturbances were only moderate. These children continued to rely on auditory, syntactical learning processes in their attempts to achieve an effective reading level. As shown by the data for normal children (see Part One), syntax in written language was achieved at about 9 years of age; a plateau followed thereafter. When a learning disability was present, however, acquisition of syntax was delayed, so processing the read word through the auditory continued until a later age.

Another outcome concerns the findings for words per sentence. This factor showed only one significant association with reading, and this was for the group with deficits in learning. In other words, as a factor of written language, sentence length was not directly related to learning to read for normal children. Therefore, though the inter-relations of read and written language have been stressed, this inter-dependence varies on the basis of the factor of written language involved. Words per sentence may involve cognitive processes that assume input in the form of reading but is more dependent on expressive developmental components. Ability to formulate ideas and convert them into sentence form may be critical to this aspect of written language. But this is true only when learning processes are not disturbed. When even moderate disabilities of learning occur, then the number of words written per sentence, to a degree, is determined by ability to read; bypassing, as in the normal, is much more restricted, so expressive performance remains more bound to the receptive level of functioning.

Total words and total sentences, together with abstract meaning, make up a significant factor of written language. Hence, it is of importance that the scores on these three attributes showed the greatest correlation with the reading-test scores. But, again, the pattern of the relations varied by group. For these three scales the control group had 11 correlations and the group with learning deficits had 7. The pattern of the associations for abstract-concrete is illus-trative of the differences by group, of the ways in which even a moderate disturbance of learning impedes cognitive processes. For normal children use of abstract meaning was related to four out of the seven reading skills measured: oral reading, accuracy, compre-hension, and vocabulary. There were only two such associations for the poor learners: oral reading and nonsense words. These findings reveal that ability to convey abstract meaning (inner language) is dependent on vocabulary and on ability to comprehend what is read, which in turn are reflected in the skills of accuracy and oral reading. Thus, as emphasized in the discussion of the other groups of excep-tional children, depth of meaning may be fostered through develop-ment of vocabulary and ability to comprehend. Conversely, children with disturbances in learning are deficient in inner language because of their limitations in these aspects of reading. When the level of reading is high, as reflected by oral reading, accuracy, comprehension, and vocabulary, then ability to express abstract meaning in the written form also is high. These findings provide insights into the associations between read and written language and into the basic manner in which a learning disability disrupts normal cognitive processes.

Severe-Learning-Disability Group

The pattern of the intercorrelations between read and written language for those with severe deficits in reading varied from that for the moderate group (see Table 82). This variation may be partially explained by the greater impact of the disability on cognitive processes.

Though the pattern for the experimental groups varied, there were similarities. For example, words per sentence showed no associations with read language. In the discussion for the moderately involved group it was suggested that ability to formulate and generate sentences seems essentially unrelated to visual receptive language and hence functions as an expressive component of the visual language system.

The results for syntax also were similar for the experimental groups, but there were fewer significant correlations for the severely involved children. Components that were correlated with syntax (oral reading and syllabication) are functions that directly entail auditory processing. The primary associations between read and written language were those that evolved for Factor 1, as measured by PSLT (total words, total sentences, and abstract-concrete). This factor was closely related to reading ability for those with marked deficits in learning. Fluency of output and depth of meaning again emerged as being of consequence in acquisition of read and written language.

Because of the differing pattern of relation for the moderate and severe groups, further interpretation is difficult. Nevertheless, the degree of the impact of the disability on the severe group seems of utmost importance. The magnitude of the correlations between certain reading skills and total words is indicative. Reading comprehension showed the greatest relation (.51), followed by syllabication (.45) and oral reading (.43); these exceed the equivalent correlations for those with moderate involvement. These results indicate that when a severe learning disability is present, use of the written word is bound directly to facility in reading. The written is restricted to being processed through the auditory and read forms to an unusual extent. Compared with the controls, there was little or no bypassing; the control group for the severely involved children was highly successful in bypassing the auditory; hence, the fewer correlations.

Because of the extent of the impact of the severe involvement on cognitive functions, remediation for this group should be more basic. The program should stress all aspects and levels of language learning, but with the hierarchy of the verbal systems serving as a foundation.

Attention to auditory language should be given first, followed by emphasis on conversion of this form to the read, and then to the written. Emphasis on vocabulary and meaning seems urgent; until inner language is adequate, other aspects cannot develop satisfactorily.

There is another implication. The remediation programs for children with moderate, as compared with severe, learning disabilities should not be identical. The greater the impact on learning, the more cognitive processes are disturbed. This more pervasive disturbance must be considered if these children are to reap essential benefits from special education. This difference on the basis of degree of involvement was a primary concern of the present investigation; classification was made acocrding to the extent of the disability. The two experimental groups (moderate and severe) were similar in other respects—for example, levels of intelligence. Thus the findings indicate that though disability is extensive and cognitive processes are disturbed in specific ways, these children have needs that can be differentiated, and that must be met through the realization that their needs are not synonymous with those having less severe disabilities.

Factor Analysis and Acquisition of Written Language

The study of normal children revealed that there are three factors of written language as determined by the PSLT: story length (total words and total sentences) and meaning (abstract-concrete), syntax, and sentence length (words per sentence). This factor-analysis approach also was used in the investigation of written language acquisition by third- and fourth-grade learning-disability public-school children. The purpose was to compare the cognitive learning styles of normal children with those of children who had deficits in learning. The results for both the moderately and severely involved are shown in Table 83.

The pattern of the factors involved in acquisition of the written word varied for the experimental and control groups; the learning disability affected the ways in which the child acquired facility with the written word. However, there also were similarities. Both groups, the moderately and severely involved, were equivalent to the normal on Factor 1. This factor (productivity and meaning) remained paramount irrespective of the presence of learning disabilities. Facility in producing a story of normal length and conveyance of meaning were critical to learning to use the written language form whether or not the child had deficits in learning.

The other factors, words per sentence and syntax, were disarranged by the learning disabilities, but this cognitive disturbance varied by the degree of the disability. For those with moderate involvement the same three factors appeared, but the order of these factors was different. Words per sentence shifted and became the second most critical factor, which, in turn, made syntax appear in third place. Therefore, as for the controls, the same three factors evolved but their order was modified. Presumably, the cognitive processes involved also were modified. Generation of ideas and sentence formulation became a higher-order process, perhaps related to inner language facility; syntax followed in the cognitive processing sequence.

A more substantial disarrangement of the three factors occurred for the group having severe deficits in learning. Factor 1 remained of paramount significance, for the controls and for the moderate-disability group. But, although words per sentence and syntax again evolved as the next most obvious loadings, they were amalgamated, appearing as only one factor. In other words, the impact of severe learning disabilities on the cognitive processes was considerable, altering the total configuration of the factors involved in acquisition of the written word. The cognitive processes, under these circumstances, were more global. It must be inferred that the change represents a significant handicap to this group of children with severe learning disabilities. They could not differentiate between syntax and sentence formulation. Normal children and those with moderate deficits in learning, distinguished cognitively between formulation of ideas in sentence form and the syntactical aspects of such a sentence. The children with severe deficits could not do so. Therefore, generation of language in sentence form and the structure of the sentence were unduly associated. A direct implication is that development of remediation programs should focus on assisting these children to correct their disturbed cognitive processes so that written language can be acquired in a more normal manner.

PSLT and Other Measures of the Written Word

The study of learning disabilities in third- and fourth-grade children provided an opportunity for comparing performance on the PSLT with two subtests on the Metropolitan Achievement Test, each of which involves use of the written word. On the spelling test, the child writes words dictated by the examiner; on the language test, the child reads sentences in which certain words have been underlined, decides whether these words have been used correctly, and for the incorrectly used words writes the correct one and provides the necessary punctuation. These tests, used separately or in combination, cannot be considered adequate measures of written language. But because there are few achievement tests that involve the written word, other than spelling, the intercorrelation of these test scores with the PSLT scores was analyzed. The results are shown in Tables 84 and 85; the correlations were significant at the .01 level of confidence.

A consistent relation appeared for total words and spelling; story length and ability to spell were correlated for both experimental and both control groups. Hence, when spelling ability is enhanced, output also is enhanced. The results for syntax were consistent; correct usage was correlated with scores on the Metropolitan language subtest for all groups. This subtest concerns the correct use of words and punctuation, variables that are included on the syntax scale. Therefore, the syntax scale, as a measure of correct usage, is supported by the results for the Metropolitan language subtest. Words per sentence was correlated with spelling ability for both control groups, but not for those with learning disabilities; this is another indication of the variations that occur when cognitive functions have been disturbed.

These data serve to clarify the usefulness of the PSLT. All three factors of written language measured by the PSLT correlated with the two subtests of the Metropolitan Achievement Test that involve use of the written word. This is evidence that the PSLT is a valid test of written language.

PSLT and Identification of Learning-Disability Children

A major problem for research is development of tests for identification of learning-disability children (Myklebust, 1968, 1971c, 1972). A number of techniques have been suggested but rarely has written language been mentioned. In the study of third- and fourth-graders, 47 psychoeducational tests were administered (Myklebust, 1972), one of which was the PSLT. The effectiveness of each of these 47 tests in identifying children with learning deficits was determined by the discriminant-analysis technique. The findings for both experimental groups are presented in Table 86. The ranks for the five PSLT scores are shown; the F values are significant at the .01 level of confidence.

All five of the PSLT scores on written language differentiated between normal and learning-disability children, irrespective of the degree of the disability. On the other hand, the pattern of significance (the effectiveness of each of these five scores) varied according to the extent of the disability. For children having moderate deficits, meaning ranked highest as a discriminator; it was eighteenth out of 47 test scores. For those with severe deficits in learning, syntax was the most effective discriminator; it ranked ninth out of 47 scores. Inasmuch as syntax is a reflection of the adequacy of auditory receptive language, children with marked disabilities were characterized mainly by this type of language disorder. Thus, syntax ability is critical to identification of children with severe deficits in language, and this ability can be ascertained by the PSLT.

In contrast, inability to acquire and use abstract meanings was the most effective discriminator when the learning disability was moderate. But the rankings for the five PSLT scores were lower for this group. Apparently, the greater the learning disability, the greater the deficiency in written language, and the greater the ease with which these disorders can be identified. To summarize further, children with moderate deficiencies in learning are most successful on the technical facets of written language, showing primary need in the area of meaning. Those having severe deficiencies are still struggling with skill components, even at the level of acquiring auditory functions. Because of these positive findings, it is apparent that the PSLT is of value in the identification of learning disabilities.

Part Three

DIAGNOSIS
REMEDIATION
CLASSIFICATION

Chapter IX

Comparison and Classification of Exceptional Children

The desirability of adhering to categories and classification on the basis of the major handicap was not a primary focus of this research. But studies have shown that the learning pattern and type of disability are intimately associated (Myklebust, 1964, 1973). Thus, irrespective of categorization, extensive knowledge concerning the handicap is necessary before programs of maximum benefit can be instituted. The educational implication, though the psychology of *similarity* is relevant, is that the psychology of *difference* is basic to understanding the cognitive disturbances of exceptional children. Moreover, there is need to recognize that handicaps often occur in multiples, with overlapping impacts on learning and cognition.

A significant approach to gaining knowledge of the learning styles of exceptional children is to compare them type by type. Yet this rarely has been done. The design of the investigations reported in this volume stressed matching of the groups of exceptional children so such comparisons could be made. This plan was only partially successful because of variations in sample size and chronological age. But the children, normal and exceptional, were mainly from the same schools and were equivalent in other respects. Therefore, a comparative analysis was made by type of disability. The results revealed group differences important to education of exceptional children.

READING-DISABILITY CHILDREN AND CHILDREN WITH ARTICULATION DISORDERS

There has been interest in possible relations between reading disabilities and speech disorders (Monroe, 1932), but this concern has been directed to the questions of whether children with speech defects are also deficient in reading or whether children with reading disabilities also have speech defects. McGrady (1968) showed that children with articulation disorders were below average in reading ability. Comparison of the written language of these groups of exceptional children seems not to have been studied previously; however, Arnold (1966) investigated the written language proficiency of stutterers and found it deficient in various respects. Such studies are of theoretical interest and have practical implications for speical education.

The reading-disability children were compared with the articulation-disorders group at the ages of 9, 11, and 13 years; there were no reading-disability children at 7 years and too few with articulation defects at 15 years. The number of children with speech disorders at 13 years was small but these data were included because they are useful in illustrating trends. The comparative results for written language are given in Table 87; there were only two significant differences.

Total Words

The articulation-disorders group was superior to the reading-disability children at 9 years of age; this was one of the two significant differences. Though the trend was for the speech-handicapped to write longer stories, essentially the groups wrote stories of equal length. Both groups were inferior, as indicated by the fact that at 13 years the level of proficiency was below that achieved by the average 9-year-old child.

Both groups made gains with age but the developmental rates varied. The reading-disability children were substantially below the speech-handicapped at 9 years; the increment from 9 to 11 years was 20 points for the former group and only 11 points for the latter. Both groups made progress through 13 years of age and this growth may have continued into the upper high-school years. The need for assistance with written language proficiency is apparent.

Total Sentences

No differences appeared for number of sentences. The children with reading disabilities and those with defects of articulation were equally inferior. The output level for sentences was between one-third and one-half of normal.

Words per Sentence

The equivalent performance of these groups of exceptional children was shown also in sentence length. At 13 years of age both groups attained a level equal to that of the average child of 11 years. The extent of the inferiority was less than for story length: in words per sentence the deficit was 2 years, and for total words it was 4 years. Both groups were equivalent in performance but the extent of their language deficiency varied on the basis of the factor involved. Their success was greater on sentence formulation than on story length. Another indication of the need for remediation was the rate of growth. Normal children made a gain of one word per sentence per year. This rate was exceeded by these groups of exceptional children only to a minor degree, the reading-disability group making the most rapid progress. To achieve normal levels of words per sentence, the exceptional children would have to make consistent gains of more than one word per sentence per year—at least one and a half words per year for 4 years.

Syntax

The groups were uniform also with respect to accuracy of the language written; the speech handicapped were more correct in syntax at 13 years of age. The variability of their performance was great at 9 years, indicating disturbance in acquisition of syntax that continued throughout the age range.

Abstract-Concrete

No differences appeared between the groups in communication of meaning; they were equally inferior, with a retardation of approximately 4 years. These results are in close agreement with those for total words and sentences; these exceptional children were seriously deficient in acquiring those aspects of written language represented by Factor 1. They are in need of remediation especially in word meaning, vocabulary, fluency, and inner language.

Summary

The reading-disability and speech-handicapped children were essentially equal in the extent of their deficiency in written language. This equivalent performance occurred although the group with articulation defects was superior in cognitive abilities, as shown by the Primary Mental Abilities (PMA) Test. Symptomatically, the speech-handicapped had deficits in output of the auditory language form, whereas those with reading disabilities had deficits in the input processes of visual language. Nevertheless, common factors may have been present. Auditory and visual integration is critical to achievement in written language. Both groups had disturbances in auditory and visual receptive language; therefore though the speech-handicapped group was most successful in reading, both might have had deficiencies at the level of the written word. This suggests that reading-disability and speech-handicapped children are homogeneous in regard to needs for remediation in written language, but heterogeneous in regard to primary symptomatologies. It seems, therefore, that their education-remediation needs can be met only when both similarities and differences are given adequate consideration.

MENTALLY RETARDED AND READING-DISABILITY CHILDREN

Emotional and other factors are important, but cognitive ability is a basic correlate of learning to read. The ways in which retarded and reading-disability children differ, however, have not been well documented. A mentally retarded child may be dyslexic, but other similarities and differences in learning patterns should be clarified in the interest of better understanding of both groups. The data presented below (see Table 88) indicate that these populations are widely different, with idiosyncratic styles of learning and with differing educational requirements.

Total Words

The stories written by the reading-disability group were much longer than the stories written by the retarded children. At 9 and 11 years the poor readers wrote three times as many words and at 13 years they wrote twice as many. The retarded made gains at each of the age levels but their rate of growth was slower. A reading disability markedly impedes acquisition of written language but, comparatively, mental retardation places a much greater restriction on this type of learning.

Total Sentences

Number of sentences also showed the reading-disability children to be superior. However, the degree of difference was not as great because the retarded continued to write short sentences as they became older. Both groups reached a plateau at 13 years of age.

Words per Sentence

Gains in the number of words written per sentence were made by both types of exceptional children, but those with reading disabilities wrote sentences more normal in length. The retarded gained 1.3 words per sentence from 9 to 11 years, 2.4 words from 11 to 13, and 1.9 words from 13 to 15 years. The highest single gain made by the reading-disability group was 1.7 words per sentence; this gain occurred between 11 and 13 years. Although the retarded made wider gains developmentally, by 15 years of age they wrote sentences equal to those of the reading-disability children of 9 years.

Syntax

The mentally retarded were inferior also in syntax. At 9 years their level of accuracy was approximately one-half that achieved by the poor readers. However, by 11 years they attained a level two-thirds that of the children with deficits in reading, and by the age of 13 their ratio of success was even higher. The rate of growth was greater for the retarded than for those having a more normal learning configuration for syntax. Like the normals, the poor readers reached a plateau at an early age, attaining maximum function at approximately 11 years of age. The retarded continued to make gains in correct usage until 15 years, but at that age their level of success was equivalent only to that of a 9-year-old child with a reading disability.

The differences in the pattern of learning for syntax suggest that these groups of exceptional children did not have the same primary type of disability. The poor readers were disturbed in ability to acquire the normal relations among words, a relation determined largely by the auditory language form. On the other hand, the retarded had a developmental delay: they continued to acquire syntax usage as they increased in age, even up to 15 years, and did not reach a plateau. So far as written language is concerned, these cognitive learning problems are different in nature and require different educational approaches.

Abstract-Concrete

It was predicted that ability to communicate meaning would be associated with type of disability in exceptional children. In the analysis of the results for normal children, depth of meaning expressed was correlated with mental ability. The results for the retarded also showed this correlation; they made no gains in use of abstraction after 11 years of age, a pattern that was in contrast to their performance on total words, words per sentence, and syntax. The profile for the poor readers was essentially opposite. Except at 15 years, they made excellent progress in communication of abstract meaning, but reached a plateau on productivity and syntax. Their deficiency was mainly in verbal functions, whereas for the retarded the greatest lack was in acquisition of meaning.

These data are revealing with respect to the impact of each of these disabilities. With mental retardation, the primary problem is integration of experience, the development of inner language. But a reading disability primarily impedes transducing of experience into verbal language symbols. In other words, the child with a reading disability finds it most difficult to express experience through language, but the retarded child's greatest problem is acquisition of meaning, learning to understand the significance of what happens to him. The task of fostering learning differs substantially for these two types of exceptional children. Only when these differences are fully recognized can educational planning be most effective.

Summary

This comparative analysis disclosed that reading disabilities, as well as mental retardation, impede acquisition of written language. Of the two, however, mental retardation imposed the greater limitation. But the deficiencies that derived from these disabilities brought about problems in learning that varied not only in degree but also in quality. As suggested in Chapter V, the mentally retarded encountered a generalized disability, encompassing all aspects of learning. Theirs was a uniform deficiency, with a developmental pattern paralleling the normal except that progress was at a slower rate. In contrast, the reading-disability children were deficient mainly in language.

MENTALLY RETARDED CHILDREN AND CHILDREN WITH ARTICULATION DISORDERS

To investigate further the developmental pattern for written language as it relates to type of exceptionality, a comparative analysis was made of the scores for the mentally retarded and the children with disorders of articulation. Both groups were deficient in language learning, but their characteristics varied widely, as shown by the data in Table 89.

Total Words

Although the children with disturbances of articulation were inferior in number of words written, the retarded were relatively much less proficient; the latter wrote 31 words less per story at 9 years, 34 words less at 11 years, and 30 words less at 13 years. However, the gains made by age were not equivalent, and at 9 years the retarded performed at a level one-third that of the speech handicapped. By 13 years this variation was reduced to one-half, but at that age the retarded performed less well than a 9-year-old with an articulation disorder.

Total Sentences

These two types of exceptional children were more equal on number of sentences written per story, especially at the upper age of 13 years. Because the retarded continued to write short sentences, they achieved a higher level of output as measured by this scale of productivity. Nevertheless, their marked inferiority was apparent.

Words per Sentence

The children with articulation disorders performed within normal limits on words per sentence; their deficiency in output was primarily in total words and total sentences. The mentally retarded, like the speech-handicapped and the normals, made uniform and equivalent gains from one age level to the next, maintaining the same degree of inferiority throughout the age range. They wrote approximately six words less per sentence than children with speech defects at 9 years of age, and this same degree of deficiency prevailed at 11 and 13 years.

As shown by the data in Part One, normal children gained one word per sentence per year. This rate of growth was shown by the speech-handicapped as well as by the retarded. Neither the retarded nor those with disorders of articulation differed from the normal in developmental pattern. The level attained by the articulation-deficient children was equivalent to that of the controls, but the level of the retarded was markedly below normal and remained so from one age to the next. These results, like those for the other comparisons, reveal the stability of words per sentence and illustrate the developmental deficits present in the mentally retarded.

Syntax

The retarded achieved greater success in syntax than in the other facets of written language, and their facility in correct usage increased with age. At 9 years their proficiency was one-half the level reached by the speech-handicapped, but at 13 years it was three-fourths this level. Though the difference between the retarded and those with deficits in articulation was highly significant, syntax was not the fundamental problem for either group. The speech-disorder children performed below normal but they made gains and achieved essentially average competence by 13 years of age. The pattern for the retarded was similar but their ultimate level of success was substantially lower.

Abstract-Concrete

Both disorders of articulation and mental retardation had an impact on use of abstraction in the story. But, as in the other aspects of written language, the impact resulting from mental retardation was greatest. The speech-handicapped scored from 3 to 5 points lower than the controls, and the retarded scored from 9 to 10 points lower —approximately twice as low as the speech-disorder group.

To some extent these results are surprising, inasmuch as both an articulation defect and mental retardation were associated with deficits in use of abstraction, albeit the impact of the mental retardation was greater. Since the speech-handicapped were not inferior to normal in cognitive ability, their limitation cannot be explained in this way. Moreover, on the PMA Test the retarded scored at a level two-thirds of average, but their level of function on abstract meaning ranged from one-fourth to one-half of average. Because of the wide differences between the retarded and speech-handicapped, these groups must be considered as having different educational needs. On the other hand, emphasis on development of meaning is a requirement of both groups. Those with disorders of articulation, because of their basic integrity, should be expected to achieve normal levels of function. If they do not, they must be suspected of having a primary deficit in inner language, one of the most limiting of all handicaps. The outlook for the mentally retarded is less favorable, but effective remediation should raise their level of function to be commensurate with their cognitive ability rather than 4 years below average. The intensive nature of their educational needs suggests that they would benefit most from programs developed specifically for them, without regard for other types of involvement.

Summary

The mentally retarded differed from the speech-handicapped in that their limitations were more generalized, but the differences were not only of degree. The two groups varied also in patterns of development. Comparatively, both groups had disorders of language, with maximum effect on the written form. For the mentally retarded, poor performance was characterized by developmental delay, and achievement of a level of proficiency more in agreement with their cognitive abilities seemed possible. For those with articulation disorders poor performance was related to disturbed cognitive functioning, with greatest effect on Factor 1 of written language; the deficit was largely in fluency, output, and meaning.

SOCIALLY-EMOTIONALLY DISTURBED CHILDREN AND CHILDREN WITH ARTICULATION DISORDERS

A major purpose of these comparative analyses was to achieve further insights relative to the characteristics of each of the groups of exceptional children and how these characteristics vary from one group to another. The study of the group with articulation disorders showed that the speech disability was not a unitary problem, though it served as the basis for classification for specialized remediation. Likewise, the socially-emotionally disturbed did not deviate in behavior only. Both organic and nonorganic abnormalities have been indicated as the primary defect in articulation disorders, and nonorganic factors have been assumed to be of major consequence in the socially-emotionally disturbed. Comparison of these groups attempted to provide information that would elucidate each type of disability, particularly whether the disorders engender similar or different patterns of language learning. If overlapping characteristics evolved, a basis for more effective programming for both groups might be developed. Since the greatest incidence of children in these groups was concentrated at the extremes of the age range, comparison could be made only at the ages of 9, 11, and 13 years. The results for written language are shown in Table 90.

Total Words

Both groups were inferior in story length, but those with speech disorders were superior at 9 and 11 years. The developmental pattern also varied by group. The children with disturbances in articulation gained approximately 11 words per story between 9 and 11 years, and 8 words between 11 and 13 years. The socially-emotionally disturbed gained only 7 words between 9 and 11 years but 32 words between 11 and 13 years. Though substantially below the speech-handicapped group initially, the disturbed achieved equal proficiency at the age of 13. Both groups were deficient in output of written language, with the emotionally disturbed showing greatest strides toward overcoming this limitation.

Total Sentences

The trends observed for total words appeared again in the results for number of sentences. At 9 and 11 years those with disorders of articulation were distinctly superior, but because the disturbed made greater strides developmentally, there were no differences at 13 years. Both groups were substantially below average, showing an inability to write stories of normal length in terms of number of words as well as number of sentences.

Words per Sentence

The group with deficits in articulation was superior in sentence length, but except at 11 years, the difference was not significant. Basically, these types of exceptional children were equal in the number of words written per sentence. Compared with the normal, the children deficient in speech were seriously disturbed in words per sentence at the lower age levels but attained more normal function by 11 years of age. A similar trend occurred for the disturbed but their rate of growth was slower. To a degree, the pattern that emerged by group was equivalent; both matured at a slower rate than the normal, with the developmental progression characterizing the disturbed being most deviate. The deficits in learning concomitant to the social-emotional disturbance were more generalized, causing greater retardation in all aspects of language. But ability to formulate and execute sentences in written form was not a factor that clearly differentiated these groups. As a common denominator it revealed the maturational delay in both groups and illustrated a similar remediation requirement despite the difference in symptomatologies.

Syntax

The differences in productivity between the groups occurred at the lower age levels, with more equivalent outcome at the older ages. The results for syntax fell in the opposite order; there were no differences at the younger ages, but at 13 years the variation favored the speech-handicapped. The disturbed were at least 2 years inferior, whereas the speech group had achieved normal levels of function. Acquiring facility in correct usage of written language was more difficult for the socially-emotionally disturbed. Because syntax is acquired largely through auditory language, this group must have had a greater disturbance of processes basic to learning. Hence, remediation for these two types of children should not be identical.

Abstract-Concrete

Both groups were unusually inferior in communication of abstract meaning; the only difference occurred at 9 years. Because the symptomatologies of these two types of children varied widely, and because those with speech defects had normal cognitive abilities, this marked inferiority in use of abstraction as a common factor was not anticipated. Neither deficits in articulation nor disturbances in social-emotional adjustment had heretofore been associated with limitations in attainment of meaning, in acquisition of inner language.

The similarity of these types of exceptional children with respect to poor achievement in expression of meaning cannot be explained at this time. The speech-handicapped present the more difficult pattern to understand. They exceeded the disturbed in output of words and sentences, yet were severely deficient in meaning, a component of the same factor (Factor 1). The performance of the socially-emotionally disturbed was more consistent in that they were developmentally inferior in all facets of written language. It is in this regard that the two groups are not equivalent. The speech-handicapped attained essentially normal function in certain areas but were markedly deficient in others. The socially-emotionally disturbed were delayed in all areas but showed continued growth from one age to the next. These variations should serve as a basis for differentiating the remediation programs for these groups.

Summary

The socially-emotionally disturbed were inferior to those with disorders of articulation primarily on story length and number of sentences. These groups, generally, were more equal on sentence length, syntax, and use of abstraction, but the disturbed had the greatest deficiency in written language. Developmental patterns also varied, the speech-handicapped children being most inconsistent and different by area of function; for example, they achieved normal facility in syntax, but at a much later age than the normals. The emotionally disturbed followed a pattern of extensive inferiority in early life, with developmental progression from one age to the next. Although they had characteristics in common, these groups presented disturbances in learning and adjustment that were dissimilar and that require specialized programming. A psychoneurological and developmental approach might be advantageous. Neither group, if considered only in terms of its primary symptomatology, would be benefited to the extent required, and both need remediation for deficits in language.

SOCIALLY-EMOTIONALLY DISTURBED AND
READING-DISABILITY CHILDREN

Emotional disturbance often is considered a primary factor in reading disabilities; only meager attention has been given to psychoneurological involvements, such as dyslexia. Moreover, written language rarely has been studied in conjunction with reading disabilities.

In comparing the socially-emotionally disturbed and those with deficits in reading, a major question was whether emotional factors were primary to both groups, the difference being in the pervasiveness of the involvement—one group showing only poor reading ability and the other poor reading and social-emotional maladjustment. The previous analysis, however, suggests that to regard either group only in terms of emotional factors might be a serious oversimplification (see Chapters IV and VII). Direct comparison of these types of exceptional children was made to gain further insights into the ways language disorders might be influential in both. The results are given in Table 91.

Total Words

All the groups of exceptional children were limited in output of written language, especially as measured by story length. This is shown again by these results. Both the reading-disability and the disturbed children were inferior in total words, but the socially-emotionally disturbed had the greatest deficiency; this difference was most marked at 11 years of age. The developmental pattern for both groups indicated progression, the poor readers making most increment between 9 and 11 years. The disturbed children, in contrast, achieved their greatest advance between 11 and 13 years of age; they disclosed a pattern of developmental delay compared with the other group. By 13 years of age the groups were equivalent.

Total Sentences

The group variations in number of sentences followed the pattern for total words. The reading-disability children exceeded the emotionally disturbed at 9 and 11 years; no differences occurred between the groups at 13 and 15 years. The principal variation was the slower rate of growth on the part of children classified as socially-emotionally disturbed.

Words per Sentence

The only significant difference for sentence length was at 11 years; the disturbed wrote fewer words per sentence. Again, the poor readers made their biggest increment between 9 and 11 years and the disturbed between 11 and 13 years. Because of this difference in rate of growth, these groups were not equivalent at the lower age levels, but because they both reached plateaus, they were equivalent at 13 and 15 years of age.

Syntax

The difference between these groups was not only in productivity —the quantity of output—but also in ability to use written language correctly. The pattern of this difference varied; at the ages of 9, 11, and 13 years the socially-emotionally disturbed were inferior, but by 15 years they attained a level slightly above that of the poor readers.

The findings for syntax again point to the variations in developmental pattern by group. The reading-disability children were severely deficient at 9 years, then achieved a more normal level at 11 years. This level, though below average, remained essentially stationary for the next 6 years. The disturbed children also were markedly inferior at 9 years but progressed from one age to the next throughout the following 6 years. Because of these variations it is unlikely that these types of exceptional children have identical deficiencies in learning. The reading-disability group performed in a manner typical of children with language disorders, including dyslexia; hence, the poor progress in syntax. The socially-emotionally disturbed performed in a manner typical of children who are delayed developmentally, whose growth rate varies from normal. These patterns by group suggest that neither of these types of children should be regarded as atypical only in emotional behavior.

Abstract-Concrete

The reading-disability children were superior in acquisition and use of meaning, but the difference reached significance only at 13 years. Compared with the normal, the socially-emotionally disturbed ranged from six to eight points below the norm and the poor readers only four to five points below (with the exception of the 15-year-olds).

It is apparent that the disturbed group encountered greater difficulty in achieving normal expression of meaning, but their rate of progression from one age level to the next was equivalent to that of the reading-disability children, as well as to that of the normals. Comparatively, a deficit in reading was less of an imposition on this facet of language.

Summary

The reading-disability and socially-emotionally disturbed children differed with respect to acquisition of written language. The greatest variation was for story length and number of sentences, but the reading-disability group was superior on all aspects. These differences occurred largely because of variations in developmental pattern. The poor readers reached a plateau at 11 to 13 years, but the disturbed group attained maximum performance between 13 and 15 years and for syntax and abstract-concrete had not yet reached a plateau at 15 years. Their pattern thus varied from the pattern of the reading-disability children.

Both groups were markedly deficient in written language, but they varied from each other in a manner suggesting that they were not homogeneous populations. Though both groups were inferior in reading (input), their use of written language (output) indicated that the basis of their disability was not identical. The reading-disability children seemed deficient in the written word *because* they were unable to learn to read; they were more characteristic of those with language disorders, having greater integrity in other respects. The socially-emotionally disturbed presented a pattern of generalized developmental retardation. That these groups are parallel in type, both being unable to learn because of emotional conflicts, is not indicated. Social-emotional maladjustment occurs with and without effects on acquisition of language, and reading disabilities occur with and without social-emotional maladjustment. A principal implication of this comparative analysis is that to consider either group only in terms of emotional factors is to overlook basic disturbances in their patterns of learning. If these disturbances are recognized, and if remediation is provided specifically in relation to the type of disability present in each group, the outlook is favorable. If the similarities between these types of exceptional children are stressed unduly, their idiosyncratic needs will not be provided for and their ultimate potential will be minimized.

MENTALLY RETARDED AND SOCIALLY-EMOTIONALLY DISTURBED CHILDREN

The question of equivalency is raised frequently in regard to the mentally retarded and the socially-emotionally disturbed. The analysis described below was made to compare their homogeneity, mainly in acquisition of written language; there is need to establish the characteristics that differentiate these types of exceptional children, as well as those that disclose similarities. Little is known about the ways the learning patterns for these groups vary or are similar. The results of the comparative analysis of their proficiency with written language are shown in Table 92.

Total Words

Both groups were inferior to the controls, but the mentally retarded scored below the socially-emotionally disturbed; the difference at 11 years was not significant. The severe limitation in written language shown by these groups is one of the most significant outcomes of this investigation. At 15 years of age the retarded wrote stories about one-third the length of the average 9-year-olds, and the disturbed children wrote stories slightly more than one-half the length of the average 9-year-old's story.

Nevertheless, the performances of these groups differed. For example, the disturbed made a gain of 32 words per story from 11 to 13 years of age, and the retarded gained only 12 words during this 2-year interval. Moreover, like the normals, the children with behavior disturbances reached a plateau at 13 years, but the retarded continued to make a modest gain from 13 to 15 years. Another indication of the variation by group is the fact that the retarded performed at a level from 2 to 3 years below that of the socially-emotionally disturbed throughout the age range; the span of this difference increased with age. These results, like those from the other analyses, disclosed that the disturbed were far below average in early life (though not to the degree found for the retarded) but made notable gains with age; hence, at the upper age level they were more equal to the normal. This was not true of the mentally retarded.

Total Sentences

No differences appeared for total sentences, an unusual finding that highlights the results for words per sentence. Though equal in the number of sentences they contained, stories written by the socially-emotionally disturbed were significantly longer. Thus, a diagnostic differentiation between these groups can be made on the basis of sentence usage. The retarded wrote many fewer words per story but an equivalent number of sentences because their sentences lacked complexity.

Words per Sentence

The most consistent variation between these types of exceptional children was in words per sentence, the retarded being inferior to the disturbed at all age levels. However, the developmental pattern varied by group. The retarded made uniform increments in growth from one age to the next, a configuration parallel to the normal. In contrast, the disturbed group made no growth from 9 to 11 years, then gained four words per sentence from 11 to 13 years. This pattern again indicated the marked delay in early life, with increments later, especially between the ages of 11 and 13 years. Because of these gains, the differences between the groups were greatest at the upper age levels; at 15 years the retarded were approximately 3 years below the socially-emotionally disturbed.

Though they shared common elements, these groups differed in significant ways. The learning rate of the disturbed exceeded that of the retarded and their level of achievement was far greater. Moreover, the factor of sentence length clearly differentiated the groups. The retarded were unable to formulate and execute sentences in a manner equal to the disturbed; they were able to produce only short sentences devoid of complex language. The inference is that the learning processes and cognitive functions also were different in the two groups.

Syntax

Of the five scores on the Picture Story Language Test, the mentally-retarded were most successful on acquisition of syntax. Nevertheless, they were inferior to the socially-emotionally disturbed, especially at 9 and 15 years of age. Again, these results provide insights into the differences between the groups. The variations were not equal in degree for each of the factors of written language. Words per sentence, as a factor, clearly differentiated the groups, but syntax, another factor, showed them to be more equivalent. Therefore, in terms of written language, the two types of children were more similar in certain respects than in others, but the ways in which they were most dissimilar may be indicative of the basic variations in learning patterns that characterize each of the groups.

Abstract-Concrete

Use of abstraction (depth of meaning), together with total words and total sentences, make up Factor 1. It is on this factor, and the factor of words per sentence, that these groups differed most. The mentally retarded were unusually deficient in communication of meaning; they reached a plateau at 13 years, having attained a level equivalent to that of the average child of 7 years. In contrast, the disturbed children made their greatest gain between 11 and 15 years. Again, this variation in developmental pattern resulted in wider group differences as age increased. The retarded remained more concrete, more bound to the observable. The inner language of the disturbed was more flexible; they integrated experience more meaningfully and were more able to express imaginative thoughts and ideas.

Summary

The comparative analysis of the written language for the mentally retarded and the socially-emotionally disturbed disclosed that the retarded were inferior and the patterns of development were dissimilar. The retarded showed a uniform deficiency from one age level to the next, but the disturbed, though initially far below average, made greater growth increments, especially from 11 to 13 years of age.

On the other hand, these groups were more similar than the mentally retarded and the children with disorders of articulation, and than the retarded and those with reading disabilities. To an extent, the basic defect in the mentally retarded and in the socially-emotionally disturbed was generalized developmental retardation. However, these groups presented widely different needs educationally; they differed in severity of defect and, apparently, in mode of learning. Emphasis on language development is indicated for both groups, but the levels at which they function differ, and programs are needed that relate to the specific deficits that characterize each group of exceptional children.

Chapter X

Disorders of Written Language —
Diagnosis and Remediation

The child is not born with language. This unique human characteristic is acquired gradually over a period of several years. The ontogenetic sequence is for the auditory form to be acquired first, followed by the read and written. The studies reported in the preceding chapters indicate that, because the written form is acquired last, its analysis provides evidence of disorders in the auditory and read forms as well. These studies also demonstrate the importance of regarding language as composed of two types, auditory and visual. Diagnosticians consider the auditory form as involving two fundamental processes—input and output, receptive and expressive. These differentiations have been made for the spoken form for decades, and have served as the basis for gaining knowledge of language-learning processes.

Evaluation of the visual language system has not been approached in terms of receptive and expressive functions. Study of reading has gone forth essentially without concern for the relevance of output. The Picture Story Language Test (PSLT) was developed to provide an achievement test for written language which, together with tests of reading, would permit appraisal of both fundamental processes of the visual language form, input and output. In the course of test development it became advantageous to investigate the relations between auditory and visual language. From these investigations came evidence that study of the last form acquired (visual expressive) was useful in evaluating the other language functions, the spoken and read.

This chapter discusses the cognitive abilities primary to gaining facility with the written word. The frame of reference emphasizes the necessity for determining precisely the type of disorder that exists because only then can remediation be effective. The need is great for such studies covering all types of exceptional children, irrespective of their classification for schooling. Such classification does not necessarily mean that the children's strengths and weaknesses, abilities and disabilities, are being considered as fundamental to an understanding of their deficiencies and a determination of the type of remediation that would be most beneficial. Diagnostic evaluations must be made and specific programs evolved according to the cognitive deficits and disturbances present. Only then can prescriptive teaching fulfill its promise for all exceptional children. It is in these terms that certain processes prerequisite to learning to use the written word are considered.

DEVELOPMENTAL PREREQUISITES FOR WRITTEN LANGUAGE

To investigate the developmental sequence of language learning, a pilot study was undertaken of 500 children aged 8 and 9 years. The learning-quotient technique (Myklebust, 1968, 1973) was used in comparing acquisition of written language with other types of school achievement. The results disclosed a hierarchy of developmental relations.

Learning quotients (LQ) were computed for reading, spelling, arithmetic, and written language; an LQ above 90 indicates that potential and attainment are equivalent. The order of the quotients from highest to lowest was: reading, 90; spelling (writing words from dictation), 85; arithmetic (including reading of problems), 75; written language (measured by the PSLT), 65. Only in reading were the children achieving at their level of potential. For the other subjects, because of their immaturity (8 and 9 years of age), their LQ's fell below 90. For our purposes, however, the more significant outcome was the low score for written language. Because we had not corrected (in the formula) for physiological maturity (chronological age), the quotients for use of the written word were far below average.

This pilot study made clear that developmental hierarchies must be taken into consideration. Substantially more maturation is required for acquisition of written than of read language. This finding was confirmed by the data for normal children (Part one). Reading scores were considerably above writing scores; the redundancy phenomenon was operative. Educational programming and management must consider the significance of these ontogenetic aspects. The studies of exceptional children (Part Two) showed that these aspects vary by type of disability. Ignoring these variations, and the developmental sequences that are disturbed leads to remediation that is ineffective or even detrimental to the child's well-being.

Auditory Processes

The processes whereby auditory language is converted to the visual were stressed by Gates (1947). He stated that "during this stage the typical child will reveal considerable inner speech in his reading. There may or may not be visible movements of the lips. The pupil is still, in a sense, translating the printed word into a spoken word to get the meaning fully" (p. 32). The child first learns one language, the auditory, and then a second language, the visual. He learns the second by translating it into its auditory equivalents. Gradually, as the visual is acquired he has less and less need to translate. He no longer finds it necessary to relate the usual to the auditory; the latter can be bypassed. So long as the words are familiar he can read by using the visual form alone. But when he encounters unfamiliar words again (even as a sophisticated adult), he translates from the auditory by "sounding out" the word. Only through this means can he fix the word in mind and relate it meaningfully to experience.

The field of biomedical engineering has provided the term *transducing*, which refers to converting one form of energy into another. The circumstances are not identical, but this concept illuminates the psychoneurological processes of learning to read and to write. After the learning has occurred, transducing no longer is necessary and the individual *in fact* engages in silent reading. In language pathology it is not uncommon to encounter persons in whom this transducing process is deficient. In adults this condition may result from cerebral vascular illness, and in children it may be due to developmental deviations or to dysfunctions in the brain that result from accident or illness. Thus in terms of diagnosis there exist people who have normal use of the spoken word but cannot give the sound for a letter seen, and people who can give the sound but cannot identify the letter from sight. The first cannot transduce from the visual to the auditory; the second cannot transduce from the auditory to the visual. Though he attributed it to other causations, Gates, to a remarkable degree, recognized this before many of the current diagnostic procedures were available.

In learning to read, it is not sufficient to be able to discriminate auditory and visual sensations separately. Intersensory synesthesia is required. Accordingly, study of written language is intriguing because facility with this verbal system includes motor function, still another factor. After the visual and auditory facets have been attained the brain must combine these and convert them into motor equivalents. Writing is an audio-visual-motor performance, so even if the auditory and visual prerequisites have been attained there may be a deficiency in converting these into a motor pattern: though there is no paralysis, the individual cannot write. This condition, known in neurology for decades, is designated *agraphia* or *dysgraphia* (see Volume One* for examples). To expedite learning of written language the level of function in each of the systems—auditory, visual and motor—must be examined.

In earlier investigations a major concern was with the ways in which auditory disorders modify the behavior of young children (Myklebust, 1954). The outcome was an approach to differential diagnosis that stressed the behavioral symptomatology that characterizes various types of exceptional children. Later the role of audition in determining patterns of behavior was studied through research on the psychological impact of early-life deafness (Myklebust, 1964). That audition has a prominent role in establishing cognitive patterns cannot be questioned. Disturbance or deprivation of auditory sensation results in a variety of behavioral modifications, including a profound alteration of learning itself (Myklebust and Neyhus, 1970; Hughes, 1971). In Volume One examples are presented of the ways in which a disturbance of auditory processing affects acquisition of the written word. Here the purpose is to indicate ways in which certain of these processes are prerequisite to development of this language system. These prerequisites serve as the basis for planning educational programs to meet the urgent needs of children with disorders of written language.

Memory

Virtually every mental act entails memory of some type and degree, so study of any aspect of learning implicates this facet of behavior. Perhaps no other cognitive function more completely combines the

---

* *Development and Disorders of Written Language,* Volume One, *Picture Story Language Test* (Myklebust, 1965).

efforts of psychologists, biomedical engineers, and neurologists; it incorporates many psychoneurosensory processes. Terms such as *retrieval, storage, span,* and *sequence* are in common usage in many fields.

Psychologically, auditory memory often has been viewed as ability to reproduce sequences, one of the most common being digit span—ability to repeat digits in the order presented or in reverse order. Many children who have language disorders are deficient in this capacity, as indicated by the work of Binet and Simon (1916), Monroe (1932), and Gates (1947). Binet showed that at 2.5 years of age the average child is capable of repeating a sequence of two digits; at 3 years, three digits; at 4.5 years, four digits; at 7 years, five digits; at 10 years, six digits. At 7 years, the age when use of the written word is beginning, the child is capable of repeating five digits. Though the degree of correlation between digit span and use of the written word is not known, writing is related to this type of memory ability.

Other facets of auditory memory are word and sentence span. Binet devised tests for both and these have been extended by Baker and Leland (1959). Spencer (1958) in a study of auditory perception used these tests with children below 6 years of age. Word span was measured by having the child repeat unrelated words, and sentence span by having him repeat sentences of increasing length. The average child of 4 years repeats a sentence of 9 to 10 words. Baker found that at 8 years the child repeats sentences of 12 to 13 words; at 11 years, 15 to 16 words; at adulthood, 18 to 19 words. This evidence shows the high levels of auditory memory function at the age when a child begins to use written language. Also, the average adult writes approximately 21 words per sentence (see Volume One), a finding that is remarkably similar to the number of words per sentence repeated by the average adult. Up to adulthood the average length of sentences repeated is greater than the number of words written per sentence. This relation discloses the greater maturity required for written language. Moreover, it is logical that by adulthood the number of words recallable by sentence in the spoken form is equivalent to the average number of words written per sentence.

Syllable Sequence and Recall of Nonsense Syllables

Though ability to repeat words that have an increasing number of syllables is not included in mental tests, it is an important function; it provides evidence of auditory maturation and psychoneurological integrity. Ability to repeat words is appraised by having the child repeat words of different lengths syllabically. The word *yet* consists of only one syllable, *after* is made up of two, and *octogenarian* has six syllables. As emphasized in Volume One in the discussion of differential diagnosis, ability to repeat words of several syllables (ability to syllabicate) is of substantial consequence in learning to read, write, and spell (see also Myklebust *et al.,* 1971). More information is necessary concerning the developmental nature of this attribute and its specific relation to facility with spoken, read, and written language.

Recall of nonsense syllables also has proved useful in evaluating auditory perceptual and memory capacities. Gates (1947) considers this function important in appraising reading readiness and in studying reading disabilities. Spencer (1958) has found that this function, as an aspect of auditory perception, matures with age. McGrady (1964) has demonstrated its usefulness in showing differences among speech-defective, aphasic, and normal children. In study of written language, developmentally and diagnostically, it is included as an indication of the level of auditory function attained. Ability to repeat nonsense syllables is related to the auditory processes necessary for acquisition of written language (see illustrations on pages 31 and 32 in Volume One).

Syllable Blending

Another facet of auditory integrity, not measured on mental tests, is ability to synthesize syllables into words. Monroe (1932) recognizes the importance of this capacity in relation to reading readiness and reading disabilities. The syllables are given with a time delay between each, for example, *tor—na—do*. The cognitive task is to retain each syllable sequentially until all have been presented and then synthesize them into the proper word. Spencer has revealed the maturational aspect of this auditory process and McGrady has shown that children with aphasia are deficient in this capacity.

Studies of the disorders of written language suggest that a child who cannot retain syllables sequentially and blend them into words cannot use the written word normally, even though he has average ability to read (see examples in Volume One). Children are unable to learn to read unless they can reauditorize and revisualize letters simultaneously. However, these functions seem unrelated to ability to synthesize expressively. Therefore, facility with reading may be attained but facility with the written word is not. Nevertheless, in this case it is *spelling* which is deficient, not written language per se. Spencer's work suggests that unless the child can synthesize at least three syllables to form a word, he lacks the necessary prerequisite for writing (spelling) words. Auditory cognitive disturbances of this type predominate in children with learning disabilities (Myklebust *et al.*, 1971).

Discrimination

Ability to distinguish among sounds—those that are alike or even those that are widely different—is a basic aspect of all auditory behavior. One of the early investigations of capacity to discriminate among speech sounds was made by Monroe (1932). She states that "inaccurate articulation and reading disability may come from a common cause, the inability to discriminate successfully the sounds of words. The child models his articulation to match the auditory pattern of the word as presented by another. When he can give himself the same auditory stimulus which is given by another person, the word will appear to himself to be correctly articulated. If his auditory discrimination is poor, he may confuse similar words in both speech and reading without recognizing the error" (p. 93). She found children with reading defects inferior to a normal control group in auditory word discrimination as well as in visual-auditory learning.

Templin (1957) considers speech sound discrimination as ability to make auditory distinctions among the different speech sounds, an auditory perceptual skill. She reports that ability to discriminate among speech sounds increases with age, but the rate of growth decelerates after 5 years of age. Spencer (1958) has come to the same conclusion, indicating that the average child achieves the adult level in this facet of auditory functioning before 6 years of age. Her study also indicates that other facets of auditory behavior reach maturity early in life. In agreement with these findings are the results of McGrady's work with children with receptive aphasia. When such a basic function as sound discrimination is disturbed, both learning and adjustment are impeded. If auditory discrimination is grossly deficient in early life all language behavior, including the written, is affected. Discrimination is one of the most basic and consequential of all auditory processes.

Scrambled Sentences

Another language facility, evidenced by the scrambled sentence test, which entails auditory maturational processes, is ability to formulate sentences from words presented in a scrambled order. This is referred to as dissected sentences by Binet and Simon (1916). The cognitive task consists of forming sentences out of words that appear to be random. At a simple level the following words might be presented: *town I yesterday to went*. The solution requires retention of the words while arranging them in the proper relation to each other so that a sentence is formed. This performance necessitates knowledge of syntax, an aspect of verbal learning often deficient in children with language disorders. The scrambled sentence function (if the words are presented visually) comprises both auditory and visual processes but is included here inasmuch as syntactical ability is an auditory aspect of language; the written follows the syntax structure of the spoken. Facility with scrambled sentences has developmental and diagnostic implications.

Oral Commissions: Following Directions

In the evaluation of auditory processes, ability to follow directions in the order given is of critical importance. Binet first recognized the value of this function as an aspect of intelligence and devised the three commissions test to measure it; Baker and Leland (1959) extended its usefulness through the oral commissions test. By the age of 4 years the average child is capable of following directions such as *put the book on the table, then get your pencil, and bring your chair over here*. Successful performance assumes competence in understanding what is said and maintaining the sequence and structure of the ideas until they have been carried out in the order stipulated. In terms of auditory cognition, this is a complex process, necessitating a long period of maturation before adult level of capacity is attained. Memory is involved but in a way unlike that measured by the digit span test. Many children having disorders in written language show deficits in this ability.

Auditory Association: Rhyme

Ability to relate one sound with another, including parts of words, is referred to as auditory association. Ability to associate sounds properly assumes integrity of auditory learning and experience. The identification of words that rhyme, a test designed by Binet, is an aspect of this capacity. The child is asked to think of a word that sounds like another word. Successful performance incorporates capacity to identify the primary auditory characteristics of the stimulus word and from memory to match these characteristics with another word; the words are associated only by the fact that they sound alike. Spencer's procedure differs in that she asked the child to select a picture of something that sounded like the stimulus word: "show me a picture of something that sounds like *up*."

Word association ability has not been studied extensively but available evidence suggests that it does not become functional until approximately 6 years of age and then shows maturation over a period of several years. This ability provides an indication of the richness and fluidity of auditory language, without involving syntax and other aspects of structure. Study of children with disorders of written language suggest that a child who has no recognition of rhyme is deficient in a prerequisite for acquisition of this language form.

Auditory Equivalents

As suggested previously, ability to transduce information received through one sensory modality into the equivalents of another is critical not only to learning to read and to write but to many aspects of everyday life. In planning remediation, therefore, it is important to ascertain the capacity to produce the auditory equivalents of both visual and tactile sensations. Birch's (1964) work on intersensory perception is relevant; however, it is significant that Binet also includes kinesthetic judgment in his tests of mental ability. Unfortunately, few standardized tests specifically measure ability to transduce intersensorially. One of the reasons a child can earn high scores on tests such as the Wechsler Intelligence Scale for Children, yet be seriously deficient on certain aspects of learning, is that measures of intersensory functions largely are omitted. Gates (1947) has incorporated visual-to-auditory conversion measures in his tests of reading readiness, and these have proved useful in the evaluation of learning disabilities (Myklebust *et al.*, 1971), but definitive tests of intersensory processes remain to be developed and standardized. Nevertheless, one is impressed with the extent of this deficiency in those who cannot learn to read and to use the written word, as shown by the studies of exceptional children (see Part Two). It is important that this function be appraised in all children who have disorders of language.

Summary

The auditory processes involved in learning are more inclusive than is indicated by this discussion. Emphasis is here given only to the fact that extensive auditory development must have occurred before acquisition of the written word is possible. Facility with the spoken word must have been well established and reading must have begun. There is general agreement concerning the basic stages of growth in ability to use auditory language. Babbling has special significance, not only in the initiation of speech but as a means through which the infant begins to organize his perceptual world (Mowrer, 1952; Myklebust, 1954). These auditory factors form the basis of experience, of inner language, of verbal reception and expression.

Auditory and visual language are not separated dichotomously; there is a period (before 6 years of age) when the child's verbal behavior is auditory in nature. Likewise, there is a period during which the child acquires the read and written language forms. The optimum age for acquiring this second-order system has not been adequately determined, but gradually more evidence is forthcoming.

Visual Processes

Much of the work on the developmental aspects of language, especially in relation to reading, has concerned visual processes. However, often this work has been limited to visual acuity or to eye movements and has not considered the neurology or the psychology of learning. Unless ability to hear and to see is adequate, learning to read and write will be impeded. All clinical teachers should be aware of the importance of visual acuity, fusion, stereopsis, and other factors constituting normal vision. Despite the relevance of these factors, and their possible significance to acquisition of language, they are frequently unrelated to learning disabilities (Myklebust, 1973). As in the case of auditory processes, this discussion is limited to the more developmental aspects.

Gesell and Amatruda (1947) give major attention to visual processes in relation to total development of the child and stress the long period of evolution required to bring vision to its advanced status as a sensory modality in man. Moreover, they stated that "seeing is not a separate isolable function: it is profoundly integrated with the total system of the child—his posture, his manual skills and coordination, his intelligence, and even his personality make-up. Indeed vision is so intimately identified with the whole child that we cannot understand its economy and its hygiene without investigating the whole child" (p. 255).

Others have highlighted the role vision plays in human development and learning. Charcot (1887) ascertained that some persons could see but not recognize what they were seeing. Freud (1953) coined the term *agnosia* for such conditions; this term is added to the term designating the modality involved, i.e., visual agnosia, auditory agnosia, and tactile agnosia. Morgan (1896) and Hinshelwood (1895) were among the first to apply this concept to diagnosis of dyslexia, to recognize the relation between dysfunctions in the brain and certain types of reading disabilities in children. Though many controversies have intervened, gradually we are becoming aware of the significance of these insightful observations (Money, 1966; Young and Lindsley, 1970). Gerstmann (1940) has added to these observations by noting that, after sustaining brain damage, some persons can no longer read, write, calculate, or perform other previously learned everyday routines, although a high level of intellectual capacity is retained.

Psychologists have enhanced understanding of the maturational processes of vision largely through studies of perception. Among the notable contributions are those of Solley and Murphy (1960), Bartley (1958), Witkin *et al.* (1954), and Gibson (1966). The most prevalent sources of information are mental and reading-readiness tests. Much of what we know about the development of visual processes and school achievement is derived from these. Despite a broad body of knowledge, categories or types of visual learning deficits are not well defined. Thus, in the following discussion operational classifications developed largely through clinical experience are stressed, with cognizance that audition and vision are not dichotomous, but semi-autonomous, functions. They are separate entities which must be integrated psychologically and neurologically. A deficit in one may have a direct effect, such as inability to learn and to remember what letters look like. An indirect effect occurs when the input cannot be integrated with the experience gained through other modalities. Clinical work, as well as research evidence, suggests the seriousness of such deficits and the necessity to appraise learning in terms of the channels through which the information is received. This frame of reference serves as a guide to the following discussion of the visual processes that seem most related to acquisition of written language.

Orientation: Scanning

Of the early workers, Pavlov (1928) and Gesell and Amatruda (1947) emphasized the role of the senses in keeping the individual in contact with and informed about his environment; among those providing more recent evidence are Mark and Hardy (1958), Baker and Leland (1959), and Benton (1959). Elsewhere hearing and vision are discussed according to their roles in serving the human organism (Myklebust, 1964; Johnson and Myklebust, 1967). From the point of view of self-preservation, hearing functions as a background sense, providing information from all directions simultaneously, whereas vision is a foreground sense providing information mainly about that which is in the mind, about that to which attention is directed. As the child is born with ability to hear but must *learn to listen,* he is born with ability to see but must *learn to look.* He can neither scan nor focus visually until he has attained a degree of oculomotor control and until he can direct his attention selectively.

Diagnostic studies of children with disorders of written language often detect those who are deficient in ability to scan and to focus. They can *see* but cannot *look.* Cattell (1940) has found that at 2 months of age the average infant begins to visually inspect and scan his environment. Gesell and Amatruda (1947) have shown that the child has ability to focus selectively and to look at a cube by 3 months of age. Such basic aspects as scanning and focusing are essential to the development of other visual processes. When these abilities do not ensue normally, a gross deficiency, often of the neurogenic type, is suspected. Reading and writing assume that these visual functions have been established developmentally.

Visual Perception

As a cognitive process perception has been studied principally through vision; this is shown by the work of Witkin *et al.* (1954), Allport (1955), Bartley (1958), Solley and Murphy (1960), Gibson (1966), and in relation to handicapped children by Strauss and Lehtinen (1947) and Frostig (1968). Though the literature is extensive, perception has been variously defined. Moreover, studies of this aspect of behavior have not emphasized maturational factors or the role of perception in learning. Without attempting an inclusive analysis, this discussion encompasses certain of the fundamentals that appear consequential to acquisition of facility with the written word.

Discrimination. What cannot be discriminated cannot be perceived. Bartley states that unless the discriminatory process is present the behavior is below the level of perception, presumably at the level of sensation. If what is being seen is to be recognized and identified, it must be distinguished as distinct from other aspects of the visual world; it must be discriminated from the background. This facility may entail selecting features such as contour, size, shape, space and time relations, color, and position. The importance of figure and ground has been emphasized by various workers, notably Strauss and Lehtinen (1947) and Cruickshank *et al.* (1961). Perceptual disturbances are of considerable consequence, but it is erroneous to assume that all learning disabilities derive from perceptual dysfunction. Other levels of integration may be involved. On the other hand, as emphasized by Bartley, it is through perception that the organism maintains *ongoing* contact with its environment; hence, perception is one of the most basic of all aspects of behavior. Writing is not possible until letters can be discriminated; words cannot be written until letters can be distinguished one from the other (Gibson, 1969). Some children substitute incorrect for correct letters, particularly those that appear alike; presumably these are the most difficult to discriminate.

Recognition. Recognition and discrimination are not identical processes. Some children can identify likenesses and differences; they can match forms, even letters, but are unable to recognize them; they can discriminate between *M* and *W* but do not recognize them as letters. This function has been emphasized on reading-readiness tests. Ability to ascribe meaning, however, encompasses pervasive aspects of learning, verbal and nonverbal. It is involved in responses to tests such as picture memory, picture completion, pictorial absurdities, and picture identification. As a process, recognition assumes integration and memory.

Meaning. Acquisition of meaning is receiving greater attention from a number of disciplines, albeit as a psychoneurosensory process this function presents many difficulties. As yet, knowledge is limited regarding this component of behavior. Perhaps most study of meaning has been accomplished in relation to verbal behavior; spoken, read, and written. Meaning as a criterion of successful use of the written word is discussed in Volume One; the abstract-concrete scale of the PSLT was developed to measure this aspect of written language.

Considerable insight into acquisition of meaning as a process has been gained through study of its pathology. Charcot (1887) observed that not all patients who failed to associate meaning with what they saw were suffering from hysteria. He said that their "blindness" resulted from a dysfunction in the brain; when reading was involved he classified the condition as *word-blindness*. But this disturbance might also encompass objects, not only the written word. More than a century ago Jackson referred to such disturbances as *imperception*, an apt term (Taylor, 1958). It was Freud, however, who coined the term used most extensively at this time; his term is *agnosia*. Primarily through neurology, this term has come to mean an inability to perceive and to recognize as the result of dysfunction in the brain. It is prefixed by a sensory modality; commonly used for diagnostic purposes are tactile agnosia, auditory, agnosia, and visual agnosia.

In this discussion our concern is to indicate that even though certain perceptual skills, such as discrimination, are excellent the child may be unable normally to associate meaning with what he discriminates. At the level of the spoken word he repeats precisely what is heard, but without meaning; this is referred to as *echolalia*. In reading he is able successfully to read passages but cannot associate meaning with what he reads: this often is designated *word-calling*. The equivalent condition is seen in use of the written word when the child successfully writes words, or even sentences, but has no knowledge of what he has written; this may be referred to as *word-writing*. Perhaps one of the most consequential considerations in relation to perception is that development of meaning is assumed.

Visual Memory

The study of memory has attained vast proportions in recent years, perhaps because of extensive research on brain function and on learning. Indeed, as a process memory is of great moment and is involved in all behavior. Often it is viewed as comprising three distinct aspects: recording, storing, and retrieving. These distinctions are relevant to consideration of learning, especially in terms of psychoneurology. Some children are unable to "register" normally what they see (or hear); for example, they cannot remember what letters look like. They see them and recognize them but the images are not recorded. Others remember them, but only for brief periods. The process of storing is deficient, so the images are not retained; the same material must be learned day after day. Still others have normal recording and storing ability but are deficient in recall, in retrieval of what has been learned. These children know they have learned a given type of information, they know they know it, but they cannot reproduce it. Expressive memory—memory for output—is disturbed.

Because memory as an attribute is of such pervasive influence it is involved in many aspects of acquiring facility with the written word. Such facility assumes that the words have been learned auditorially, visually, and in a sense, motorically. Stated differently, the words must have been recorded and stored auditorially and visually, then must be retrievable auditorially, visually, and motorically. Only when all these processes function normally can the child produce the written word (see Volume One for examples of deficiencies).

Visual memory has been studied in various ways—through tests of picture (object) span, letter span, attention span, memory for designs, visual digit span, and object location. All these may be useful in appraisal of maturational levels or specific deficits in visual memory. It is critical, however, to be aware that both auditory and visual memory may be adequate intrasensorially but deficient intersensorially; the child may not be able to learn and remember the auditory equivalents of letters as seen or the visual equivalents of letters as heard. It is in these inclusive terms that developmental prerequisites must be ascertained. Unfortunately, through lack of proper diagnosis, many children reach high-school age without having the precise nature of their problem determined and appropriate remedial education inaugurated. Minimal integrity and attainment are essential before written language can be mastered.

Imagery

There is a relation between imagery and memory which, perhaps, is best described by the statement that there can be no imagery without memory. Imagery, however, has been studied much less than memory and, particularly in recent years, has been neglected; for exceptions see Bruner (1966), Penfield (1969), Pribram (1969), and Richardson (1969). Increasingly, investigators are demonstrating the importance of imagery in the study of learning, psychologically and neurologically.

Imagery, as a cognitive function, usually refers to ability to recall experience auditorially or visually; it is defined as ability to recall

all or parts of an actual experience, picturing it in the mind. This process has been referred to as *revisualization* (Johnson and Myklebust, 1967). Studies in language pathology show that much learning is dependent on the processes of reauditorization and revisualization. The extent to which certain sophisticated dyslexics describe how they cannot picture what letters and words look like is remarkable. A brilliant university student, who had residual dyslexia, said, "I read auditorially—I can't read visually." Diagnostic studies usually confirm these subjective reports; both picture- and letter-completion tests are useful for such studies. For example, in a letter-completion test to evaluate these prerequisites for writing the child is given parts of letters and is asked to complete them. Often, though a part already has been shown to him, he cannot internalize this part and associate it with the other parts to complete the letter; hence, he cannot write. Until such revisualization is possible, at least at a rudimentary level, the child is unable to use the written word. Sometimes copying assists in establishing this facility.

Unfortunately, standardized procedures designed specifically for determining imagery levels developmentally have not been evolved for either auditory or visual functioning. However, the work of Ilg and Ames (1964) is relevant and their techniques for determining visual readiness deserve wider application. Diagnosticians can also use the various picture-completion tests included in mental test batteries, as well as improvised clinical techniques such as the letter-completion test.

Motor Processes

Many workers in recent years have stressed motor functions in relation to learning. However, this emphasis has not been in terms of either developmental patterns or language acquisition. Another limitation is that few motor tests provide normative data so that maturational levels can be ascertained. A notable exception is the Oseretsky Test (Doll, 1946; Sloan, 1955); Boyd (1965) used items from this test in comparing the motor abilities of deaf and hearing children.

In previous chapters the usefulness of the Heath Railwalking Test for appraising locomotor coordination is indicated. This test has been used extensively for both clinical and research purposes and has been valuable in ascertaining generalized motor integrity and in revealing the motor characteristics of handicapped children (Myklebust, 1954, 1964).

Jones (1949), through studies using the dynamometer, has shown that children mature in hand and arm strength. This approach is advantageous to diagnosis, particularly in eliciting indications of a neurogenic basis for the defect. Gesell and Amatruda (1947) and Bayley (1943) also have provided normative data for determining levels of motor growth and performance.

That motor ability and facility with writing are related is apparent from observation, but the specific relations and the developmental factors of primary consequence have not been well established. Rigorous procedures for such study have been provided by Rarick and Harris (1963). They present data on the correlations between legibility and rate of development and on differences by sex (females show greater and more rapid progress in legibility from the sixth to the tenth grades). Fine motor control stands out as an important factor in legibility.

Various conditions interfere with development of the motor ability prerequisite for writing. Cobb (1958) discusses a number of these in relation to specific types of dysfunctions of the central nervous system. The most basic disturbances are those that impose limitations on fine motor coordination of the hands and fingers, though use of the arm also is critical. Serious impositions on writing derive from hemiplegia, athetosis, spasticity, rigidity, flaccidity, paralysis agitans, chorea, ataxia, and apraxia. In exceptional children it is necessary to ascertain the integrity of the motor system when determining prerequisites for writing. As shown by the examples in Volume One, serious trauma ensues when children without the necessary motor ability are required to write.

Studies using the PSLT on both normal and exceptional children show that motor maturity for writing at adult levels is not attained until substantially later than had been presumed. As the work of Rarick and Harris (1963) also suggests, an adult level of ability develops at a later age and requires a longer period for maturation than is allowed for by those who urge early teaching of writing.

Acquisition of the needed motor ability follows a sequential pattern, as shown by Gesell and Amatruda (1947) and Doll (1953). Their findings reveal that by the age of 1 year the child grasps a crayon; at 18 months he picks up and grasps the crayon with a palmar grip; at 2 years he uses the thumb more effectively, but not until 4 years does he approximate holding the pencil like an adult; from 5 to 6 years he continues to improve in both grasp and coordination and at this time can use writing tools to print simple words; at about 6 years he copies capital letters; at 7 he writes, but the script is large, awkward, uneven, and irregular in size and position—at this age he prefers to print and uses a pencil with greater adeptness (see examples in Volume One). At 9 years he can use writing more as a tool, and penmanship becomes smaller and more uniform. By 10 years of age he begins to write occasional short letters and writing finally has become a fundamental means of communication, albeit (as indicated by the data in Part Two as well as in Volume One) facility with the written word continues to mature for 7 years more. Motor ability, however, presents no further obstacle to writing after 10 to 12 years of age.

Writing is a motor act accomplished through use of the preferred hand. Though the association between handedness and development of writing is complex, it can be viewed in terms of motor behavior. Perhaps the most perplexing child is the one who writes normally (left to right) with one hand and spontaneously writes from right to left, usually in a "mirror" pattern, with the other hand. This psychomotor phenomenon is intriguing and awaits an explanation through research and diagnostic evidence. Here it is emphasized that a fundamental approach to study of motor maturity for writing includes appraisal of laterality.

Inner Language Processes

One of the most critical and least understood prerequisites for use of written language, as well as for use of the spoken and read forms, is the manner in which words become associated with meaning; this has been referred to as the inner language process (Myklebust, 1954). The abstract-concrete scale from the PSLT represents one of the ways the process may be evaluated. It is significant, however, that meaning as measured by this scale is closely related to word fluency; the greater the facility with words, the greater the facility for expression of meaning. This association is reciprocal; enhancement of vocabulary results in higher levels of meaning, and vice versa.

The studies reported in Part Two indicate that all types of disabilities affect this critical factor of language. In other words, meaning and word fluency are vulnerable to a variety of impositions. By implication, if expression of meaning is to be developed, a type of "word redundancy" must be achieved. The child must not only have an adequate vocabulary but also a pool of words available that exceeds his immediate needs. There is no more urgent requirement, so far as educational remediation is concerned, than to inaugurate programs that focus on this factor in language development.

Inner language disorders are debilitating to many aspects of learning; hence, the urgency for their more ready diagnosis and more general recognition. To better understand inner language disturbance it is only necessary to recall the common experience of reading a page only to realize suddenly that one's attention has been on something else; there is no awareness of what was read. This occurrence, though normal, illustrates that input and inner language processes do not necessarily work in unison. Rather, these processes can be detached to serve different purposes. According to clinical evidence, certain neurological disturbances produce a condition in which such detachment becomes unavoidable. When this occurs, even though receptive and expressive functions remain intact, ability to associate meaning with words is impaired. In relation to the spoken word, this is *echolalia;* that which is heard is repeated without meaning. In reading, the analogous condition is designated *word-calling.* The comparable disability in written language is *word-writing;* the words are written but have no meaning to the writer.

Word-writing must be differentiated from inability to read what one has written, a moderately common condition in children and adults who had normal language abilities before becoming dyslexic. They write meaningfully and successfully monitor the process, but cannot read what they have written. This is a receptive disorder, not a disorder of inner language. Disorders of inner language may be specific to a given verbal system (spoken, read, or written) but more often affect all language functions, albeit to varying extents.

It is not the intention in this discussion to imply that inner language deficits occur only when certain neurological insults have been sustained. The studies of written language suggest that a more common imposition is an indirect result of the handicap or disability. For example, profound early-life deafness restricts development of meaning (Myklebust, 1964). The data reported in this volume indicate that other handicaps also present an imposition on learning of this critical component of language. Social-emotional disturbances, disorders of articulation, learning disabilities, reading disabilities, and mental retardation all indirectly impose restrictions on development of inner language.

Nevertheless, it is premature to conclude that all handicapped children can be provided the most effective programs of remediation simply by grouping them together. Their deficiencies vary widely in extent and in type. To be served most adequately, each group must be appraised according to its idiosyncratic cognitive abilities and disabilities. Then programs for exceptional children will be truly meaningful.

Part Four

STATISTICAL DATA
TABLES 1 THROUGH 92

TABLE 1. Development of written language—Results for groups comprising the standardization sample

TOTAL WORDS

	Males			Females			Total		
	N	Mean	SD	N	Mean	SD	N	Mean	SD
7 Years									
Urban	46	22.4	15.6	33	28.7	18.8	79	25.1	17.2
Rural	16	21.6	10.6	28	38.4	15.6	44	32.2	16.1
Total	62	22.2	14.4	61	33.1	18.0	123	27.6	17.1
9 Years									
Urban	22	54.2	22.1	28	75.0	51.9	50	65.5	42.1
Suburban	10	122.7	33.4	14	167.4	48.1	24	148.8	47.5
Rural	29	90.2	45.6	20	80.3	27.5	49	86.2	39.2
Total	61	82.1	43.4	62	97.6	58.1	123	89.8	51.7
11 Years									
Urban	33	78.7	36.9	32	93.9	45.4	65	86.2	41.7
Suburban	9	164.7	41.3	14	191.9	51.5	23	181.3	48.7
Rural	21	126.2	45.0	18	128.7	42.4	39	127.4	43.2
Total	63	106.8	51.1	64	125.1	59.5	127	116.0	56.0
13 Years									
Urban	23	103.1	47.7	28	104.0	63.6	51	103.6	56.6
Suburban	19	165.9	62.6	13	200.4	48.6	32	180.0	59.0
Rural	21	167.4	62.0	21	196.4	61.1	42	181.9	62.6
Total	63	143.5	64.3	62	154.7	75.6	125	149.1	70.1
15 Years									
Urban	23	110.1	44.3	29	152.2	47.2	52	133.6	50.1
Suburban	27	124.3	43.3				27	124.3	43.4
Rural	13	144.1	56.1	33	154.0	37.8	46	151.2	43.3
Total	63	123.2	47.4	62	153.2	42.1	125	138.1	47.1
17 Years									
Urban	5	117.8	34.4	5	129.2	22.7	10	123.5	28.1
Suburban	40	164.4	59.2	32	168.2	60.9	72	166.1	59.6
Rural	16	156.4	70.3	26	165.6	69.6	42	162.1	69.1
Total	61	158.5	61.3	63	164.0	62.8	124	161.3	61.9

TABLE 2. **TABLE 2. Development of written language—Results for groups comprising the standardization sample**

TOTAL SENTENCES

	Males			Females			Total		
	N	Mean	SD	N	Mean	SD	N	Mean	SD
7 Years									
Urban	46	3.7	2.6	33	4.5	3.0	79	4.1	2.8
Rural	16	3.4	2.1	28	5.7	2.5	44	4.8	2.6
Total	62	3.6	2.5	61	5.0	2.8	123	4.3	2.7
9 Years									
Urban	22	5.7	2.5	28	7.7	5.1	50	6.8	4.2
Suburban	10	12.1	5.0	14	17.3	6.1	24	15.1	6.1
Rural	29	9.4	4.2	20	9.6	3.4	49	9.5	3.9
Total	61	8.5	4.4	62	10.5	6.1	123	9.5	5.4
11 Years									
Urban	33	6.9	3.5	32	8.0	4.7	65	7.4	4.1
Suburban	9	16.1	4.7	14	19.0	7.3	23	17.9	6.5
Rural	21	12.6	4.1	18	12.1	3.6	39	12.4	3.9
Total	63	10.1	5.2	64	11.5	6.7	127	10.8	6.0
13 Years									
Urban	23	7.8	3.5	28	7.6	5.1	51	7.7	4.4
Suburban	19	13.6	7.9	13	15.4	4.6	32	14.3	6.7
Rural	21	12.4	4.3	21	14.1	6.2	42	13.3	5.4
Total	63	11.1	5.9	62	11.4	6.4	125	11.2	6.1
15 Years									
Urban	23	7.1	2.5	29	10.7	4.1	52	9.1	3.9
Suburban	27	8.6	3.9				27	8.6	3.9
Rural	13	10.2	5.1	33	11.2	4.9	46	10.9	4.9
Total	63	8.4	3.8	62	10.9	4.5	125	9.7	4.4
17 Years									
Urban	5	8.6	3.7	5	8.4	3.0	10	8.5	3.2
Suburban	40	9.7	4.2	32	11.4	6.6	72	10.5	5.4
Rural	16	10.6	4.9	26	12.1	5.5	42	11.5	5.3
Total	61	9.9	4.4	63	11.5	6.0	124	10.7	5.3

TABLE 3. **Development of written language—Results for groups comprising the standardization sample**

WORDS PER SENTENCE

	Males			Females			Total		
	N	Mean	SD	N	Mean	SD	N	Mean	SD
				7 Years					
Urban	46	6.0	2.3	33	6.4	2.6	79	6.2	2.4
Rural	16	7.1	2.0	28	7.1	1.9	44	7.1	1.9
Total	62	6.3	2.2	61	6.7	2.3	123	6.5	2.3
				9 Years					
Urban	22	9.5	3.1	28	9.9	2.4	50	9.7	2.7
Suburban	10	10.7	2.8	14	9.9	1.8	24	10.3	2.3
Rural	29	9.7	2.3	20	8.6	1.7	49	9.2	2.1
Total	61	9.8	2.7	62	9.5	2.1	123	9.6	2.4
				11 Years					
Urban	33	11.9	2.7	32	12.8	3.9	65	12.4	3.3
Suburban	9	10.7	2.5	14	10.7	2.4	23	10.7	2.4
Rural	21	10.2	2.7	18	10.8	2.1	39	10.5	2.4
Total	63	11.2	2.8	64	11.8	3.3	127	11.5	3.0
				13 Years					
Urban	23	13.6	3.1	28	14.3	3.1	51	14.0	3.1
Suburban	19	14.0	4.9	13	13.4	2.3	32	13.8	4.0
Rural	21	13.7	2.9	21	14.6	3.7	42	14.1	3.3
Total	63	13.8	3.6	62	14.2	3.2	125	14.0	3.4
				15 Years					
Urban	23	15.5	3.0	29	14.8	3.0	52	15.1	3.0
Suburban	27	15.5	5.0				27	15.5	5.0
Rural	13	15.1	4.1	33	14.8	3.4	46	14.9	3.6
Total	63	15.4	4.1	62	14.8	3.2	125	15.1	3.7
				17 Years					
Urban	5	14.8	4.2	5	16.6	4.5	10	15.7	4.2
Suburban	40	17.8	4.3	32	16.0	3.8	72	17.0	4.1
Rural	16	15.1	3.0	26	14.4	3.5	42	14.7	3.3
Total	61	16.8	4.1	63	15.4	3.8	124	16.1	4.0

TABLE 4. Development of written language—Results for groups comprising the standardization sample

SYNTAX

	Males			Females			Total		
	N	Mean	SD	N	Mean	SD	N	Mean	SD
7 Years									
Urban	46	82	24	33	82	23	79	82	24
Rural	16	92	10	28	97	05	44	95	07
Total	62	85	22	61	89	19	123	87	20
9 Years									
Urban	22	91	11	28	95	05	50	93	82
Suburban	10	97	03	14	97	04	24	97	04
Rural	29	96	05	20	98	05	49	97	05
Total	61	94	08	62	96	05	123	95	07
11 Years									
Urban	33	95	05	32	97	04	65	96	04
Suburban	9	97	04	14	99	01	23	98	03
Rural	21	98	03	18	100	01	39	99	02
Total	63	97	04	64	98	03	127	97	04
13 Years									
Urban	23	97	03	28	97	04	51	97	03
Suburban	19	97	03	13	99	02	32	97	03
Rural	21	98	02	21	100	01	42	99	01
Total	63	97	03	62	98	03	125	97	03
15 Years									
Urban	23	97	04	29	99	02	52	98	03
Suburban	27	97	03				27	97	03
Rural	13	98	03	33	99	03	46	98	03
Total	63	97	04	62	99	02	125	98	03
17 Years									
Urban	5	98	02	5	100	01	10	99	02
Suburban	40	98	03	32	100	18	72	99	12
Rural	16	98	03	26	99	01	42	99	02
Total	61	98	03	63	100	13	124	99	09

TABLE 5. Development of written language—Results for groups comprising the standardization sample

ABSTRACT-CONCRETE

	Males			Females			Total		
	N	Mean	SD	N	Mean	SD	N	Mean	SD
7 Years									
Urban	46	6.7	2.4	33	7.9	3.0	79	7.1	2.7
Rural	16	9.3	5.0	28	9.0	3.0	44	9.1	3.7
Total	62	7.3	3.5	61	8.4	2.9	123	7.8	3.2
9 Years									
Urban	22	8.8	3.7	28	12.0	4.1	50	10.6	4.2
Suburban	10	18.8	1.8	14	18.1	3.4	24	18.4	2.8
Rural	29	14.1	4.2	20	13.3	4.6	49	13.8	4.3
Total	61	12.9	5.1	62	13.8	4.8	123	13.4	4.9
11 Years									
Urban	33	12.2	5.0	32	14.3	4.3	65	13.2	4.8
Suburban	9	18.6	2.3	14	20.5	1.0	23	19.8	1.9
Rural	21	17.5	4.0	18	16.2	4.1	39	16.9	4.0
Total	63	14.8	5.2	64	16.2	4.4	127	15.5	4.8
13 Years									
Urban	23	13.9	4.9	28	16.1	11.4	51	15.1	9.1
Suburban	19	18.0	3.2	13	20.0	1.7	32	18.8	2.8
Rural	21	18.0	3.1	21	18.7	2.9	42	18.4	3.0
Total	63	16.5	4.3	62	17.8	8.0	125	17.1	6.4
15 Years									
Urban	23	17.8	5.0	29	19.3	3.3	52	18.6	4.1
Suburban	27	18.3	4.5				27	18.3	4.5
Rural	13	14.8	3.7	33	19.7	4.0	46	18.3	4.4
Total	63	17.4	4.6	62	19.5	3.6	125	18.4	4.3
17 Years									
Urban	5	20.6	1.8	5	16.6	5.2	10	18.6	4.2
Suburban	40	20.2	2.7	32	19.4	4.3	72	19.8	3.5
Rural	16	17.4	5.2	26	16.8	3.6	42	17.1	4.2
Total	61	19.5	3.7	63	18.1	4.2	124	18.8	4.0

TABLE 6. Intercorrelation of auditory receptive and written language in normal children

	7 Years (N = 64)	9 Years (N = 40)	11 Years (N = 54)	13 Years (N = 39)	15 Years (N = 42)
Test One: Comprehension					
Total words	.37**	.09	.09	.16	.20
Total sentences	.20	.04	.04	.18	.21
Words per sentence	.31**	.01	.01	.07	.02
Syntax	.21*	.37**	.37**	.02	.29
Abstract-concrete	.33**	.02	.02	.24	—.43
Test Two: Auditory to Visual					
Total words	.19	.05	.05	.20	.17
Total sentences	.09	.11	.11	.16	.18
Words per sentence	.19	.15	.15	.09	.04
Syntax	.08	.20	.20	.05	.12
Abstract-concrete	.11	.40**	.40**	.32*	.08

*$p < .05$.
**$p < .01$.

TABLE 7. Intercorrelation of auditory expressive and written language in normal children

	7 Years (N = 64)	9 Years (N = 40)	11 Years (N = 54)	13 Years (N = 39)	15 Years (N = 42)
Test One: Opposites					
Total words	.27*	.12	.12	.32*	.12
Total sentences	.07	.04	.04	.29*	.02
Words per sentence	.44**	.13	.13	.05	.27
Syntax	.31**	.36*	.36**	.35*	.13
Abstract-concrete	.30*	.25	.25*	.52**	.04
Test Two: Definition of Words					
Total words	.36**	.25	.25	.09	.05
Total sentences	.25	.14	.14	.10	.04
Words per sentence	.29*	.17	.17	.05	.16
Syntax	.29*	.28*	.28*	.35	.21
Abstract-concrete	.28*	.37**	.37**	.35*	.02

*$p < .05$.
**$p < .01$.

TABLE 8. Development of written language—inter-age comparison

TOTAL WORDS

	N	Mean	SD	N	Mean	SD	t
		7 Years			9 Years		
Males	62	22.2	14.4	61	82.1	43.4	10.57**
Females	61	33.1	18.0	62	97.6	58.1	8.42**
		9 Years			11 Years		
Males	61	82.1	43.4	63	106.8	51.1	2.82**
Females	62	97.6	58.1	64	125.1	59.5	2.65**
		11 Years			13 Years		
Males	63	106.8	51.1	63	143.5	64.3	3.57**
Females	64	125.1	59.5	62	154.7	75.6	2.57*
		13 Years			15 Years		
Males	63	143.5	64.3	63	123.2	47.4	2.03*
Females	62	154.7	75.6	62	153.2	42.1	0.26
		15 Years			17 Years		
Males	63	123.2	47.4	61	158.5	61.3	3.61**
Females	62	153.2	42.1	63	164.0	62.8	1.16

$*p < .05.$
$**p < .01.$

TABLE 9. Development of written language—inter-age comparison

TOTAL SENTENCES

	N	Mean	SD	N	Mean	SD	t
		7 Years			9 Years		
Males	62	3.6	2.5	61	8.5	4.4	7.95**
Females	61	5.0	2.8	62	10.5	6.1	6.44**
		9 Years			11 Years		
Males	61	8.5	4.4	63	10.1	5.2	1.75
Females	62	10.5	6.1	64	11.5	6.7	0.88
		11 Years			13 Years		
Males	63	10.1	5.2	63	11.1	5.9	1.01
Females	64	11.5	6.7	62	11.4	6.4	0.00
		13 Years			15 Years		
Males	63	11.1	5.9	63	8.4	3.8	3.05**
Females	62	11.4	6.4	62	10.9	4.5	0.61
		15 Years			17 Years		
Males	63	8.4	3.8	61	9.9	4.4	2.06*
Females	62	10.9	4.5	63	11.5	6.0	0.64

$*p < .05.$
$**p < .01.$

TABLE 10. Development of written language—inter-age comparison

WORDS PER SENTENCE

	N	Mean	SD	N	Mean	SD	t
		7 Years			9 Years		
Males	62	6.3	2.2	61	9.8	2.7	8.48**
Females	61	6.7	2.3	62	9.5	2.1	7.05**
		9 Years			11 Years		
Males	61	9.8	2.7	63	11.2	2.8	2.73**
Females	62	9.5	2.1	64	11.8	3.3	4.68**
		11 Years			13 Years		
Males	63	11.2	2.8	63	13.8	3.6	4.53**
Females	64	11.8	3.3	62	14.2	3.2	4.15**
		13 Years			15 Years		
Males	63	13.8	3.6	63	15.4	4.1	2.33*
Females	62	14.2	3.2	62	14.8	3.2	1.04
		15 Years			17 Years		
Males	63	15.4	4.1	61	16.8	4.1	1.90
Females	62	14.8	3.2	63	15.4	3.8	0.97

$*p < .05.$
$**p < .01.$

TABLE 11. Development of written language—inter-age comparison

SYNTAX

	N	Mean	SD	N	Mean	SD	t
		7 Years			9 Years		
Males	62	84.7	21.8	61	94.3	7.8	3.26**
Females	61	88.9	18.6	62	96.4	4.7	3.05**
		9 Years			11 Years		
Males	61	94.3	7.8	63	96.8	4.1	2.22*
Females	62	96.4	4.7	64	98.1	2.9	2.43*
		11 Years			13 Years		
Males	63	96.8	4.1	63	97.4	2.7	0.97
Females	64	98.1	2.9	62	98.0	3.0	0.19
		13 Years			15 Years		
Males	63	97.4	2.7	63	97.2	3.5	0.36
Females	62	98.0	3.0	62	98.8	2.3	1.67
		15 Years			17 Years		
Males	63	97.2	3.5	61	97.8	3.3	0.98
Females	62	98.8	2.3	63	99.9	12.7	0.68

*$p < .05$.
**$p < .01$.

TABLE 12. Development of written language—inter-age comparison

ABSTRACT-CONCRETE

	N	Mean	SD	N	Mean	SD	t
		7 Years			9 Years		
Males	62	7.3	3.5	61	12.9	5.1	7.38**
Females	61	8.4	2.9	62	13.8	4.8	7.76**
		9 Years			11 Years		
Males	61	12.9	5.1	63	14.8	5.2	1.98
Females	62	13.8	4.8	64	16.2	4.4	2.96**
		11 Years			13 Years		
Males	63	14.8	5.2	63	16.5	4.3	2.02*
Females	64	16.2	4.4	62	17.8	8.0	0.89
		13 Years			15 Years		
Males	63	·16.5	4.3	63	17.4	4.6	1.13
Females	62	17.8	8.0	62	19.5	3.6	3.60**
		15 Years			17 Years		
Males	63	17.4	4.6	61	19.5	3.7	2.84**
Females	62	19.5	3.6	63	18.1	4.2	1.86

*$p < .05$.
**$p < .01$.

TABLE 13. Development of written language—sex differences

Age	Males			Females			t
	N	Mean	SD	N	Mean	SD	
Total Words							
7	62	22.2	14.4	61	33.1	18.0	3.74**
9	61	82.1	43.4	62	97.6	58.1	1.59
11	63	106.8	51.1	64	125.1	59.5	1.87
13	63	143.5	64.3	62	154.7	75.6	1.00
15	63	123.2	47.4	62	153.2	42.1	3.77**
17	61	158.5	61.3	63	164.2	62.8	0.52
Total Sentences							
7	62	3.6	2.5	61	5.0	2.8	2.98**
9	61	8.5	4.4	62	10.5	6.1	1.99*
11	63	10.1	5.2	64	11.5	6.7	1.33
13	63	11.1	5.9	62	11.4	6.4	0.37
15	63	8.4	3.8	62	10.9	4.5	3.35**
17	61	9.9	4.4	63	11.5	6.0	1.73
Words per Sentence							
7	62	6.3	2.2	61	6.7	2.3	0.98
9	61	9.8	2.7	62	9.5	2.1	0.96
11	63	11.2	2.8	64	11.8	3.3	1.11
13	63	13.8	3.6	62	14.2	3.2	0.66
15	63	15.4	4.1	62	14.8	3.2	0.91
17	61	16.8	4.1	63	15.4	3.8	1.99*
Syntax							
7	62	84.7	21.8	61	88.9	18.6	1.15
9	61	94.3	7.8	62	96.4	4.7	1.81
11	63	96.8	4.1	64	98.1	2.9	2.06*
13	63	97.4	2.7	62	98.0	3.0	1.18
15	63	97.2	3.5	62	98.8	2.3	3.03**
17	61	97.8	3.3	63	99.9	12.7	1.27
Abstract-Concrete							
7	62	7.3	3.5	61	8.4	2.9	1.96
9	61	12.9	5.1	62	13.8	4.8	0.91
11	63	14.8	5.2	64	16.2	4.4	1.64
13	63	16.5	4.3	62	17.8	8.0	0.51
15	63	17.4	4.6	62	19.5	3.6	2.84**
17	61	19.5	3.7	63	18.1	4.2	1.85

*$p < .05$.
**$p < .01$.

TABLE 14. Development of written langauge in normal children—correlation among the scores and with chronological age (N=747)

	Total words	Total sentences	Words per sentence	Syntax	Abstract-concrete
Chronological age	.59**	.28**	.71**	.31**	.61**
Total words		.83**	.46**	.31**	.70**
Total sentences			—.01	.27**	.54**
Words per sentence				.32**	.49**
Syntax					.38**

**p < .01.

TABLE 15. Development of written language in normal children—intercorrelations by age and sex

	7 Years		9 Years		11 Years		13 Years		15 Years		17 Years	
	M	F	M	F	M	F	M	F	M	F	M	F
Total Words (TW)												
TS	.93**	.87**	.86**	.93**	.89**	.91**	.85**	.89**	.76**	.75**	.81**	.80**
WPS	.24*	.14	.30*	.15	-.07	-.22	.00	.03	.19	.00	.11	-.05
Syn	.43**	.39**	.33**	.24	.28*	.19	.08	.23	.13	.06	.16	-.06
A-C	.32*	.34*	.68**	.43**	.66**	.63**	.62**	.59**	.31*	.48**	.34**	.34**
Total Sentences (TS)												
TW	.93**	.87**	.86**	.93**	.89**	.91**	.85**	.89**	.76**	.75**	.81**	.80**
WPS	-.16	.14	-.16	.14	-.44**	-.51**	-.44**	-.37**	-.42**	-.60**	-.43**	-.55**
Syn	.37**	.39**	.26*	.22	.30*	.17	.03	.15	.12	.12	.19	-.06
A-C	.27*	.34*	.61**	.39**	.67**	.52**	.51**	.50**	.23	.22	.24	.36**
Words per Sentence (WPS)												
TW	.10	.14	.30**	.15	-.07	-.22	.00	.03	.19	.00	.11	-.05
TS	-.16	-.18	-.16	-.14	-.44**	-.51**	-.44**	-.37**	-.42**	-.60**	-.43**	-.55**
Syn	.50**	.40**	.19	-.02	-.05	-.12	-.08	.18	.04	-.11	-.07	.02
A-C	.30**	.15	.19	.08	-.25*	-.01	.01	.06	.90	.30*	.15	-.13
Syntax (Syn)												
TW	.43**	.39**	.33**	.24	.28*	.19	.08	.23	.13	.06	.16	-.06
TS	.37**	.39**	.26*	.22	.30*	.17	.03	.15	.12	.12	.19	-.06
WPS	.50**	.40**	.19	.02	-.05	-.12	-.08	.18	.04	-.11	-.07	.02
A-C	.53**	.44**	.39**	.18	.25*	.05	.07	.31*	.10	-.27*	-.09	.02
Abstract-Concrete (A-C)												
TW	.32**	.34*	.68**	.43**	.66**	.63**	.62**	.59**	.31*	.48**	.34**	.34**
TS	.27*	.31*	.61**	.39**	.67**	.52**	.51**	.50**	.23	.22	.24	.36**
WPS	.30*	.15	.19	.08	-.25*	-.01	.07	.06	.09	.30*	.15	-.13
Syn	.53**	.44**	.39**	.18	.25*	.05	.07	.31*	.10	-.27*	-.09	.02

*p < .05.
**p < .01

196

TABLE 16. The development of written language in third- and fourth-grade suburban school children (mean C.A.=9.2)

	Original sample at 9 years (N = 123)		Third- and fourth-graders (N = 238)	
	Mean	SD	Mean	SD
Total words	90.4	51.5	81.5	49.5
Total sentences	9.6	5.4	8.3	5.0
Words per sentence	9.7	2.3	10.1	2.7
Syntax	95.3	6.5	94.2	4.2
Abstract-concrete	13.4	4.9	16.4	4.0

TABLE 17. Factor analysis results for the Picture Story Language Test for 238 third- and fourth-grade school children

	Factors			
	1	2	3	4
Total words	.894	.022	.078	.128
Total sentences	.885	.005	.012	.232
Words per sentence	.011	.007	.026	.927
Syntax	.042	.006	.906	.116
Abstract-concrete	.640	.012	.102	.070
Percent of variance	23.7	16.4	9.8	9.5

TABLE 18. Word-type comparison by sex on the basis of all of the words written per story ($N_{male}=20$; $N_{female}=20$)

	Males		Females		
	Mean	SD	Mean	SD	t
7 Years					
Nouns	6.5	4.0	6.5	3.0	.03
Pronouns	3.0	3.4	3.3	2.8	.30
Adjectives	1.4	1.6	2.0	1.9	1.14
Present verbs	2.4	1.9	3.8	2.5	1.87
Past verbs	0.9	2.9	0.4	1.1	.70
Future verbs	0.0	0.0	0.0	0.2	1.02
Infinitives	0.2	0.7	0.6	1.2	1.06
Adverbs	0.5	0.8	1.1	1.6	1.41
Articles	3.1	3.4	3.3	2.9	.19
Prepositions	1.9	2.4	2.0	1.7	.15
Conjunctions	1.2	2.4	1.2	1.6	.06
Interjections	0.0	0.0	0.0	0.0	.00
9 Years					
Nouns	13.0	4.8	16.4	8.2	1.58
Pronouns	5.4	4.2	9.6	6.6	2.36*
Adjectives	5.6	3.5	6.9	3.8	1.09
Present verbs	3.6	3.2	3.8	3.4	.24
Past verbs	2.2	3.7	6.4	8.0	2.10*
Future verbs	0.0	0.0	0.1	0.4	1.00
Infinitives	0.4	0.6	1.2	2.3	1.49
Adverbs	1.6	1.8	6.0	4.9	3.74**
Articles	7.4	3.1	7.3	4.5	.04
Prepositions	3.9	3.2	6.0	3.5	2.03*
Conjunctions	3.4	2.6	6.0	4.8	2.16*
Interjections	0.0	0.0	0.1	0.4	1.00
11 Years					
Nouns	16.0	5.4	17.9	7.6	.88
Pronouns	8.6	5.1	8.6	5.4	.00
Adjectives	7.8	4.0	9.5	5.2	1.16
Present verbs	3.9	3.9	3.4	4.3	.42
Past verbs	4.8	6.0	6.0	5.1	.71
Future verbs	0.0	0.0	0.0	0.0	.00
Infinitives	1.6	2.2	1.5	1.8	.23
Adverbs	3.3	3.4	4.0	3.6	.68
Articles	7.8	3.4	8.5	4.6	.58
Prepositions	7.2	3.1	6.9	2.6	.33
Conjunctions	4.9	3.2	6.2	3.4	1.20
Interjections	0.0	0.0	0.1	0.3	.59

TABLE 18—Continued

	Males		Females		
	Mean	SD	Mean	SD	t
13 Years					
Nouns	18.5	6.7	23.0	13.5	1.34
Pronouns	11.0	6.1	11.2	10.8	.04
Adjectives	9.1	5.0	12.2	5.6	2.47*
Present verbs	4.6	5.3	6.3	4.4	1.07
Past verbs	6.8	7.2	7.1	9.6	.13
Future verbs	0.0	0.0	0.1	0.3	.59
Infinitives	1.4	1.4	2.1	2.9	.97
Adverbs	5.5	2.9	8.2	6.8	1.64
Articles	9.4	5.2	10.2	5.3	.45
Prepositions	8.8	2.2	9.4	5.6	.40
Conjunctions	6.0	3.9	8.0	5.6	1.28
Interjections	0.1	0.4	0.1	0.4	.00
15 Years					
Nouns	20.0	8.6	32.1	9.6	4.19**
Pronouns	14.3	10.0	22.0	9.6	2.47*
Adjectives	11.8	4.8	17.2	5.5	3.31**
Present verbs	6.1	6.8	10.6	8.4	1.88
Past verbs	8.6	9.1	11.2	8.3	.98
Future verbs	0.4	1.4	0.7	1.3	.73
Infinitives	1.7	1.1	3.4	2.4	2.83**
Adverbs	8.3	6.2	14.0	8.8	2.40*
Articles	8.9	4.7	12.6	5.6	2.26*
Prepositions	8.9	3.7	14.1	4.2	4.12**
Conjunctions	8.4	5.7	12.4	4.7	2.42*
Interjections	0.0	0.0	0.6	1.0	2.09*

*$p < .05$.
**$p < .01$.

TABLE 19. Word-type comparison by sex on the basis of the number of different words written per story ($N_{male}=20$; $N_{female}=20$)

	Males		Females		
	Mean	SD	Mean	SD	t
7 Years					
Nouns	5.6	3.2	5.8	2.9	.12
Pronouns	1.5	1.3	1.8	1.2	.68
Adjectives	1.2	1.4	1.8	1.6	1.34
Present verbs	1.8	1.4	2.5	1.8	1.28
Past verbs	0.2	0.7	0.4	0.9	.53
Future verbs	0.0	0.0	0.0	0.0	.00
Infinitives	0.2	0.7	0.4	0.7	.63
Adverbs	0.4	0.7	0.8	1.1	1.43
Articles	1.0	0.7	1.2	0.8	1.07
Prepositions	1.2	1.4	1.3	0.9	.24
Conjunctions	0.5	0.5	0.5	0.5	.18
Interjections	0.0	0.0	0.0	0.0	.00
9 Years					
Nouns	10.6	3.1	12.9	5.3	1.65
Pronouns	2.4	1.4	4.0	1.8	3.19**
Adjectives	4.4	2.8	5.4	2.9	1.12
Present verbs	2.4	2.1	2.8	2.2	.74
Past verbs	1.4	2.5	5.0	6.1	2.38
Future verbs	0.0	0.0	0.0	0.0	0.00
Infinitives	0.4	0.6	1.0	1.9	0.00
Adverbs	1.5	1.7	5.1	4.2	3.60**
Articles	2.2	2.0	1.8	0.4	.98
Prepositions	2.8	1.9	3.5	1.6	1.34
Conjunctions	1.4	1.0	2.0	1.0	1.86
Interjections	0.0	0.0	0.1	0.4	1.00
11 Years					
Nouns	13.2	4.0	14.4	5.0	.80
Pronouns	3.9	2.0	3.9	1.2	.00
Adjectives	6.2	3.2	7.4	4.4	1.03
Present verbs	2.5	2.2	2.6	3.0	.06
Past verbs	3.8	4.5	4.5	4.0	.52
Future verbs	0.0	0.0	0.0	0.0	.00
Infinitives	1.2	1.7	1.3	1.6	.30
Adverbs	3.0	2.7	3.6	3.3	.62
Articles	1.8	0.4	2.2	1.2	1.30
Prepositions	4.5	2.0	4.2	1.5	.63
Conjunctions	2.1	1.1	3.2	1.3	2.84*
Interjections	0.0	0.0	0.1	0.3	.59

TABLE 19—Continued

	Males		Females		
	Mean	SD	Mean	SD	t
13 Years					
Nouns	15.0	4.9	15.6	6.2	.37
Pronouns	4.6	1.9	5.2	3.0	.81
Adjectives	6.8	3.1	9.7	4.3	2.52*
Present verbs	3.4	3.8	4.5	3.0	.96
Past verbs	5.4	5.3	4.9	6.4	.24
Future verbs	0.0	0.0	0.1	0.3	.59
Infinitives	1.2	1.2	1.9	2.5	1.20
Adverbs	4.6	2.6	5.8	4.6	.97
Articles	1.9	0.3	2.0	0.2	.59
Prepositions	5.0	1.0	5.2	2.6	.49
Conjunctions	3.2	2.0	3.7	1.8	.90
Interjections	0.1	0.4	0.1	0.4	.00
15 Years					
Nouns	15.0	5.8	23.2	7.8	3.75**
Pronouns	5.1	2.3	7.8	3.5	2.83**
Adjectives	9.8	3.7	14.4	4.9	3.34*
Present verbs	4.8	4.8	8.4	6.7	1.96
Past verbs	7.0	7.0	9.4	6.8	1.09
Future verbs	0.4	1.1	0.6	1.0	.60
Infinitives	1.4	1.0	3.0	2.2	3.04**
Adverbs	6.6	4.8	11.0	6.0	2.53*
Articles	2.0	0.5	2.2	0.4	1.76
Prepositions	5.2	1.7	7.4	1.7	4.05**
Conjunctions	5.2	2.4	6.0	2.0	1.15
Interjections	0.0	0.0	0.4	0.8	2.26*

*$p < .05$.
**$p < .01$.

TABLE 20. Intercorrelations by word type for normal males and females combined

7 YEARS

	Pronouns	Adjectives	Present verbs	Past verbs	Future verbs	Total verbs	Infinitives	Adverbs	Articles	Prepositions	Conjunctions	Interjections	Total words
Nouns	.44	.27		.49		.52			.84	.54	.26		.86
Pronouns			.34	.61		.79	.27	.31	.31	.54			.72
Adjectives									.30	.36			.38
Present verbs				—.29		.63	.36	.45					.39
Past verbs						.55			.43	.31			.57
Future verbs													
Total verbs							.41	.45	.46	.46			.80
Infinitives								.45					.28
Adverbs										.39			.47
Articles										.47			.76
Prepositions													.70
Conjunctions													
Interjections													

Critical value at $p < .05$: $r = .26$.
Critical value at $p < .01$: $r - .37$.

202

TABLE 21. Intercorrelations by word type for normal males and females combined

9 YEARS

	Pronouns	Adjectives	Present verbs	Past verbs	Future verbs	Total verbs	Infinitives	Adverbs	Articles	Prepositions	Conjunctions	Interjections	Total words
Nouns	.55	.65		.54	.38	.61	.62	.39	.72	.80	.49		.85
Pronouns		.56		.78	.31	.89	.50	.77	.30	.49	.53		.85
Adjectives				.44	.34	.54	.44	.39	.49	.71	.27		.73
Present verbs				−.49									
Past verbs						.86	.50	.82	.30	.40	.66		.80
Future verbs									.58		.29		.35
Total verbs							.58	.82	.31	.47	.65		.88
Infinitives								.47	.26	.52	.42		.67
Adverbs										.39	.63		.75
Articles										.49	.38		.59
Prepositions											.31		.74
Conjunctions													.69
Interjections													

Critical value at $p < .05$: $r = .26$.
Critical value at $p < .01$: $r = .37$.

203

TABLE 22. Intercorrelations by word type for normal males and females combined

11 YEARS

	Pronouns	Adjectives	Present verbs	Past verbs	Future verbs	Total verbs	Infinitives	Adverbs	Articles	Prepositions	Conjunctions	Interjections	Total words
Nouns	.50	.48		.41		.63		.44	.63	.48	.61		.85
Pronouns		.49		.61	.38	.85	.34	.70			.67	.30	.77
Adjectives				.34		.57	.45	.51			.56		.70
Present verbs				−.63									
Past verbs					.39	.68	.47	.60			.57		.64
Future verbs						.47		.43					.39
Total verbs							.48	.75			.76		.88
Infinitives								.44			.58		.50
Adverbs											.60		.71
Articles										.57			.43
Prepositions													.43
Conjunctions												.53	.83
Interjections													.26

Critical value at $p < .05$: $r = .26$.
Critical value at $p < .01$: $r = .37$.

204

TABLE 23. Intercorrelations by word type for normal males and females combined

13 YEARS

	Pronouns	Adjectives	Present verbs	Past verbs	Future verbs	Total verbs	Infinitives	Adverbs	Articles	Prepositions	Conjunctions	Interjections	Total words
Nouns	.52	.67		.69	.41	.84	.65	.76	.72	.88	.62	.50	.93
Pronouns		.47		.63	.75	.79	.57	.71		.40	.59	.70	.71
Adjectives			.32	.40	.56	.64	.37	.60	.42	.48	.60	.52	.75
Present verbs				-.41									
Past verbs					.46	.81	.56	.75	.30	.63	.65	.59	.78
Future verbs						.60	.49	.64		.33	.57	.80	.61
Total verbs							.68	.88	.36	.71	.79	.67	.95
Infinitives								.71	.31	.61	.39	.48	.71
Adverbs									.31	.69	.72	.63	.90
Articles										.68			.53
Prepositions											.43	.48	.81
Conjunctions												.59	.77
Interjections													.66

Critical value at $p < .05$: $r = .26$.
Critical value at $p < .01$: $r = .37$.

205

TABLE 24. Intercorrelations by word type for normal males and females combined

15 YEARS

	Pronouns	Adjectives	Present verbs	Past verbs	Future verbs	Total verbs	Infinitives	Adverbs	Articles	Prepositions	Conjunctions	Interjections	Total words
Nouns	.75	.75	.43	.49	.41	.84	.40	.70	.74	.80	.76		.94
Pronouns		.41	.38	.56	.50	.88	.54	.72	.50	.51	.80	.37	.87
Adjectives				.50		.58		.58	.63	.62	.53	.43	.72
Present verbs				−.40	.55	.52		.45	.28	.32	.50		.47
Past verbs						.56	.28	.41	.47	.32	.46		.56
Future verbs						.53	.41	.36	.29	.27	.49		.47
Total verbs								.78	.69	.58	.89	.33	.94
Infinitives								.36		.29	.32	.27	.45
Adverbs									.61	.48	.76	.40	.84
Articles										.54	.62		.76
Prepositions											.59	.32	.72
Conjunctions													.88
Interjections													.35

Critical value at $p < .05$: $r = .26$.
Critical value at $p < .01$: $r = .37$.

7 YEARS

	Pronouns	Adjectives	Present verbs	Past verbs	Future verbs	Total verbs	Infinitives	Adverbs	Articles	Prepositions	Conjunctions	Interjections	Total words
Nouns	m = .59	m = .43		m = .65				m = .55	m = .84, f = .84	m = .66			m = .91, f = .80
Pronouns			f = .38	m = .83		m = .91, f = .65	m = .43	m = .40	m = .52	m = .56, f = .51			m = .78, f = .64
Adjectives			m = .52, f = .58					m = .53	m = .50	m = .79			m = .61
Present verbs						f = .90				m = .40			f = .67
Past verbs						m = .77		f = .44	m = .58	m = .40			m = .71
Future verbs													
Total verbs							m = .45, f = .39	m = .59, f = .38	m = .67	m = .68			m = .84, f = .75
Infinitives								f = .48					
Adverbs									m = .68	m = .61	f = .46		m = .67, f = .41
Articles										m = .68			m = .89, f = .56
Prepositions													m = .79, f = .53
Conjunctions													
Interjections													

Critical value at $p < .05$: $r = .38$.
Critical value at $p < .01$: $r = .52$.
m = males; f = females.

TABLE 26. Intercorrelations of word type by age and sex for normal children

9 YEARS

	Pronouns	Adjectives	Present verbs	Past verbs	Future verbs	Total verbs	Infinitives	Adverbs	Articles	Prepositions	Conjunctions	Interjections	Total words
Nouns	f = .58	m = .55 f = .71		m = .42 f = .52	f = .41	m = .46 f = .62			m = .71 f = .76	m = .72 f = .84	f = .56		m = .82 f = .86
Pronouns		m = .55 f = .54		m = .64 f = .80	f = .44	m = .80 f = .90		m = .59 f = .79	f = .45	m = .37	f = .59		m = .73 f = .86
Adjectives				f = .48 m = -.48		m = .53 f = .54	f = .68	m = .49		f = .46			m = .76 f = .75
Present verbs				f = -.61		m = .39	f = .55						
Past verbs						m = .60 f = .91	f = .50	m = .70 f = .83	f = .67	m = .68 f = .73	f = .45		m = .57 f = .82
Future verbs							f = .55	f = .45	f = .38	f = .39	f = .78		
Total verbs							f = .63	m = .57 f = .84	f = .72		f = .77		m = .72 f = .90
Infinitives								f = .45		m = .51 f = .58	f = .44		m = .38 f = .69
Adverbs										m = .40	f = .66		m = .66 f = .71
Articles										m = .36 f = .62	f = .44		m = .57 f = .68
Prepositions													m = .75 f = .73
Conjunctions													f = .77
Interjections													

Critical value at p < .05: r = .38.
Critical value at p < .01: r = .51.
m = males; f = females

TABLE 27. Intercorrelations of word type by age and sex for normal children

11 YEARS

	Pronouns	Adjectives	Present verbs	Past verbs	Future verbs	Total verbs	Infinitives	Adverbs	Articles	Prepositions	Conjunctions	Interjections	Total words
Nouns	m = .73	m = .61 / f = .40		m = .65	m = .47	m = .73 / f = .58	m = .41	m = .55	m = .44 / f = .73	m = .61 / f = .44	m = .64 / f = .58	f = .43	m = .90 / f = .83
Pronouns		m = .68 / f = .38		m = .72 / f = .52	m = .47	m = .92 / f = .80		m = .79 / f = .63			m = .60 / f = .75	f = .63	m = .86 / f = .70
Adjectives			f = .38	m = .55	m = .42	m = .56 / f = .59	m = .43 / f = .52	m = .49 / f = .52			m = .52 / f = .57		m = .74 / f = .67
Present verbs				m = −.63 / f = −.63									
Past verbs					m = .55	m = .76 / f = .58	m = .57	m = .57 / f = .64			m = .57 / f = .56	f = .56	m = .76 / f = .49
Future verbs						m = .64		m = .66			m = .38		m = .61
Total verbs							m = .46 / f = .52	m = .82 / f = .67			m = .71 / f = .84	f = .59	m = .89 / f = .88
Infinitives								f = .53			m = .74 / f = .45		m = .56 / f = .46
Adverbs											m = .58 / f = .60	f = .42	m = .75 / f = .67
Articles										m = .70 / f = .50		m = .39	
Prepositions													f = .47 / m = .52
Conjunctions												f = .78	m = .79 / f = .86
Interjections													f = .58

Critical value at *p* < .05: *r* = .38.
Critical value at *p* < .01: *r* = .52.
m = males; f = females.

TABLE 28. Intercorrelations of word type by age and sex for normal children

13 YEARS

	Pronouns	Adjectives	Present verbs	Past verbs	Future verbs	Total verbs	Infinitives	Adverbs	Articles	Prepositions	Conjunctions	Interjections	Total words
Nouns	f = .63	m = .44 f = .78		f = .86		m = .64 f = .88		f = .85	m = .81 f = .74	m = .69	f = .72	f = .85	m = .82 f = .96
Pronouns		m = .48 f = .51		m = .62		m = .57 f = .71		m = .68		f = .94	m = .77 f = .54	m = .57 f = .82	m = .67 f = .74
Adjectives			f = .42	f = .64	m = .42 f = .65	m = .52 f = .72		f = .75	f = .59	f = .51	m = .58 f = .59	m = .42 f = .66	m = .67 f = .82
Present verbs				f = .61 m = −.76	f = .40			f = .71					
Past verbs					f = .51	m = .68 f = .89		m = .67 f = .83	f = .49	f = .81	m = .53 f = .72	f = .78	m = .56 f = .89
Future verbs						f = .69		m = .45 f = .72		f = .49	m = .66	f = .68	f = .70
Total verbs								m = .62 f = .93	f = .40	f = .80	m = .77	m = .89	m = .89
Infinitives								f = .84	f = .43	f = .77	m = .80 f = .61	f = .87	m = .96 f = .88
Adverbs									f = .46	f = .81	m = .69 f = .73	m = .45 f = .82	m = .64 f = .94
Articles										m = .59 f = .79		f = .47	m = .53 f = .59
Prepositions											f = .56		m = .42 f = .89
Conjunctions												m = .66 f = .73	m = .73 f = .79
Interjections													f = .88

Critical value at $p < .05$: $r = .38$.
Critical value at $p < .01$: $r = .52$.

TABLE 25. Intercorrelations of word type by age and sex for normal children

15 YEARS

	Pronouns	Adjectives	Present verbs	Past verbs	Future verbs	Total verbs	Infinitives	Adverbs	Articles	Prepositions	Conjunctions	Interjections	Total words
Nouns	m = .86, f = .58	m = .71, f = .64		m = .59, f = .40	m = .60	m = .86, f = .80	m = .51	m = .65, f = .65	m = .78, f = .64	m = .73, f = .69	m = .83, f = .62		m = .95, f = .89
Pronouns		m = .41		m = .76	m = .53, f = .45	m = .93, f = .79	m = .42, f = .52	m = .55, f = .79	m = .61	m = .58	m = .83, f = .70		m = .89, f = .81
Adjectives			f = .38	f = .61		m = .52, f = .48		m = .72	m = .69, f = .49	m = .50, f = .48	m = .58	f = .42	m = .71, f = .57
Present verbs				m = .37	m = .80	m = .65, f = .51		f = .40	f = .48		m = .56		m = .40, f = .39
Past verbs					f = −.56	m = .65, f = .40		m = .46, f = .44	m = .47, f = .44		m = .48, f = .38	f = .46	m = .64, f = .47
Future verbs						m = .68		m = .48, f = .58	m = .58		m = .74		m = .66
Total verbs							f = .37	m = .73, f = .81	m = .73, f = .57	m = .53, f = .43	m = .93, f = .79		m = .95, f = .94
Infinitives								m = .37	m = .37	m = .45			m = .46
Adverbs									m = .75, f = .44	f = .38	m = .72, f = .78	m = .48	m = .79, f = .87
Articles										m = .57, f = .57	m = .72, f = .43		m = .84, f = .63
Prepositions											m = .50, f = .51		m = .66, f = .58
Conjunctions													m = .92, f = .83
Interjections													

Critical value at $p < .05$: $r = .38$.
Critical value at $p < .01$: $r = .52$.
m = males; f = females.

TABLE 30. Number of significant intercorrelations of word type by age and sex

Word type	7 Years M	F	9 Years M	F	11 Years M	F	13 Years M	F	15 Years M	F
Nouns	8	4	6	10	11	7	5	12	9	11
Pronouns	8	4	6	10	8	7	8	11	9	11
Adjectives	7	0	6	10	9	8	8	11	6	8
Present verbs	2	5	2	1	1	2	1	2	6	5
Past verbs	6	0	6	11	10	7	6	12	7	8
Future verbs	0	0	0	3	8	0	4	12	1	9
Total verbs	9	6	7	10	9	9	7	12	10	11
Infinitives	2	2	3	9	6	5	1	11	1	6
Adverbs	7	5	6	6	8	8	7	12	8	10
Articles	8	2	3	9	3	3	3	9	7	11
Prepositions	9	2	7	8	3	2	3	12	6	9
Conjunctions	0	1	0	9	9	9	8	11	8	11
Interjections	0	0	0	0	1	7	4	12	2	1
Total words	8	7	9	10	10	10	9	12	10	12
	74	38	61	106	96	84	74	151	90	123

TABLE 31. Development of written language—a cross-cultural comparison

TOTAL WORDS

	U.S. N	Mean	SD	Uruguay N	Mean	SD
			7 Years			
Males	62	22.2	14.4	13	33.4	15.8
Females	61	33.1	18.0	6	38.7	22.6
Total	123	27.6	17.1	19	35.4	18.8
			9 Years			
Males	61	83.1	43.1	89	80.7	38.9
Females	62	97.6	58.1	74	94.0	47.6
Total	123	90.4	51.5	163	87.4	43.5
			11 Years			
Males	63	106.8	51.1	74	113.8	58.4
Females	64	125.1	59.5	90	129.8	60.5
Total	127	116.0	56.0	164	123.9	60.6

TABLE 32. Development of written language—a cross-cultural comparison

TOTAL SENTENCES

	U.S.			Uruguay		
	N	Mean	SD	N	Mean	SD
7 Years						
Males	62	3.6	2.5	13	5.4	2.5
Females	61	5.0	2.8	6	5.9	3.0
Total	123	4.3	2.7	19	5.6	2.7
9 Years						
Males	61	8.6	4.3	89	9.9	5.1
Females	62	10.5	6.1	74	11.0	5.2
Total	123	9.6	5.4	163	10.4	5.1
11 Years						
Males	63	10.1	5.2	74	9.9	4.5
Females	64	11.5	6.7	90	12.0	6.6
Total	127	10.8	6.0	164	10.8	6.5

TABLE 33. Development of written language—a cross-cultural comparison

WORDS PER SENTENCE

	U.S.			Uruguay		
	N	Mean	SD	N	Mean	SD
7 Years						
Males	62	6.3	2.2	13	6.1	2.8
Females	61	6.7	2.3	6	6.5	2.1
Total	123	6.5	2.3	19	6.2	2.8
9 Years						
Males	61	9.9	2.5	89	8.2	2.4
Females	62	9.5	2.1	74	8.9	2.3
Total	123	9.7	2.3	163	8.5	2.4
11 Years						
Males	63	11.2	2.8	74	11.8	3.1
Females	64	11.8	3.3	90	11.8	3.9
Total	127	11.5	3.0	164	11.8	3.5

TABLE 34. Development of written language—a cross-cultural comparison

SYNTAX

	U.S.			Uruguay		
	N	Mean	SD	N	Mean	SD
Males	62	84.6	21.9	13	84.3	22.2
Females	61	88.9	18.7	6	84.0	24.2
Total	123	86.7	20.4	19	84.2	23.0
		9 Years				
Males	61	94.3	7.8	89	95.0	5.5
Females	62	96.4	4.7	74	96.9	4.5
Total	123	95.3	6.5	163	95.9	5.2
		11 Years				
Males	63	96.7	4.1	74	95.2	4.7
Females	64	98.1	2.9	90	96.5	3.5
Total	127	97.4	3.6	164	95.9	4.1

TABLE 35. Development of written language—a cross-cultural comparison

ABSTRACT-CONCRETE

	U.S.			Uruguay		
	N	Mean	SD	N	Mean	SD
		7 Years				
Males	62	7.3	3.5	13	6.4	3.5
Females	61	8.4	2.9	6	6.8	3.6
Total	123	7.8	3.2	19	6.5	2.8
		9 Years				
Males	61	13.0	5.1	89	11.5	4.4
Females	62	13.8	4.8	74	11.7	5.7
Total	123	13.4	4.9	163	11.5	4.3
		11 Years				
Males	63	14.8	5.2	74	14.9	4.3
Females	64	16.2	4.4	90	16.0	4.3
Total	127	15.5	4.8	164	15.4	4.5

TABLE 36. Development of written language—a cross-cultural comparison of children aged 8 and 10 years

	8 Years		10 Years	
	U.S. mean	Uruguay mean	U.S. mean	Uruguay mean
	Total Words			
Males	52	67	94	86
Females	65	74	111	105
	Total Sentences			
Males	6.1	5.4	9.3	10.5
Females	7.7	5.9	11.0	11.5
	Words per Sentence			
Males	8.1	8.3	10.6	8.8
Females	8.1	9.0	10.5	9.5
	Syntax			
Males	89	93	95	95
Females	92	95	97	96
	Abstract-Concrete			
Males	10	9.6	14	14
Females	11	10.0	15	14

TABLE 37. Comparison of Primary Mental Abilities IQ scores for normal and reading-disability children

	Normal			Reading Disability			
Age	N	Mean	SD	N	Mean	SD	U
			Verbal Words				
9	43	106	12.9	14	85	6.9	4.91**
11	32	108	12.7	17	88	14.2	4.11**
			Verbal Pictures				
9	43	113	17.9	14	108	12.8	1.21
11	32	112	12.5	17	91	14.4	3.94**
			Reasoning (Reading)				
9	43	111	16.4	14	82	9.1	4.74**
11	32	109	16.7	17	84	13.9	4.12**
			Reasoning (Nonreading)				
9	43	107	23.2	14	96	18.6	1.85
11	32	101	13.8	17	93	11.6	2.32*
			Reasoning (Words and Figures)				
9	43	109	16.1	14	87	10.4	4.02**
11	60	109	23.6	44	89	20.8	4.42**
13	49	121	24.7	58	82	21.3	6.71**
15	47	122	20.3	10	63	20.1	4.63**
			Perceptual Speed				
9	43	106	19.7	14	93	16.0	2.47*
11	32	101	16.7	17	90	16.6	2.07*
			Verbal Ability				
9	43	109	13.1	14	94	5.0	4.29**
11	60	109	16.8	44	96	14.3	6.57**
13	49	109	18.9	58	81	15.2	6.74**
15	47	121	16.4	10	65	13.9	4.88**
			Space				
9	43	101	19.0	14	91	15.7	1.79
11	60	94	23.3	44	77	15.0	4.11**
13	49	111	29.4	58	82	26.9	5.12**
15	47	108	26.9	10	66	34.1	3.22**
			Number				
9	43	108	12.3	14	95	11.4	3.02**
11	60	107	20.6	44	96	24.8	3.40**
13	49	118	22.8	58	89	23.5	5.58**
15	47	114	18.5	10	72	22.3	4.20**
			Word Fluency				
11	27	112	28.1	27	87	13.5	3.53**
13	49	108	21.6	58	83	19.3	5.52**
15	47	113	22.3	10	61	10.4	4.67**

*$p < .05$.
**$p < .01$.

TABLE 38. Comparison of Draw-a-Man IQ scores for normal and reading-disability children

Age	Normal			Reading Disability			
	N	Mean	SD	N	Mean	SD	U
9	43	104	14.6	14	90	12.0	3.06**
11	60	96	12.7	44	83	19.5	4.37**
13	49	82	8.6	58	78	13.2	3.27**
15	47	93	10.7	10	68	8.3	4.56**

**$p < .01$.

TABLE 39. Comparison of normal and reading-disability children on auditory receptive language

Age	Normal			Reading Disability			
	N	Mean	SD	N	Mean	SD	U
Test One: Comprehension							
9	43	14.3	2.3	14	10.6	3.0	3.81**
11	60	16.0	2.4	44	12.8	2.4	5.90**
13	49	16.9	2.1	58	14.2	3.0	4.91**
15	47	16.3	1.9	10	13.7	2.4	3.14**
Test Two: Auditory to Visual							
9	43	20.7	4.6	14	17.5	5.4	2.17*
11	60	24.3	4.4	44	19.6	5.2	4.57**
13	49	25.9	4.2	58	22.5	5.1	4.32**
15	47	26.7	1.8	10	24.8	4.3	1.58

*$p < .05$.
**$p < .01$.

TABLE 40. Comparison of normal and reading-disability children on auditory expressive language

Age	Normal			Reading Disability			U
	N	Mean	SD	N	Mean	SD	
			Test One: Opposites				
9	43	40.0	8.7	14	27.3	8.5	4.08**
11	60	50.9	8.3	44	32.6	8.3	7.59**
13	49	53.3	3.0	58	40.9	8.6	6.24**
15	47	61.6	6.5	10	36.7	6.6	4.93**
			Test Two: Definition of Words				
9	43	10.0	3.2	14	6.0	1.9	3.84**
11	60	13.8	2.6	44	10.0	3.2	5.86**
13	49	16.7	1.8	58	12.3	3.1	7.16**
15	47	18.9	2.1	10	12.3	2.9	4.82**

**$p < .01$.

TABLE 41. Comparison of normal and reading-disability children on read language

Age	Normal			Reading Disability			U
	N	Mean	SD	N	Mean	SD	
11	60	33.4	10.5	44	17.1	7.6	7.31**
13	49	43.1	8.1	58	24.5	8.3	7.99**
15	47	63.3	11.8	10	21.1	11.5	4.92**

**$p < .01$.

TABLE 42. Comparison of normal and reading-disability children on written language

Age	Normal			Reading Disability			
	N	Mean	SD	N	Mean	SD	U
Total Words							
9	123	90.4	51.4	14	28.7	13.8	5.52***
11	127	116.0	56.0	45	49.0	26.1	7.60***
13	125	149.7	70.0	59	58.2	25.2	9.20***
15	125	138.0	47.1	12	35.0	25.6	5.42***
Total Sentences							
9	123	9.5	5.3	14	3.3	1.8	5.19***
11	127	10.8	6.0	45	4.8	2.5	6.53***
13	125	11.2	6.1	59	5.0	2.3	7.81***
15	125	9.6	4.3	12	3.5	2.2	4.86***
Words per Sentence							
9	123	9.6	2.3	14	8.8	4.3	1.01
11	127	11.4	3.0	45	10.2	2.8	2.58**
13	125	13.9	3.3	59	11.9	2.7	3.85***
15	125	15.0	3.6	12	10.0	2.6	4.48***
Syntax							
9	123	95.4	6.5	14	78.2	26.0	4.49**
11	127	97.5	3.7	45	91.2	7.1	6.34***
13	125	97.7	2.9	59	91.8	6.5	6.79***
15	125	98.0	3.1	12	89.8	5.6	4.55***
Abstract-Concrete							
9	123	13.4	4.9	14	8.5	4.0	3.48***
11	127	15.5	4.8	45	10.3	4.6	5.79***
13	125	16.7	4.3	59	12.5	4.7	5.35***
15	125	18.4	4.2	12	9.3	3.9	4.87***

**p < .01.
***p < .001.

TABLE 43. Intercorrelation of auditory receptive and written language for children with reading disabilities

	9 Years (N = 14)	11 Years (N = 44)	13 Years (N = 57)	15 Years (N = 10)
	Test One: Comprehension			
Total words	.24	.11	.13	.04
Total sentences	.43	.06	.04	—.02
Words per sentence	.03	.12	.14	.48
Syntax	.53*	.07	.31**	—.55**
Abstract-concrete	.06	.04	.07	.17
	Test Two: Auditory to Visual			
Total words	.06	.06	.04	.20
Total sentences	.18	—.01	.04	.28
Words per sentence	.26	.12	.00	.00
Syntax	.65**	.03	.20	.12
Abstract-concrete	.22	—.06	.09	.03

$*p < .05.$
$**p < .01.$

TABLE 44. Intercorrelation of auditory expressive and written language for children with reading disabilities

	9 Years (N = 14)	11 Years (N = 44)	13 Years (N = 57)	15 Years (N = 10)
Test One: Opposites				
Total words	—.20	.11	—.03	.54
Total sentences	—.13	.00	—.03	.44
Words per sentence	.04	.18	—.04	.02
Syntax	.24	.17	.13	.15
Abstract-concrete	.16	.21	.28*	.29
Test Two: Definition of Words				
Total words	—.10	.23	.03	.42
Total sentences	—.29	.16	.00	.44
Words per sentence	—.13	.06	.03	—.19
Syntax	—.46*	.13	—.11	.30
Abstract-concrete	—.07	.29*	.26*	.17

*p < .05.

TABLE 45. Comparison of normal and reading-disability children on locomotor coordination

	Normal			Reading Disability			
Age	N	Mean	SD	N	Mean	SD	U
9	43	77.2	30.4	14	57.6	23.0	2.02*
11	60	82.9	31.0	44	65.3	29.9	2.59**
13	49	97.8	32.4	58	77.4	33.6	2.95**
15	47	118.1	23.8	10	95.0	22.2	2.63**

*p < .05.
**p < .01.

TABLE 46. Comparison of normal and dyslexic children on written language

		Normal			Dyslexic		
Age	N	Mean	SD	N	Mean	SD	U
			Total Words				
7	83	24.5	17.0	9	10.3	7.2	2.46*
9	54	65.3	41.4	18	19.6	17.7	4.25**
11	71	88.7	49.4	16	45.5	31.3	2.76**
13	62	99.0	52.9	8	60.3	39.8	3.33**
15	56	129.4	51.1	7	97.7	35.2	2.24*
17	10	123.5	28.1	8	86.5	43.4	10.00
			Total Sentences				
7	83	4.0	2.7	9	1.5	0.8	2.74**
9	54	6.8	4.1	18	2.6	2.2	3.41**
11	71	6.8	5.1	16	4.0	2.9	2.61**
13	62	7.4	4.1	8	4.8	2.8	1.59
15	56	8.8	3.9	7	5.7	2.5	1.03
17	10	8.5	3.2	8	5.6	2.1	9.50
			Words per Sentence				
7	83	6.1	2.4	9	6.3	2.1	0.44
9	54	9.7	2.6	18	5.4	3.6	3.48**
11	71	12.1	3.3	16	11.4	6.4	0.67
13	62	13.7	3.0	8	10.8	6.4	1.21
15	56	15.2	3.2	7	18.3	7.3	1.05
17	10	15.6	4.2	8	14.6	4.4	20.00
			Syntax				
7	83	81.0	21.5	9	75.8	16.0	1.46
9	54	91.0	14.0	18	64.3	36.4	3.30**
11	71	95.5	4.9	16	79.0	30.0	2.52*
13	62	96.5	3.6	8	82.7	28.8	1.18
15	56	98.5	2.2	7	96.5	3.8	1.47
17	10	98.9	1.6	8	96.2	4.3	15.00
			Abstract-Concrete				
7	83	7.0	2.6	9	6.1	2.4	.34
9	54	10.3	4.1	18	7.9	5.8	.15
11	71	13.2	4.7	16	11.6	6.7	.20
13	62	13.9	5.0	8	11.8	6.6	.59
15	56	18.5	4.1	7	17.0	6.2	.15
17	10	18.6	4.7	8	17.2	5.6	14.00

[1] For 7- through 15-year groups the z score is reported from the Mann-Whitney U computation. For the 17-year group the U is reported directly due to smaller N's.
    *$p < .05$.
    **$p < .01$.

222

TABLE 47. Intercorrelation among scores for written language for dyslexic children (N=64)

	Total sentences	Words per sentence	Syntax	Abstract-concrete
Total words	.88**	.77**	.57**	.78**
Total sentences		.53**	.65**	.74**
Words per sentence			.69**	.72**
Syntax				.71**

**p < .01.

TABLE 48. Intercorrelation among scores for written language in dyslexic group by age (N=64)

	7 Years	9 Years	11 Years	13 Years	15 Years	17 Years
			Total Words			
Total sentences	.91**	.92**	.92**	.92**	.67*	.89**
Words per sentence	.68*	.79**	.46*	.80**	.41	.73*
Syntax	.56	.64**	.65**	.79**	.52	.10
Abstract-concrete	.76**	.67**	.64**	.93**	.74*	.33
			Total Sentences			
Total words	.91**	.92**	.92**	.92**	.67*	.89**
Words per sentence	.43	.68**	.26	.65*	—.36	.38
Syntax	.62*	.71**	.65**	.82**	.58	.40
Abstract-concrete	.71*	.57*	.64**	.91**	.64	.27
			Words per Sentence			
Total words	.68*	.79**	.46*	.80**	.41	.73*
Total sentences	.43	.68**	.26	.64*	—.36	.38
Syntax	.63*	.83**	.65**	.86**	—.12	—.16
Abstract-concrete	.76**	.84**	.62**	.73*	.104	.55
			Syntax			
Total words	.56	.64**	.65**	.79**	.52	.10
Total sentences	.62	.71**	.65**	.82**	.58	.40
Words per sentence	.63**	.83**	.78**	.86**	—.12	—.16
Abstract-concrete	.91**	.74**	.75**	.82**	.74*	.22
			Abstract-Concrete			
Total words	.76**	.67**	.64**	.93**	.74*	.33
Total sentences	.71*	.57*	.62**	.91**	.64	.27
Words per sentence	.76**	.84**	.57*	.73*	.10	.55
Syntax	.91**	.74**	.75**	.82**	.74*	.22

*p < .05.
**p < .01.

TABLE 49. Intercorrelation between written language and auditory abilities for dyslexic children (N=64)

Total words		Total sentences		Words per sentence		Abstract-concrete		Syntax	
.82**	Verbal opposites	.66**	Verbal opposites	.72**	Verbal opposites	.67**	Verbal opposites	.52**	Orientation
.72**	Orientation	.62**	Orientation	.67**	Orientation	.67**	Free associations	.50**	Verbal opposites
.72**	Like-differences	.60**	Like-differences	.63**	Like-differences	.61**	Orientation	.50**	WISC verbal
.67**	Auditory span, syllables	.54**	Auditory span, syllables	.63**	Free associations	.61**	Like-differences	.46**	Social adjustment
.65**	Verbal absurdities	.54**	Verbal absurdities	.60**	Social adjustment	.58**	Social adjustment	.45**	Like-differences
.64**	Free associations	.50**	Free associations	.56**	Verbal absurdities	.54**	Verbal absurdities	.45**	Free associations
.61**	Social adjustment	.48**	Social adjustment	.54**	Auditory span, syllables	.53**	Auditory span, syllables	.44**	Verbal absurdities
.60**	Attention span, words	.48**	Attention span, words	.54**	Oral directions	.46**	Attention span, words	.33**	Auditory span, syllables
.60**	Oral directions	.44**	WISC verbal	.54**	WISC verbal	.45**	Oral directions	.33**	Attention span, words
.55**	WISC verbal	.43**	Oral directions	.52**	Attention span, words	.38**	WISC verbal	.28*	Oral directions
.34**	Oral commands	.17	Oral commands	.36**	Oral commands	.23*	Oral commands	.08	Oral commands

*p < .05.
**p < .01.

224

TABLE 50. Intercorrelation between written language and visual abilities for dyslexic children (N = 64)

Total words		Total sentences		Words per sentence		Abstract-concrete		Syntax	
.68**	Picture absurdities	.52**	Picture absurdities	.62**	Picture absurdities	.56**	Picture absurdities	.46**	Visual span, letters
.60**	Designs	.49**	Visual span, letters	.60**	Visual span, letters	.54**	Visual span, letters	.35**	Picture absurdities
.58	Visual span, letters	.44**	Designs	.58**	Visual span, objects	.47**	Designs	.28*	Designs
.57**	Visual span, objects	.39**	Visual span, objects	.48**	Designs	.42**	Visual span, objects	.27**	Visual span, objects
.47**	WISC performance	.31**	WISC performance	.48**	WISC performance	.38**	WISC performance	.24*	WISC performance
.00	Draw-A-Man	−.02	Draw-A-Man	.00	Draw-A-Man	−.04	Draw-A-Man	−.05	Draw-A-Man

*p < .05.
**p < .01.

225

TABLE 51. Comparison of Primary Mental Abilities IQ scores for normal and mentally retarded children

	Normal			Retarded		
N	Mean	SD	N	Mean	SD	t
			Verbal Words			
97	108.2	11.9	70	65.4	6.9	29.23**
			Verbal Pictures			
139	111.7	15.6	99	71.7	12.5	21.94**
			Reasoning (Reading)			
120	104.7	16.2	77	60.3	9.1	24.54**
			Reasoning (Nonreading)			
127	110.8	22.4	79	65.9	11.3	19.00**
			Reasoning (Words and Figures)			
208	110.7	21.6	95	60.2	8.2	29.47**
			Perceptual Speed			
134	106.2	18.8	116	66.1	14.0	19.28**
			Verbal Ability			
218	107.6	15.6	127	67.1	9.3	30.18**
			Space			
187	107.2	23.4	98	68.0	14.2	17.58**
			Number			
212	108.8	18.2	91	71.1	12.0	21.27**
			Reading IQ			
87	109.7	11.8	55	65.8	5.8	29.51**
			Nonreading IQ			
122	111.3	13.8	78	69.1	9.3	25.79**
			Arithmetic IQ			
129	105.7	10.2	78	67.2	8.0	30.23**

**$p < .01$.

TABLE 52. IQ Scores for mentally retarded children on the Draw-A-Man Test

		Males			Females			Total	
Age	N	Mean	SD	N	Mean	SD	N	Mean	SD
9	11	81.8	13.9	9	82.0	10.7	20	81.9	12.3
11	12	67.4	17.0	9	71.4	18.2	21	69.1	17.2
13	28	63.8	12.6	18	65.3	14.0	46	64.4	13.0
15	19	69.3	15.0	16	59.6	13.8	35	64.9	15.0

TABLE 53. Comparison of normal and mentally retarded children on auditory receptive language

		Normal			Retarded		
Age	N	Mean	SD	N	Mean	SD	t
			Test One: Comprehension				
9	46	13.5	2.8	21	5.5	2.3	12.31**
11	60	16.0	2.4	22	6.4	3.4	12.18**
13	52	16.8	2.2	46	7.9	3.9	13.68**
15	47	16.3	1.9	35	8.8	4.0	10.26**
			Test Two: Auditory to Visual				
11	60	24.3	4.4	22	13.2	5.6	8.39**
13	52	25.6	4.4	46	14.6	6.5	9.68**
15	47	26.8	1.8	35	18.1	6.4	7.82**

**p < .01.

TABLE 54. Comparison of normal and mentally retarded children on auditory expressive language

Age	Normal			Retarded			
	N	Mean	SD	N	Mean	SD	t
Test One: Opposites							
11	60	50.9	8.3	22	11.8	9.0	17.79**
13	52	53.1	9.0	46	20.5	11.4	15.57**
15	47	61.6	6.5	35	25.3	10.5	18.04**
Test Two: Definition of Words							
11	60	13.8	2.6	22	4.3	2.6	14.66**
13	52	16.5	2.4	46	5.5	2.8	20.75**
15	47	18.9	2.1	35	7.8	3.4	17.05**

**$p < .01$.

TABLE 55. Comparison of normal and mentally retarded children on read language

Age	Normal			Retarded			
	N	Mean	SD	N	Mean	SD	t
13	52	42.9	9.0	32	12.2	13.2	11.55**
15	47	63.3	11.9	31	7.7	7.2	25.75**

**$p < .01$.

TABLE 56. Comparison of normal and mentally retarded children on written language

Age	N	Mean	SD	N	Mean	SD	U
		Normal			Retarded		
				Total Words			
9	123	90.4	51.5	20	9.0	12.7	6.98***
11	127	116.0	56.0	21	17.4	16.1	7.15***
13	125	149.7	70.1	46	29.6	27.0	9.43***
15	125	138.1	47.1	35	32.0	25.6	8.65***
				Total Sentences			
9	123	9.6	5.4	20	1.5	2.3	6.57***
11	127	10.8	6.0	21	2.5	2.3	7.32***
13	125	11.3	6.1	46	3.9	3.6	7.73***
15	125	9.7	4.4	35	3.5	2.6	7.55***
				Words per Sentence			
9	123	9.7	2.3	20	2.8	3.5	6.39***
11	127	11.5	3.0	21	4.1	3.3	6.96***
13	125	14.0	3.4	46	6.5	2.9	9.46***
15	125	15.1	3.7	35	8.4	3.9	7.33***
				Syntax			
9	123	95.4	6.5	20	40.2	41.2	6.24***
11	127	97.5	3.7	21	59.4	37.2	6.95***
13	125	97.7	2.9	46	73.4	28.0	8.03***
15	125	98.0	3.1	35	76.3	26.8	7.72***
				Abstract-Concrete			
9	123	13.4	4.9	20	6.0	5.3	6.40***
11	127	15.5	4.8	21	7.7	5.2	6.54***
13	125	16.7	4.4	46	9.4	3.9	9.10***
15	125	18.4	4.3	35	7.1	2.9	8.59***

***$p < .001$.

TABLE 57. Intercorrelation of auditory receptive and written language for mentally retarded children

	11 Years (N = 11)	13 Years (N = 28)	15 Years (N = 29)
Test One: Comprehension			
Total words	—.09	.25	.25
Total sentences	—.35	.24	.12
Words per sentence	—.37	.17	.51**
Syntax	—.38	.28	.41*
Abstract-concrete	—.12	.07	.53**
Test Two: Auditory to Visual			
Total words	.18	—.01	.18
Total sentences	—.24	—.05	.24
Words per sentence	—.28	.20	.12
Syntax	—.29	.19	.40*
Abstract-concrete	.03	—.11	.34*

*p < .05.
**p < .01.

230

TABLE 58. Intercorrelation of auditory expressive and written language for mentally retarded children

	11 Years (N = 11)	13 Years (N = 28)	15 Years (N = 29)
	Test One: Opposites		
Total words	—.07	—.12	—.14
Total sentences	—.23	—.13	—.15
Words per sentence	—.23	—.10	.20
Syntax	—.23	—.21	.20
Abstract-concrete	—.03	—.25	.18
	Test Two: Definition of Words		
Total words	.30	.19	—.03
Total sentences	—.04	.20	.00
Words per sentence	—.06	.00	.10
Syntax	—.07	.20	.15
Abstract-concrete	.18	.36*	.22

*$p < .05$.

TABLE 59. Comparison of normal and mentally retarded children on locomotor coordination

Age	Normal			Retarded			t
	N	Mean	SD	N	Mean	SD	
9	46	72.2	30.8	20	37.8	17.0	5.79**
11	60	82.9	31.0	20	49.8	36.5	3.64**
13	52	96.7	34.0	42	60.5	36.7	4.91**
15	47	118.2	23.9	34	62.2	39.8	7.30**

**$p < .01$.

TABLE 60. Comparison of Primary Mental Abilities IQ scores for normal children and children with articulation disorders

Age	\	Normal		\	Articulation disorders		U
	N	Mean	SD	N	Mean	SD	
			Verbal Words				
7	67	101.9	12.0	75	97.2	10.7	2.55
9	43	106.7	12.9	31	100.1	13.9	2.61**
11	32	108.9	12.7	12	93.0	15.8	2.95**
			Verbal Pictures				
7	67	114.6	14.2	75	106.2	16.4	3.25**
9	43	112.9	17.9	31	108.2	16.5	1.48
11	32	112.7	12.5	12	103.4	21.2	1.69
			Reasoning (Reading)				
7	67	95.9	17.7	75	86.6	21.2	3.10**
9	43	111.0	16.4	31	100.1	17.7	2.78**
11	32	109.0	16.7	12	87.8	19.1	2.99**
			Reasoning (Nonreading)				
7	67	109.4	28.3	75	98.3	30.2	2.00
9	43	107.4	23.2	31	99.5	18.0	2.08*
11	32	101.1	13.8	12	94.5	25.1	0.49
			Reasoning (Words and Figures)				
7	67	102.3	16.3	75	93.1	20.6	2.71**
9	43	109.4	16.1	31	99.0	14.5	2.75**
11	60	109.4	23.6	12	91.0	20.3	2.41*
13	49	121.9	24.7	9	120.8	34.5	0.05
			Perceptual Speed				
7	67	106.8	20.2	75	104.3	17.3	0.49
9	43	106.8	19.7	31	97.9	16.8	2.14*
11	32	101.0	16.7	12	92.2	17.2	1.36
			Verbal Ability				
7	67	107.3	11.1	75	99.2	15.3	3.48**
9	43	109.3	13.1	31	103.2	12.9	2.38*
11	60	109.9	16.8	12	96.9	16.5	2.35*
13	49	109.0	18.9	9	107.6	12.3	0.18
			Space				
7	67	103.0	11.1	75	93.8	31.5	1.86
9	43	101.5	19.0	31	90.1	20.4	2.36*
11	60	94.2	23.3	12	73.4	21.8	2.49*
13	49	111.6	29.4	9	90.7	32.4	2.19*
			Number				
7	67	102.1	12.6	75	96.9	18.0	2.15*
9	43	108.4	12.3	31	103.8	11.9	1.42
11	60	107.8	20.6	12	96.1	15.6	1.79
13	49	118.1	22.8	9	120.2	23.5	0.24

*$p < .05$.
**$p < .01$.

TABLE 61. Comparison of Draw-A-Man IQ Scores for normal children and children with articulation disorders

Age	Normal			Articulation disorders			U
	N	Mean	SD	N	Mean	SD	
7	67	108.8	17.8	75	104.1	15.7	1.49
9	43	104.0	14.7	31	97.9	15.4	1.81
11	60	96.2	12.7	12	77.4	15.3	3.64**
13	49	82.3	8.7	9	83.3	10.8	0.80

$**p < .01.$

TABLE 62. Comparison of normal children and children with articulation disorders on auditory receptive language

Age	Normal			Articulation disorders			U
	N	Mean	SD	N	Mean	SD	
	Test One: Comprehension						
7	67	9.5	3.4	75	9.7	2.7	1.21
9	43	14.3	2.3	31	13.1	3.7	2.38*
11	60	16.0	2.4	12	13.9	2.0	2.50*
13	49	16.9	2.1	9	16.2	2.6	1.68
	Test Two: Auditory to Visual						
7	67	15.6	5.0	75	14.5	5.0	1.21
9	43	20.7	4.6	31	18.2	4.7	2.38*
11	60	24.3	4.4	12	19.8	7.4	2.50*
13	49	25.9	4.2	9	24.6	4.2	1.68

$*p < .05.$

TABLE 63. Comparison of normal children and children with articulation disorders on auditory expressive language

Age	Normal			Articulation disorders			U
	N	Mean	SD	N	Mean	SD	
Test One: Opposites							
7	67	22.7	8.4	75	21.4	9.0	0.65
9	43	40.0	8.7	31	32.4	9.8	3.10**
11	60	50.9	8.3	12	34.5	13.3	3.81**
13	49	53.3	3.0	9	54.0	8.7	0.39
Test Two: Definition of Words							
7	67	5.6	2.4	75	5.1	1.9	1.16
9	43	10.0	3.2	31	7.9	3.6	2.41*
11	60	13.8	2.6	12	9.7	4.3	3.31**
13	49	16.7	1.8	9	15.1	5.3	0.08

*$p < .05$.
**$p < .01$.

TABLE 64. Comparison of normal children and children with articulation disorders on read language

Age	Normal			Articulation disorders			U
	N	Mean	SD	N	Mean	SD	
9	60	21.1	7.9	31	12.9	8.1	4.12**
11	49	33.4	10.5	12	20.8	12.0	2.87**
13	47	43.1	8.2	12	40.3	8.5	1.30

**$p < .01$.

TABLE 65. Comparison of normal children and children with articulation disorders on written language

Age	Normal			Articulation disorders			
	N	Mean	SD	N	Mean	SD	U
Total Words							
7	123	27.6	17.1	79	17.5	15.5	4.47***
9	123	90.4	51.4	35	40.5	25.5	6.56***
11	127	116.0	56.0	15	51.0	23.9	4.67***
13	125	149.7	70.0	9	59.7	43.7	3.83***
Total Sentences							
7	123	4.3	2.7	79	2.5	2.4	4.79***
9	123	9.5	5.3	35	4.8	2.9	5.77***
11	127	10.8	6.0	15	5.3	2.3	3.82***
13	125	11.2	6.1	9	5.1	3.0	3.47***
Words per Sentence							
7	123	6.5	2.2	79	4.9	3.6	3.69***
9	123	9.6	2.3	35	8.2	2.4	2.94***
11	127	11.4	3.0	15	10.1	3.8	1.86
13	125	13.9	3.3	9	11.4	2.7	2.26*
Syntax							
7	123	86.8	20.5	79	65.0	38.0	5.16***
9	123	95.4	6.5	35	83.3	17.0	6.09***
11	127	97.5	3.7	15	88.5	10.4	4.43***
13	125	97.7	2.9	9	95.8	5.0	1.67
Abstract-Concrete							
7	123	7.8	3.2	79	5.5	3.8	3.93***
9	123	13.4	4.9	35	9.7	5.1	4.13***
11	127	15.5	4.8	15	9.8	4.4	3.92***
13	125	16.7	4.3	9	11.1	4.9	2.93***

*p < .05.
**p < .01.
***p < .001.

235

TABLE 66. Intercorrelation of auditory receptive and written language for children with articulation disorders

	7 Years (N = 71)	9 Years (N = 30)	11 Years (N = 11)
Test One: Comprehension			
Total words	.22*	.44**	.53*
Total sentences	.17	.45**	.00
Words per sentence	.25*	.15	.64*
Syntax	.31**	.35*	.51
Abstract-concrete	.18	.09	.24
Test Two: Auditory to Visual			
Total words	.34**	.24	.49
Total sentences	.32**	.19	.20
Words per sentence	.18	.13	.42
Syntax	.31**	.30	.14
Abstract-concrete	.23	.19	.29

*$p < .05$.
**$p < .01$.

TABLE 67. Intercorrelation of auditory expressive and written language for children with articulation disorders

	7 Years (N = 71)	9 Years (N = 30)	11 Years (N = 11)
Test One: Opposites			
Total words	.39**	.25	.87**
Total sentences	.33**	.09	.41
Words per sentence	.25*	.41*	.48
Syntax	.31**	.27	.57
Abstract-concrete	.32**	.21	.46
Test Two: Definition of Words			
Total words	.29**	.17	.57*
Total sentences	.28**	.06	.03
Words per sentence	.30**	.31*	.59*
Syntax	.30**	.33*	.49
Abstract-concrete	.28**	.05	.37

*p < .05.
**p < .01.

TABLE 68. Comparison of normal children and children with articulation disorders on locomotor coordination

Age	Normal			Articulation disorders			
	N	Mean	SD	N	Mean	SD	U
7	67	53.8	21.3	75	42.2	18.1	3.28**
9	43	77.2	30.4	31	51.2	21.4	3.56**
11	60	82.9	31.0	12	65.0	28.1	1.58
13	49	97.9	32.4	9	66.2	44.2	2.16*

*p < .05.
**p < .01.

237

TABLE 69. Comparison of Primary Mental Abilities IQ scores for normal and socially-emotionally disturbed children

	Normal			Disturbed			
Age	N	Mean	SD	N	Mean	SD	U
			Verbal Words				
9	43	106.7	12.9	11	88.9	20.0	3.32**
11	32	108.9	12.7	13	69.1	14.6	4.90**
			Verbal Pictures				
9	43	112.9	17.9	11	97.8	20.7	2.35**
11	32	112.7	12.5	13	88.2	12.8	4.21**
			Reasoning (Reading)				
9	43	111.0	16.4	11	76.2	31.0	3.34**
11	32	109.0	16.7	13	61.4	30.6	4.15**
			Reasoning (Nonreading)				
9	43	107.4	23.2	11	85.3	30.6	2.34*
11	32	101.1	13.8	13	75.6	20.4	3.66**
			Reasoning (Words and Figures)				
9	43	109.4	16.1	11	81.1	23.3	3.50**
11	60	109.4	23.6	13	68.0	17.9	4.79**
13	49	121.9	24.7	11	72.2	17.6	4.47**
15	47	122.8	20.3	16	84.0	18.1	4.98**
			Perceptual Speed				
9	43	106.8	19.7	11	92.3	14.6	2.32*
11	32	101.0	16.7	13	80.5	20.6	3.06**
			Verbal Ability				
9	43	109.3	13.1	11	92.3	19.5	3.28**
11	60	109.9	16.8	13	79.3	11.1	7.80**
13	49	109.0	18.9	11	81.1	15.2	3.83**
15	47	121.7	16.4	16	89.5	18.0	4.86**
			Space				
9	43	101.5	19.0	11	91.9	16.9	1.68
11	60	94.2	23.3	13	82.0	21.5	1.29
13	49	111.6	29.4	11	76.7	10.5	3.81**
15	47	108.1	26.9	16	97.7	24.6	1.41
			Number				
9	43	108.4	12.3	11	98.0	13.0	2.47*
11	60	107.8	20.6	13	80.6	9.8	4.71**
13	49	118.1	22.8	11	90.1	27.7	2.96**
15	47	114.4	18.5	16	93.4	22.5	3.08**
			Word Fluency				
13	49	108.4	28.1	11	79.9	13.3	4.10**
15	47	113.4	22.3	16	89.3	11.0	3.32**

*p < .05.
**p < .01.

TABLE 70. Comparison of Draw-A-Man IQ scores for normal and socially-emotionally disturbed children

Age	Normal			Disturbed			U
	N	Mean	SD	N	Mean	SD	
9	43	104.0	14.6	11	78.4	13.5	4.14**
11	60	96.1	12.7	13	74.2	16.7	4.08**
13	49	82.2	8.6	11	78.3	11.0	2.41**
15	47	92.9	10.7	16	68.8	10.8	5.18**

$**p < .01.$

TABLE 71. Comparison of normal and socially-emotionally disturbed children on auditory receptive language

Age	Normal			Disturbed			U
	N	Mean	SD	N	Mean	SD	
			Test One: Comprehension				
9	43	14.3	2.3	11	8.7	3.7	4.12**
11	60	16.0	2.4	13	7.9	2.6	5.59**
13	49	16.9	2.1	11	14.6	3.3	2.98**
15	47	16.3	1.9	16	16.0	2.7	0.23
			Test Two: Auditory to Visual				
9	43	20.7	4.6	11	15.2	4.6	3.26**
11	60	24.3	4.4	13	14.3	5.2	4.89**
13	49	25.9	4.2	11	24.7	9.6	2.47*
15	47	26.7	1.8	16	24.4	3.4	2.53*

$*p < .05.$
$**p < .01.$

TABLE 72. Comparison of normal and socially-emotionally disturbed children on auditory expressive language

Age	Normal			Disturbed			U
	N	Mean	SD	N	Mean	SD	
			Test One: Opposites				
9	43	40.0	8.7	11	23.3	11.0	4.02**
11	60	50.9	8.3	13	24.6	11.3	5.35**
13	49	53.3	3.0	11	43.0	6.9	3.61**
15	47	61.6	6.5	16	49.4	5.2	5.13**
			Test Two: Definition of Words				
9	43	10.0	3.2	11	6.8	3.0	2.57**
11	60	13.8	2.6	13	8.6	2.6	5.15**
13	49	16.7	1.8	11	13.2	2.7	3.69**
15	47	18.9	2.1	16	14.3	2.6	5.32**

**p < .01.

TABLE 73. Comparison of normal and socially-emotionally disturbed children on read language

Age	Normal			Disturbed			U
	N	Mean	SD	N	Mean	SD	
13	49	43.1	8.1	13	30.8	6.5	4.05**
15	47	63.3	11.8	16	38.8	11.0	5.47**

**p < .01.

TABLE 74. Comparison of normal and socially-emotionally disturbed children on written language

Age	Normal			Disturbed			
	N	Mean	SD	N	Mean	SD	U
			Total Words				
9	123	90.4	51.4	12	15.9	11.8	5.54***
11	127	116.0	56.0	18	22.6	20.8	6.47***
13	125	149.7	70.0	18	54.3	42.7	5.24***
15	125	138.0	47.1	20	53.8	31.3	6.24***
			Total Sentences				
9	123	9.5	5.3	12	1.6	1.3	5.52***
11	127	10.8	6.0	18	2.6	1.9	6.07***
13	125	11.2	6.1	18	4.9	3.4	4.67***
15	125	9.6	4.3	20	4.3	2.2	5.55***
			Words per Sentence				
9	123	9.6	2.3	12	6.5	4.5	2.26*
11	127	11.4	3.0	18	6.9	3.5	4.84***
13	125	13.9	3.3	18	10.6	3.9	3.36***
15	125	15.0	3.6	20	11.9	5.4	4.48***
			Syntax				
9	123	95.4	6.5	12	67.8	35.5	4.06***
11	127	97.5	3.7	18	76.0	29.4	5.98***
13	125	97.7	2.9	18	86.0	9.4	5.53***
15	125	98.0	3.1	20	90.4	21.7	3.31***
			Abstract-Concrete				
9	123	13.4	4.9	12	6.0	5.2	4.24***
11	127	15.5	4.8	18	7.6	5.2	5.09***
13	125	16.7	4.3	18	9.4	3.9	5.28***
15	125	18.4	4.2	20	11.9	5.4	4.92***

*p < .05.
***p < .001.

TABLE 75. Intercorrelation of auditory receptive and written language for socially-emotionally disturbed children

	9 Years (N = 11)	11 Years (N = 11)	13 Years (N = 11)	15 Years (N = 16)
Test One: Comprehension				
Total words	.53*	.16	.34	.07
Total sentences	.54*	.25	.07	.36
Words per sentence	.62*	—.14	.64*	—.39
Syntax	.57*	—.04	—.06	.08
Abstract-concrete	.55	—.27	.29	—.23
Test Two: Auditory to Visual				
Total words	.45	—.17	.45	.46*
Total sentences	.53*	—.18	.37	.01
Words per sentence	.70**	.28	.22	.46*
Syntax	.76**	.49	.35	.20
Abstract-concrete	.48	—.03	—.12	.68**

*$p < .05$.
**$p < .01$.

TABLE 76. Intercorrelation of auditory expressive and written language for socially-emotionally disturbed children

	9 Years (N = 11)	11 Years (N = 11)	13 Years (N = 11)	15 Years (N = 16)
Test One: Opposites				
Total words	—.05	.08	—.23	—.05
Total sentences	—.15	.05	—.29	—.22
Words per sentence	.11	.01	—.36	.36
Syntax	.25	.25	.28	—.15
Abstract-concrete	—.02	.25	—.28	.45*
Test Two: Definition of Words				
Total words	.23	—.13	—.32	.10
Total sentences	.14	—.16	—.26	.18
Words per sentence	.45	—.26	—.57*	.19
Syntax	.54*	—.10	.57*	.02
Abstract-concrete	.33	.05	—.16	.09

*$p < .05$.

242

TABLE 77. Comparison of normal and socially-emotionally disturbed children on locomotor coordination

	Normal			Disturbed			
Age	N	Mean	SD	N	Mean	SD	U
9	43	77.2	30.4	11	59.4	30.9	1.48
11	60	82.9	31.0	13	51.9	28.0	2.99**
13	49	97.8	32.4	11	82.5	30.3	1.40
15	47	118.1	23.8	16	90.1	32.5	3.30**

**p < .01.

TABLE 78. Reading scores for learning disability and control groups

Test	Moderate (N = 116)		Control (N = 116)			Severe (N = 112)		Control (N = 112)		
	Mean	SD	Mean	SD	t	Mean	SD	Mean	SD	t
Gates-MacGinitie accuracy	9.6	2.1	11.1	2.6	4.47***	8.6	1.4	11.1	2.9	7.36***
Gates-MacGinitie comprehension	9.3	1.6	11.2	2.1	6.86***	8.3	1.2	11.0	2.1	10.48***
Gates-MacGinitie vocabulary	9.5	1.6	11.2	1.7	6.62***	8.5	1.5	11.0	1.8	10.06***
Wide-range oral reading	10.2	1.8	11.9	2.4	6.07***	9.0	1.3	11.6	2.2	10.89***
Gates-McKillop word parts	10.2	1.3	11.2	0.9	6.64***	9.3	1.5	11.2	1.0	11.68***
Gates-McKillop nonsense words	9.6	0.9	10.2	0.6	5.41***	8.9	1.0	10.1	0.6	10.43***
Gates-McKillop syllabication	9.7	1.4	10.9	0.9	7.51***	8.7	1.3	10.8	1.0	13.23***

***p < .001.

TABLE 79. Written language age scores for the moderate-learning-disability and control groups

	Moderate (N = 116)		Control (N = 116)		
	Mean	SD	Mean	SD	*t*
Total words	9.2	2.3	10.1	2.9	2.57*
Total sentences	9.8	3.6	10.7	3.9	1.61
Words per sentence	9.8	2.2	10.5	2.7	2.29*
Syntax	10.4	3.2	11.7	3.7	2.85**
Abstract-concrete	12.6	3.9	13.9	3.6	2.67**

*$p < .05$.
**$p < .01$.

TABLE 80. Written language age scores for the severe-learning-disability and control groups

	Severe (N = 112)		Control (N = 112)		
	Mean	SD	Mean	SD	*t*
Total words	8.9	2.1	10.1	2.7	3.54***
Total sentences	9.5	3.1	10.4	3.6	1.88
Words per sentence	9.3	1.9	10.7	2.7	4.49***
Syntax	9.0	2.2	11.7	3.6	6.67***
Abstract-concrete	11.9	4.2	14.0	3.7	3.97***

***$p < .001$.

244

TABLE 81. Intercorrelation of read and written language for moderate-learning-disability (N=116) and control (N=116) groups

	Total words	Total sentences	Words per sentence	Syntax	Abstract-concrete
Wide-range oral reading	m = .35 c = .31			m = .33	m = .24 c = .36
Gates-MacGinitie accuracy	m = .32 c = .37	c = .27	m = .29	m = .32	c = .36
Gates-MacGinitie comprehension	c = .44	c = .30		m = .37	c = .41
Gates-MacGinitie vocabulary	c = .31			m = .37	c = .34
Gates-McKillop word parts				m = .29 c = .33	
Gates-McKillop nonsense words	m = .33	m = .30			m = .27
Gates-Mckillop syllabication	m = .31 c = .29			m = .27 c = .26	

m = moderate group; c = control group.

TABLE 82. Intercorrelation of read and written language for severe-learning-disability (N=112) and control (N=112) groups

	Total words	Total Sentences	Words per sentence	Syntax	Abstract-concrete
Wide-range oral reading	s = .43	s = .40		s = .28	s = .30
Gates-MacGinitie accuracy	c = .28				c = .28
Gates-MacGinitie comprehension	s = .51 c = .33	s = .37			s = .31 c = .29
Gates-MacGinitie vocabulary	s = .39	s = .36			s = .34
Gates-McKillop word parts	s = .25				
Gates-McKillop nonsense words	s = .29	s = .33			s = .26
Gates-McKillop syllabication	s = .45	s = .34		s = .26	s = .28

s = severe group; c = control group.

TABLE 83. Factor analysis results for written language for learning-disability children

	Moderate (N = 116) Factor				Severe (N = 112) Factor			
	1	2	3	4	1	2	3	4
Total words	.852	.032	.067	.028	.775	.086	.030	.364
Total sentences	.845	.020	.184	.024	.857	.069	.071	.002
Words per sentence	.178	.004	.786	.059	.096	.028	.079	.850
Syntax	.183	.045	.210	.865	.134	.006	.148	.657
Abstract-concrete	.788	.053	.263	.071	.756	.083	.126	.025

TABLE 84. Intercorrelation of Picture Story Language Test with other measures of the written word for moderate-learning-disability and control groups

	Metropolitan spelling	Metropolitan language
Total words	m = .30	
	c = .39	
Total sentences		c = .35
Words per sentence	c = .32	
Syntax	m = .43	m = .42
		c = .29
Abstract-concrete		c = .32

m = moderate group; c = control group.

TABLE 85. Intercorrelation of Picture Story Language Test with other measures of the written word for severe-learning-disability and control groups

	Metropolitan spelling	Metropolitan language
Total words	s = .54	
	c = .32	c = .31
Total sentences	s = .49	
Words per sentence	c = .27	
Syntax		s = .31
	c = .30	c = .31
Abstract=concrete	s = .34	s = .28
		c = .28

s = severe group; c = control group.

TABLE 86. Rank for Picture Story Language Test scores out of 47 measures as determined by discriminant analysis

	Moderate (N = 90)			Severe (N = 88)	
	Rank	F		Rank	F
Abstract-concrete	18th	6.10	Syntax	9th	25.35
Syntax	27th	4.32	Total words	15th	18.27
Words per sentence	34th	3.39	Total sentences	18th	15.49
Total sentences	42nd	2.78	Abstract-concrete	37th	6.54
Total words	43rd	2.70	Words per sentence	41st	5.79

TABLE 87. Comparison of reading-disability children and children with articulation disorders on written language

	Reading disability			Articulation disorders			
Age	N	Mean	SD	N	Mean	SD	U
			Total Words				
9	14	28.7	13.8	35	40.5	25.5	2.06*
11	45	49.0	26.1	15	51.0	23.9	0.45
13	59	58.2	25.2	9	59.7	43.7	0.89
			Total Sentences				
9	14	3.3	1.8	35	4.8	2.9	1.83
11	45	4.9	2.5	15	5.3	2.3	0.65
13	59	5.0	2.3	9	5.1	3.0	0.29
			Words per Sentence				
9	14	8.8	4.3	35	8.2	2.4	0.55
11	45	10.2	2.8	15	10.1	3.8	0.48
13	59	11.9	2.7	9	11.4	2.7	0.51
			Syntax				
9	14	78.2	26.0	35	83.3	17.0	0.25
11	45	91.2	7.1	15	88.5	10.4	0.71
13	59	91.8	6.5	9	95.8	5.0	1.97*
			Abstract-Concrete				
9	14	8.5	4.0	35	9.7	5.1	0.68
11	45	10.3	4.6	15	9.8	4.4	0.32
13	59	12.5	4.7	9	11.1	4.9	0.79

*$p < .05$.

TABLE 88. Comparison of reading-disability and mentally retarded children on written language

Age	Reading disability			Mentally retarded			
	N	Mean	SD	N	Mean	SD	U
Total Words							
9	14	28.7	13.8	20	9.0	12.7	37.00**
11	45	49.0	26.1	21	17.4	16.1	4.76***
13	59	58.2	25.2	46	29.6	27.0	5.61***
15	12	35.0	25.6	35	32.0	25.6	0.45
Total Sentences							
9	14	3.3	1.8	20	1.5	2.3	61.00*
11	45	4.9	2.5	21	2.5	2.3	3.52***
13	59	5.0	2.3	46	3.9	3.6	2.88**
15	12	3.5	2.2	35	3.4	2.6	0.13
Words per Sentence							
9	14	8.8	4.3	20	2.8	3.5	41.50**
11	45	10.2	2.8	21	4.1	3.3	5.71***
13	59	11.9	2.7	46	6.5	2.9	7.57***
15	12	10.0	2.6	35	8.4	3.9	1.33
Syntax							
9	14	78.2	26.0	20	40.2	41.2	61.00*
11	45	91.2	7.1	21	59.4	37.2	4.20***
13	59	91.8	6.5	46	73.4	28.0	4.33***
15	12	89.8	5.6	35	76.3	26.8	1.39
Abstract-Concrete							
9	14	8.5	4.0	20	6.0	5.3	54.50*
11	45	10.3	4.6	21	7.7	5.2	3.97
13	59	12.5	4.7	46	9.4	3.9	6.30
15	12	9.3	3.9	35	7.1	2.9	1.58

*p < .05.
**p < .01.
***p < .001.

TABLE 89. Comparison of mentally retarded children and children with articulation disorders on written language

Age	Mentally retarded			Articulation disorders			U
	N	Mean	SD	N	Mean	SD	
			Total Words				
9	20	9.0	12.7	35	40.5	25.5	4.78***
11	21	17.4	16.1	15	51.0	23.9	3.77***
13	46	29.6	27.0	9	59.7	43.7	2.34*
			Total Sentences				
9	20	1.5	2.3	35	4.8	2.9	4.32***
11	21	2.5	2.3	15	5.3	2.3	3.01**
13	46	3.9	3.6	9	5.1	3.0	1.27
			Words per Sentence				
9	20	2.8	3.5	35	8.2	2.4	4.52***
11	21	4.1	3.3	15	10.1	3.8	3.91***
13	46	6.5	2.9	9	11.4	2.7	3.90***
			Syntax				
9	20	40.2	41.2	35	83.3	17.0	3.58***
11	21	59.4	37.2	15	88.5	10.4	2.73**
13	46	73.4	28.0	9	95.8	5.0	3.25***
			Abstract-Concrete				
9	20	6.0	5.3	35	9.7	5.1	4.47***
11	21	7.7	5.2	15	9.8	4.4	2.90***
13	46	9.4	3.9	9	11.1	4.9	3.38***

*$p < .05$.
**$p < .01$.
***$p < .001$.

TABLE 90. Comparison of socially-emotionally disturbed children and children with disorders of articulation on written language

Age	N	Mean	SD	N	Mean	SD	U
		Articulation disorders			Disturbed		
	N	Mean	SD	N	Mean	SD	*U*
			Total Words				
9	35	40.5	25.5	12	15.9	11.8	3.45***
11	15	51.0	23.9	18	22.6	20.8	46.00**
13	9	59.7	43.7	18	54.3	42.7	71.00
			Total Sentences				
9	35	4.8	2.9	12	1.6	1.3	3.69***
11	15	5.3	2.4	18	2.6	1.9	50.00**
13	9	5.1	3.0	18	4.9	3.4	74.00
			Words per Sentence				
9	35	8.2	2.4	12	6.5	4.5	0.81
11	15	10.1	3.8	18	6.9	3.5	77.00*
13	9	11.4	2.7	18	10.6	3.9	66.50
			Syntax				
9	35	83.3	17.0	12	67.8	35.5	0.61
11	15	88.5	10.4	18	76.0	29.4	96.50
13	9	95.8	5.0	18	86.0	9.4	26.00*
			Abstract-Concrete				
9	35	9.7	5.1	12	6.0	5.2	2.32*
11	15	9.8	4.4	18	7.7	5.2	108.50
13	9	11.1	4.9	18	9.4	3.9	55.00

*$p < .05$.
**$p < .01$.
***$p < .001$.

251

TABLE 91. Comparison of reading-disability and socially-emotionally disturbed children on written language

Age	Reading disability			Disturbed			U
	N	Mean	SD	N	Mean	SD	
			Total Words				
9	14	28.7	13.8	12	15.9	11.8	40.00*
11	45	49.0	26.1	18	22.7	20.8	3.63***
13	59	58.2	25.2	18	54.3	42.7	0.98
15	12	35.0	25.6	20	53.8	31.3	66.50*
			Total Sentences				
9	14	3.3	1.8	12	1.6	1.3	39.50*
11	45	4.9	2.5	18	2.6	1.9	3.48***
13	59	5.0	2.3	18	4.9	3.4	0.77
15	12	3.5	2.2	20	4.3	2.2	92.50
			Words per Sentence				
9	14	8.8	4.3	12	6.5	4.5	65.00
11	45	10.2	2.8	18	6.9	3.5	3.34***
13	59	11.9	2.7	18	10.6	3.9	1.49
15	12	10.0	2.6	20	11.9	5.4	100.50
			Syntax				
9	14	78.2	26.0	12	67.8	35.5	73.00
11	45	91.2	7.1	18	76.0	29.4	2.54*
13	59	91.8	6.5	18	86.0	9.4	2.27*
15	12	89.8	5.6	20	90.4	21.7	63.00*
			Abstract-Concrete				
9	14	8.5	4.0	12	6.0	5.2	56.50
11	45	10.3	4.6	18	7.7	5.2	1.60
13	59	12.5	4.7	18	9.4	3.9	2.67*
15	12	9.3	3.9	20	11.9	5.4	86.00

*$p < .05$.
***$p < .001$.

TABLE 92. Comparison of mentally retarded and socially-emotionally disturbed children on written language

	Mentally retarded			Disturbed			
Age	N	Mean	SD	N	Mean	SD	*U*
			Total Words				
9	20	9.0	12.7	12	15.9	11.8	65.00*
11	21	17.4	16.1	18	22.6	20.8	0.64
13	46	29.6	27.0	18	54.3	42.7	2.17*
15	35	32.0	25.6	20	53.8	31.3	2.68**
			Total Sentences				
9	20	1.4	2.3	12	1.6	1.3	91.50
11	21	2.5	2.2	18	2.6	1.9	0.17
13	46	3.9	3.6	18	4.9	3.4	1.25
15	35	3.4	2.5	20	4.3	2.2	1.44
			Words per Sentence				
9	20	2.8	3.5	12	6.5	4.5	63.00*
11	21	4.1	3.3	18	6.9	3.5	2.28*
13	46	6.5	2.9	18	10.6	3.9	3.48***
15	35	8.4	3.9	20	11.9	5.4	2.53*
			Syntax				
9	20	40.2	41.2	12	67.8	35.5	67.50*
11	21	59.4	37.2	18	76.0	29.4	1.49
13	46	73.4	28.0	18	86.0	9.4	1.39
15	35	76.3	26.8	20	90.4	21.7	3.53***
			Abstract-Concrete				
9	20	6.0	5.3	12	6.0	5.2	77.00*
11	21	7.7	5.2	18	7.6	5.2	1.67
13	46	9.4	3.9	18	9.4	3.9	2.43*
15	35	7.1	2.9	20	11.9	5.4	3.34***

*$p < .05$.
**$p < .01$.
***$p < .001$.

References

Allport, F. Theories of Perception and the Concepts of Structure. New York: Wiley, 1955.

Arnold, G. Stuttering as a language problem: The written language of stutterers. Paper presented at American Speech and Hearing Convention, Washington, D.C., November 1966.

Baker, H., and Leland, B. Detroit Tests of Learning Aptitude. Indianapolis: Bobbs-Merrill, 1959.

Barnhart, C. (ed.). The American College Dictionary. New York: Random House, 1952.

Bartley, S. Principles of Perception. New York: Harper, 1958.

Bayley, N. Size and body build of adolescents in relation to rate of skeletal maturing. Child Dev. Monogr. 14, 1943.

Benton, A. Right-Left Discrimination and Finger Localization. New York: Hoeber, 1959.

Binet, A., and Simon, T. The Intelligence of the Feeble Minded. Baltimore: Williams & Wilkins, 1916.

Birch, H. (ed.). Brain Damage in Children: The Biological and Social Aspects. Baltimore: Williams & Wilkins, 1964.

Blank, M., and Bridger, W. Perceptual abilities and conceptual deficiencies in retarded readers. In J. Zubin and G. Jervis (eds.). Psychopathology of Mental Development. New York: Grune & Stratton, 1967.

Boder, E. Developmental dyslexia: Prevailing diagnostic concepts and a new diagnostic approach. In H. Myklebust (ed.). Progress in Learning Disabilities, Vol. II. New York: Grune & Stratton, 1971.

Boshes, B., and Myklebust, H. A neurological and behavioral study of children with learning disorders. Neurology 14:1, 1964.

Boyd, J. Motor behavior of deaf and hearing children. Unpublished doctoral dissertation, Northwestern University, 1965.

Broadbent, W. Cerebral mechanisms of speech and thought. Medicochir. Trans. 55:145, 1872.

Brown, R. Words and Things. Glencoe, Ill.: Free Press, 1958.

Bruner, J. Toward a Theory of Instruction. Cambridge, Mass.: Belknap Press, 1966.

Carroll, J. The Study of Language. Cambridge, Mass.: Harvard Univ. Press, 1953.

Cattell, P. The Measurement of Intelligence of Infants and Young Children. New York: Psychological Corp., 1940.

Charcot, J. Sur un cas de cécité verbale. In Oeuvres complètes de Charcot. Paris: Delahaye-Lecrosnier, 1887.

Chomsky, N. The formal nature of language. In E. Lenneberg (ed.). Biological Foundations of Language. New York: Wiley, 1967.

Clodd, E. The Story of the Alphabet. New York: Appleton, 1900.

Cobb, S. Foundations of Neuropsychiatry. Baltimore: Williams & Wilkins, 1958.

Cohn, R. Arithmetic and learning disabilities. In H. Myklebust (ed.). Progress in Learning Disabilities, Vol. II. New York: Grune & Stratton, 1971.

Connolly, C. Social and emotional factors in learning disabilities. In H. Myklebust (ed.). Progress in Learning Disabilities, Vol. II. New York: Grune & Stratton, 1971.

Cruickshank, W., Bentzen, F., Ratzeburg, F., and Tannhauser, M. A Teaching Method for Brain-Injured and Hyperactive Children. Syracuse: Syracuse Univ. Press, 1961.

De Saussure, F. Cours de linguistique générale (3rd ed.). Paris: Payot, 1931.

Diringer, D. Writing. New York: Praeger, 1962.

Doll, E. Anthropometry as an Aid to Mental Diagnosis. Vineland, N.J.: Vineland Training School Research Department, 1916.

Doll, E. The Oseretsky Tests of Motor Proficiency. Minneapolis: Educational Test Bureau, 1946.

Doll, E. The Measurement of Social Competence. Minneapolis: Educational Test Bureau, 1953.

Duff, M. Language functions in children with learning disabilities. Unpublished doctoral dissertation, Northwestern University, 1968.

Eisenson, J. Correlates of aphasia in adults. In L. Travis (ed.). Handbook of Speech Pathology and Audiology. New York: Appleton, 1971.

Ferguson, C. Baby talk in six languages. Am. Anthropol. 66:103–114, 1964.

Freud, S. On Aphasia. New York: International Univ. Press, 1953.

Friedrich, J. Extinct Languages. New York: Philosophical Library, 1957.

Frostig, M. Education for children with learning disabilities. In H. Myklebust (ed.). Progress in Learning Disabilities, Vol. I. New York: Grune & Stratton, 1968.

Gansl, I., and Garrett, H. Columbia Vocabulary Test. New York: Psychological Corp., 1939.

Gates, A. The Improvement of Reading. New York: Macmillan, 1947.

Gelb, I. A Study of Writing. Chicago: Univ. Chicago Press, 1963.

Gerstmann, J. Syndrome of finger agnosia, disorientation for right and left, agraphia and acalculia. Arch. Neurol. 44:389, 1940.

Geschwind, N. Neurological foundations of language In H. Myklebust (ed.). Progress in Learning Disabilities, Vol. I. New York: Grune & Stratton, 1968.

Geschwind, N. Language and the brain. Sci. Am. 226:76–83, 1972.

Gesell, A., and Amatruda, C. Developmental Diagnosis (2nd ed.). New York: Hoeber, 1947.

Gibson, E. Principles of Perceptual Learning and Development. New York: Appleton, 1969.

Gibson, J. The Senses Considered as Perceptual Systems. Boston: Houghton Mifflin, 1966.

Goetzinger, N. A reevaluation of the Heath Railwalking Test. Educ. Res. 18:1–15, 1961.

Goldfarb, W. Childhood Schizophrenia. Cambridge: Harvard Univ. Press, 1961.

Goldstein, K. Language and Language Disturbances. New York: Grune & Stratton, 1948.

Goodenough, F. The Measurement of Intelligence by Drawings. New York: World, 1926.

Heath, S. R. Railwalking performance as related to mental age and etiological type among the mentally retarded. Am. J. Psychol. 55:240, 1942.

Hebb, D. The semi-autonomous process: Its nature and nurture. Am. Psychol. 18:16–27, 1963.

Hécaen, H., and Ajuriaguerra, J. Left-handedness. New York: Grune & Stratton, 1964.

Hermann, K. Reading Disability. Springfield, Ill.: Thomas, 1959.

Hinshelwood, J. Word-blindness and visual memory. Lancet 2:1564–1570, 1895.

Hinshelwood, J. Congenital Word-Blindness. London: Lewis, 1917.

Hughes, J. Electroencephalography and learning. In H. Myklebust (ed.). Progress in Learning Disabilities, Vol. I. New York: Grune & Stratton, 1968.

Hughes, H. Electroencephalography and learning disabilities. In H. Myklebust (ed.) Progress in Learning Disabilities, Vol. II. New York: Grune & Stratton, 1971.

Ilg, F., and Ames, L. School Readiness. New York: Harper & Row, 1964.

Ingram, T. The nature of dyslexia. In F. Young and D. Lindsley (eds.). Early Experience and Visual Information Processing in Perceptual and Reading Disorders. Washington, D.C.: National Academy of Sciences, 1970.

Johnson, D., and Myklebust, H. Dyslexia in childhood. In J. Hellmuth (ed.). Learning Disorders, Vol. I. Seattle: Special Child Publications, 1965.

Johnson, D., and Myklebust, H. Learning Disabilities: Educational Principles and Practices. New York: Grune & Stratton, 1967.

Jones, H. Motor Performance and Growth. Berkeley: Univ. California Press, 1949.

Killen, J. Relationships between psychodynamic factors and nonverbal cognitive processes in normal and learning-disability children. Unpublished doctoral dissertation, Northern Illinois University, 1972.

Kinsbourne, M., and Warrington, E. Developmental factors in reading and writing backwardness. In J. Money (ed.). The Disabled Reader. Baltimore: Johns Hopkins Press, 1966.

Langer, S. Philosophy in a New Key. Cambridge: Harvard Univ. Press, 1957.

Lenneberg, E. Biological Foundations of Language. New York: Wiley, 1967.

Leopold, W. Patterning in children's language learning. In S. Saporta (ed.). Psycholinguistics: A Book of Readings. New York: Holt, 1961.

Mark, H., and Hardy, W. Orienting reflex disturbances in central auditory or language handicapped children. J. Speech Hear. Disord. 23:237–242, 1958.

Mathews, J. Communication disorders in the mentally retarded. In L. Travis (ed.). Handbook of Speech Pathology and Audiology. New York: Appleton, 1971.

McCarthy, D. Language development in children. In L. Carmichael (ed.). A Manual of Child Psychology. New York: Wiley, 1954.

McGrady, H. Verbal and nonverbal functioning in children with speech and language disorders. Unpublished doctoral dissertation, Northwestern University, 1964.

McGrady, H. Language pathology. In H. Myklebust (ed.). Progress in Learning Disabilities, Vol. I. New York: Grune & Stratton, 1968.

McNeill, D. Developmental psycholinguistics. In F. Smith and G. Miller (eds.). The Genesis of Language: A Psycholinguistic Approach. Cambridge: MIT Press, 1966.

McNeill, D. The Acquisition of Language: The Study of Developmental Psycholinguistics. New York: Harper & Row, 1970.

Meredith, H. The Rhythm of Physical Growth. Studies in Child Welfare, No. 1. Iowa City, Iowa: 1921.

Millikan, C., and Darley, F. (eds.). Brain Mechanism Underlying Speech and Language. New York: Grune & Stratton, 1967.

Money, F., (ed.). Reading Disability: Progress and Research Needs in Dyslexia. Baltimore: Johns Hopkins Press, 1962.

Money, J. (ed.). The Disabled Reader: Education of the Dyslexic Child. Baltimore: Johns Hopkins Press, 1966.

Monroe, M. Children Who Cannot Read. Chicago: Univ. Chicago Press, 1932.

Morgan, W. A case of congenital wordblindness. Br. Med. J. 2:1378, 1896.

Mountcastle, V. (ed.). Interhemispheric Relations and Cerebral Dominance. Baltimore: Johns Hopkins Press, 1962.

Mowrer, O. The autism theory of speech development and some clinical applications. J. Speech Hear. Disord. 17:263, 1952.

Mowrer, O. Learning Theory and the Symbolic Processes. New York: Wiley, 1960.

Myklebust, H. The significance of etiology in motor performance of deaf children with special reference to meningitis. Am. J. Psychol. 59:249, 1946.

Myklebust, H. Auditory Disorders in Children: A Manual for Differential Diagnosis. New York: Grune & Stratton, 1954.

Myklebust, H. The Psychology of Deafness (2nd ed.). New York: Grune & Stratton, 1964.

Myklebust, H. Development and Disorders of Written Language, Vol. I, Picture Story Language Test. New York: Grune & Stratton, 1965.

Myklebust, H. (ed.). Progress in Learning Disabilities, Vol. I. New York: Grune & Stratton, 1968.

Myklebust, H. Childhood aphasia. In L. Travis (ed). Handbook of Speech Pathology and Audiology. New York: Appleton, 1971a.

Myklebust, H. (ed.). Progress in Learning Disabilities, Vol. II. New York: Grune & Stratton, 1971b.

Myklebust, H. The Pupil Rating Scale: Screening for Learning Disabilities. New York: Grune & Stratton, 1971c.

Myklebust, H. Identification and diagnosis of children with learning disabilities. In S. Walzer and P. Wolff (eds.). Seminars in Psychiatry: Minor Cerebral Dysfunction in Children. New York: Grune & Stratton, 1973.

Myklebust, H., Bannochie, M., and Killen, J. Learning disabilities and cognitive processes. In H. Myklebust (ed.). Progress in Learning Disabilities, Vol. II, New York: Grune & Stratton, 1971.

Myklebust, H., Bannochie, M., and Killen, J. Laterality and cognitive functions in the mentally retarded. To be published in 1973.

Myklebust, H., and Boshes, B. Psychoneurological learning disorders in children. Arch. Pediatr. 77:247–256, 1960.

Myklebust, H., and Boshes, B. Minimal brain damage in children. Final Report: Minimal Brain Damage in Children. Washington, D.C.: Department of Health, Education, and Welfare, 1969.

Myklebust, H., and Johnson, D. Dyslexia in children. Except. Child. 29:14–25, 1962.

Myklebust, H., Killen, J., and Bannochie, M. Emotional aspects of learning disabilities. J. Autism Child. Schizo. 2(2):151–159, 1972.

Myklebust, H., and Neyhus, A. Diagnostic Test of Speechreading. New York: Grune & Stratton, 1970.

Neyhus, A., and Myklebust, H. Speechreading failure in deaf children. Final Report: Speechreading Failure in Deaf Children. Washington, D.C.: Department of Health, Education, and Welfare, 1969.

Orton, S. "Word-blindness" in school children. Arch. Neurol. 14:581–615, 1925.

Orton, S. Reading, Writing and Speech Problems in Children. New York: Norton, 1937.

Oseretsky, N. Psychomotorik: Methoden zur untersuchung der motoric. Beth. Z. Angew. Psychol. 17:162, 1931.

Pavlov, I. Lectures on Conditional Reflexes. (Tr. by W. Gantt.) New York: International, 1928.

Pei, M. Voices of Man: The Meaning and Function of Language. New York: Harper & Row, 1962.

Penfield, W. Consciousness, memory and man's conditional reflexes. In J. Kagen and K. Pribram (eds.). On the Biology of Learning. New York: Harcourt, 1969.

Perrin, P. Writer's Guide and Index to English. New York: Scott, Foresman, 1942.

Powers, M. Functional disorders of articulation: Symptomatology and etiology. In L. Travis (ed.). Handbook of Speech Pathology and Audiology. New York: Appleton, 1971.

Pribram, K. (ed.). On the Biology of Learning. New York: Harcourt, 1969.

Quiros, J. de. Dysphasia and dyslexia in school children. Folia Phoniatr. 16:201–222, 1964.

Rabinovitch, R. Reading and learning disabilities. In S. Arieti (ed.). American Handbook of Psychiatry, Vol. I. New York: Basic Books, 1959.

Rarick, G., and Harris, T. Physiological and motor correlates of handwriting legibility. In V. Herrick (ed.). New Horizons for Research in Handwriting. Madison: Univ. Wisconsin Press, 1963.

Richardson, S. Mental Imagery. New York: Springer, 1969.

Sapir, E. Language. New York: Harcourt, 1921.

Schiefelbusch, R., Copeland, H., and Smith, J. Language and Mental Retardation. New York: Holt, 1967.

Sloan, W. The Lincoln-Oseretsky Motor Development Scale. Genet. Psychol. Monogr. 51:183, 1955.

Slobin, D. Early grammatical development in several languages, with special attention to Soviet research. In T. Bever and W. Weksel (eds.). The Structure and Psychology of Language. New York: Holt, 1971.

Solley, C., and Murphy, G. Development of the Perceptual World. New York: Basic Books, 1960.

Spencer, R. An investigation of the maturation of various factors of auditory perception in preschool children. Unpublished doctoral dissertation, Northwestern University, 1958.

Sperry, R. Cerebral dominance in perception. In F. Young and D. Lindsley (eds.). Early Experience and Visual Information Processing in Perceptual and Reading Disorders. Washington, D.C.: National Academy of Sciences, 1970.

Strauss, A., and Lehtinen, L. Psychopathology and Education of the Brain-Injured Child. New York: Grune & Stratton, 1947.

Taylor, I. The Alphabet. London: 1883.

Taylor, J. (ed.). Selected Writings of John Hughlings Jackson, Vols. I and II. New York: Basic Books, 1958.

Templin, M. Certain Language Skills in Children. Minneapolis: Univ. Minnesota Press, 1957.

Terman, L., and Merrill, M. Stanford-Binet Intelligence Scale: Manual for Third Revision. Boston: Houghton Mifflin, 1960.

Thurstone, L., and Thurstone, T. SRA Primary Mental Abilities. Chicago: Science Research Associates, 1962.

Travis, L. (ed.). Handbook of Speech Pathology and Audiology. New York: Appleton, 1971.

Tuana, E., et al. Desarrollo del lenguaje escrito de los escolares: Estudio experimental del test "Cuento sobre una lámina." Bol. Inst. Interam. del Niño 45(179):564–640, 1971.

Vandenberg, D. The Written Language of Deaf Children. Wellington: Council for Educational Research, 1971.

Vygotsky, L. Thought and Language. Cambridge, Mass.: MIT Press, 1962.

Whorf, B. Language, Thought and Reality. New York: Wiley, 1956.

Wilson, M. A standardized method of obtaining a spoken language sample. Unpublished master's thesis, University of Nebraska, 1968.

Witkin, H., Lewis, H., Hertzman, M., Machover, K., Bretnall Meisner, P., and Wapner, S. Personality through Perception. New York: Harper, 1954.

Young, F., and Lindsley, D. (eds.). Early Experiences and Visual Information Processing in Perceptual and Reading Disorders. Washington, D.C.: National Academy of Sciences, 1970.

Zangwill, O. Cerebral Dominance and Its Relation to Psychological Function. London: Oliver & Boyd, 1960.

Name Index

Ajuriaguerra, N., 58
Allport, F., 172
Amatruda, C., 58, 170, 172, 177
Ames, L., 66, 176
Arnold, G., 144

Baker, H., 60, 165, 168, 172
Barnhart, C., 28
Bartley, S., 171, 172, 173
Bayley, N., 177
Benton, A., 172
Binet, A., 165, 168
Birch, H., 169
Blank, M., 82
Boder, E., 13, 55, 63, 71, 126
Boshes, B., 11, 78, 129
Boyd, J., 176
Bridger, W., 82
Broadbent, W., 126
Brown, R., 3, 8
Bruner, J., 175

Carroll, J., 51
Cattell, P., 172
Charcot, J., 171, 174
Chomsky, N., 28
Clodd, E., 6
Cobb, S., 177
Cohn, R., 59, 66
Connolly, C., 63
Cruickshank, W., 173

Darley, F., 46
De Saussure, F., 4
Diringer, G., 5, 6, 7
Doll, E., 97, 176, 177
Duff, M., 11

Eisenson, J., 58

Ferguson, C., 51
Freud, S., 171

Friedrich, J., 6
Frostig, M., 172

Gansl, I., 61
Garrett, H., 61
Gates, A., 163, 165, 166, 169
Gelb, I., 3, 5, 6, 7, 9
Gerstmann, J., 78, 171
Geschwind, N., 13, 55, 97
Gesell, A., 58, 170, 172, 177
Gibson, E., 173
Gibson, J., 171, 172
Goetzinger, N., 58
Goldfarb, W., 58
Goldstein, K., 8
Goodenough, F., 58

Hardy, W., 172
Harris, T., 177
Heath, S. R., 58, 77, 96
Hebb, D., 57
Hécaen, H., 58
Hermann, K., 63, 78, 126
Hinshelwood, J., 63, 171
Hughes, J., 14, 164

Ilg, F., 66, 176
Ingram, T., 63

Johnson, D., 64, 66, 78, 100, 113, 172, 176
Jones, H., 177

Killen, J., 63
Kinsbourne, M., 55, 78

Langer, S., 4
Lehtinen, L., 172, 173
Leland, B., 60, 165, 168, 172
Lenneberg, E., 28
Leopold, W., 28
Lindsley, D., 3, 55, 63, 171

261

Subject Index